D0410057

FOOTPRINTS
in SPAIN

FOOTPRINTS
in SPAIN

BRITISH LIVES IN A FOREIGN LAND

Simon Courtauld

QUARTET

First published in 2016 by Quartet Books Limited
A member of the Namara Group
27 Goodge Street, London, W1T 2LD

Copyright © Simon Courtauld 2016

The right of Simon Courtauld
to be identified as the author of this work
has been asserted by him in accordance with the
Copyright, Designs and Patents Act, 1988.

All rights reserved.
No part of this book may be reproduced in
any form or by any means without prior
written permission from the publisher.

A catalogue record for this book
is available from the British Library

ISBN 978 0 7043 7 4195

Typeset by Josh Bryson
Printed and bound in Great Britain by
T J International Ltd, Padstow, Cornwall

CORNWALL COUNTY LIBRARY		
38009048654823		
Bertrams	28/10/2016	
AN	£20.00	
WAD		

COURTAULD SIMON
Footprints in Spain
462288/00015 - 4 of 4

CONTENTS

PREFACE

John of Gaunt, George Orwell, Lord Byron, Kenneth Tynan, Charles I, Frances Partridge, the Duke of Wellington, Kim Philby, Princess Victoria Eugenie, Benjamin Disraeli. All spent time in Spain: not all of them are well known for their Spanish connection, but Spain touched them all in some way and on many left its mark. The theme of this book is not only the people of Britain who, over the centuries, have had associations with Spain, but also some of the institutions—from the Royal English College founded in Valladolid and still open today to the originally Scottish company which worked the Rio Tinto mines in the province of Huelva. Gibraltar, which was of course part of Spain until the eighteenth century, has its own chapter.

While researching the various historical links between Britain and Spain, I have found it convenient to divide them by cities, and at the same time to give some of the flavour and history of each place. This has led me indirectly to three remarkable Spanish women who, less well-known than Catherine of Aragon, also deserve to be remembered in Britain – Maria Pita, Luisa de Carvajal, Dolores Ibarruri ('La Pasionaria') – and to a notorious Carlist brigand who in later life retired to Surrey, where he is buried.

I have been surprised to learn of the number of distinguished Britons—politicians, priests, authors—who have been fascinated by the Spanish bullfight, and of the bullfighting terms which were incorporated in the *Oxford English Dictionary* in the nineteenth century. Now that bullfighting has been banned in parts of Spain, and its long-term future is uncertain, I have thought it relevant to try to place tauromachy, *la fiesta nacional*, in the life, including the religious life, and culture of Spain. It is one aspect of this country, having known so much cruelty and death in its history, which has drawn outsiders to a part of Europe which is so different from Britain.

While travelling round Spain, many people have assisted by pointing me in the right direction. However, for their helpful insights

I would like especially to thank: Javier Burrieza, Bruce McIntyre, David Penton, Monsignor John Pardo, Jennifer Ballantine Perera, Michael Wigram, Bess Twiston-Davies, Robin Gamble—and, above all, Jennie, who came with me every step of the way and to whom this book is dedicated.

HUELVA

A Huelva una vez y nunca vuelvas. 'One visit to Huelva is quite enough,' or so they say in Seville and other parts of Andalusia. True, the outskirts of the city—oil refineries, gas installations, chemical factories, hectares of plastic polytunnels for growing soft fruit— are distinctly unappealing. And, perhaps because much of the city was severely damaged by the 1755 earthquake which destroyed Lisbon, the local tourist brochure used to state that Huelva had no particular historic interest. This is not only excessively modest but in fact untrue: *circumspice* and there are hidden gems to be found.

Close to the sea, Huelva is situated at the confluence of the rivers Odiel and Tinto.* Forty miles north, and near the source of the Rio Tinto (Red River), are the now abandoned mines which a British company, Matheson & Co., together with Deutsche Bank, bought from the Spanish government in 1873 and worked for their copper deposits. The Romans had mined copper, silver and iron ore in these hills, which within a few years made Rio Tinto the world's leading producer of copper and the largest single employer of labour in Spain. (Another originally Scottish concern, the Tharsis Sulphur and Copper Company, named after the Phoenicians who had also worked these mines, was extracting copper ore and pyrites twenty miles west of Rio Tinto.)

Accommodation for the mainly Scottish workforce of the Rio Tinto company was provided in purpose-built villages near the mines and in Huelva. Management lived forty miles up country, while the houses in the city were for the workers who had to travel to and from the mines on the company's railway, and for those involved in administration and shipping the copper from the port to Britain.

---

* In his book *The Mighty Dead: Why Homer Matters*, Adam Nicolson speculates that these rivers, coloured and made toxic by the metals in the surrounding hills and valleys which have been mined since the Bronze Age, may have inspired Homer's gates of Hades.

The Barrio Obrero Reina Victoria, or Queen Victoria's Workers' District, built in the early years of the twentieth century, contrasted oddly with the local architecture and is the more striking today in the centre of a modern Spanish city. The first houses, designed by two Spanish architects under British supervision, were saddle-roofed bungalows, said to be in the English style but with elements that were recognisably Andalusian or German in their construction. After World War I, when the second, and larger, phase of building was undertaken, the English architect R. H. Morgan looked to Hertfordshire for inspiration—more specifically to the first English 'garden city' which had been built in Letchworth in 1903. By the 1920s, when the major part of the Barrio Reina Victoria project was under way, a second Hertfordshire garden city was being built at Welwyn. This was *rus in urbe*, as first envisaged by the social reformer Ebenezer Howard who wanted to provide towns where industry and residential areas would be separate—a relatively new concept at the end of the nineteenth century—and the houses would adjoin open spaces, with hedges and trees. In Huelva magnolias and mulberry trees were planted along wide avenues, and the idea was that no two houses would be the same.

The houses of the barrio have been modified and altered in some respects over the years, but the English 'garden city' style of the early twentieth century is still apparent. There are red-brick quoins against the white stucco, false chimneys and brightly painted front doors, gables and dormer windows. Blue is a popular colour, both for the woodwork under the eaves and the wooden decoration within the triangle of the gables. Bougainvillaea grows profusely in the front gardens, yellow and white gateposts and trellis fencing separate the houses from communal paths between trimmed hedges. Above the main entrance to the barrio, Queen Victoria's name, inscribed prominently on a steel arch, sits against the backdrop of a large palm tree. Queen Victoria's name is also attached, rather inappropriately one might think, to a Catholic brotherhood in Huelva. The Hermandad de la Victoria is in fact named in honour of Maria Santisima de la Victoria, but it was founded in the barrio named after our Protestant

Queen Victoria and processes through the district every year during Holy Week.

In hilly country south of Aracena, the Rio Tinto managers and engineers had larger houses of British design with chimneys, tiled and gabled roofs and bay windows. They were, according to an architectural historian, virtual replicas of houses being built at the time in Aldershot and Camberley. Lawns were laid and kept well watered, and clipped hedges enclosed the properties. However, the overhanging cloud of dust blown from the mines nearby made it very difficult to grow flowers and shrubs successfully. (Roses, crocosmia, choisya, lavender flourish today in these still 'English' gardens.) The principal houses were built round three sides of a square, all of them with front doors facing not outwards towards the town but inwards, overlooking each other and the company tennis courts (the first in Spain). It was symptomatic, according to a Spanish account, of '*la ideologia segregacionista dominante en la colonia britanica*'. A stone wall was built round the perimeter of the village: Spain and foreigners were, as far as possible, to be kept out of sight and mind. Like Wellington in the Peninsular War, the managers of the Rio Tinto looked upon the Spaniards as an inferior race. If any Rio Tinto man was heard speaking Spanish he was immediately suspect, and fraternising with Spanish women was strongly discouraged, almost to the point of being forbidden. It was said that only thirty Anglo-Spanish marriages took place in eighty years.

Social activity was centred on a club next to the tennis courts which excluded not only Spaniards but all women from its 'men only' bar. There was a theatre, library and billiard room, where sporting cups and trophies of those days are still displayed. The photographs taken at the turn of the twentieth century are reminiscent of club life in the Indian hill stations of the Raj. Members and their wives are shown celebrating Christmas at the club in fancy dress, while ladies' and children's races were held to mark Queen Victoria's birthday.

Today the 'men only' bar, still with that name on the door, has hunting prints by Herring and Aldin on its wood-panelled walls and ships' crests from Royal Naval frigates visiting the port of Huelva. A picture of Constable's *The Hay Wain* hangs on a wall of one of the original houses, now restored in the style of its first owners. Canisters labelled 'Scones' and 'Twinings Tea' stand on a shelf in the kitchen, Union Jacks, together with a portrait of Queen Victoria, hang above the fireplace in the sitting-room furnished with a chintz-covered sofa and armchairs. The overall impression conveyed is of a complete lack of interest in the people and culture of the country in which these employees of the Rio Tinto company were living. A line of smaller houses looks rather like a row of English almshouses, and some of the properties still have very Victorian verandas, their roofs supported by green-painted wooden pillars.

The company directors did at least give their settlement a Spanish name: Bella Vista, acknowledging the distant view of the hills. The distinguished British architect, Alan Brace, built more houses in the 1930s, again in the English style of the period, as well as a school and company offices. A hospital was built around this time which today houses a mining museum, opened in 1992 and named in memory of its first president, Ernest Lluch, who was murdered by ETA, the Basque separatist organisation, in 2000. One of the treasures of the museum is the Maharajah's railway carriage, built in Birmingham in 1892 for Queen Victoria's visit to India, which of course never took place. It was used instead by the Queen Regent of Spain, Maria Cristina, and Alfonso XIII when they paid a royal visit to the Rio Tinto mines.

The Scots Presbyterian chairman, Hugh Matheson, decided in 1890 that the Rio Tinto staff should have a church to serve their spiritual needs. In contrast to the country's Catholic places of worship, a kirk was built in simple, unadorned neo-Gothic style. There was no stained glass, no gilt, no altarpiece, no sculpture—just a wooden-beamed roof, wooden pews, plain walls and an organ. When the mines were returned to Spanish ownership in 1954, the Bishop of Huelva gave permission for the chapel to continue as a place of Protestant worship, though today it is used only for concerts. A cemetery nearby containing some sixty graves (British and Spanish) and a few Celtic crosses, was completely overgrown in 2015, but the regional government had apparently agreed to a project of clearance and restoration. The memorial to five named employees of the company killed in World War I has been well maintained.

In need of recreation, the managers and senior employees of the company played tennis, cricket, squash and golf, games which, it would be claimed, they introduced to Spain. More significantly, the British mineworkers were in the habit of playing informal games of football which led, in 1889, to the founding by two Scottish doctors of the first football club in Spain. The following year, under the name of Recreativo de Huelva, the club played a team from Seville. It is recorded that only two of the players were not British, but the game at which Spain would excel a century later had begun its life in the peninsula. (In the last years of the century the Eastern Telegraph Company, laying a submarine cable between Vigo and Cornwall, introduced the game to Galicia; and English miners and shipyard workers in Bilbao began playing football with local Basques and formed the Athletic Club. It still retains the English spelling of its name today. In 1907, unlikely though it may seem, a team of seminarians from the English College in Valladolid apparently defeated a team representing Real Madrid. Football may have been played in Catalonia around 1848, when British railway workers were building the first line in Spain, between Barcelona and Mataró, a few miles up the coast. And when the now world-famous club of FC Barcelona was formed fifty years later, its first president was an Englishman, Walter Wild.)

During the early years of Rio Tinto's history the problems associated with these huge open-cast copper mines—some four hundred metres deep and employing thousands of unskilled labourers—became apparent. The continuous discharge of sulphur dioxide into the air was harmful both to the workers' lungs and to the agricultural crops of local peasant farmers. Rumblings of discontent—also over working conditions and low wages—led to a strike and demonstrations at the beginning of February 1888 which became so serious that the company's general manager asked the civil authorities of the town to call in troops to restore order. A crowd of thousands, including women and children, gathered in the main square on 4 February to renew their protests, soldiers and members of the Guardia Civil opened fire and by the end of the day fifty lay dead and hundreds were wounded. It was not Amritsar, the infamous massacre which took place thirty years later in northern India, but there were parallels. (A film based on the events, *El Corazon de la Tierra*, was made in 2007.)

Further violent strikes occurred in 1920, at the mines and the port of Huelva, by which time Rio Tinto's general manager was an autocratic martinet, Walter Browning, known as *el rey de Huelva* during his twenty years running the mines. He escaped four assassination attempts and, having worked as a gold prospector in Mexico, he was always armed. But the end came for Browning in 1927 when his resignation was demanded for having lived too well at the company's expense.

A decade later, with the country ravaged by civil war and the province of Huelva having fallen to the Nationalists in the summer of 1936, many of Rio Tinto's mineworkers, supporting the Republic and the anarchists, were imprisoned and executed. Nationalist troops used the British-built school as a barracks. Mining continued, but productivity suffered, a situation which persisted throughout World War II. During this period Rio Tinto was in effect a British enclave surrounded by a supposedly neutral country infiltrated, especially in that part of Andalusia, by Nazi agents.

The mines have been closed for many years, but the vast holes in the ground remain. The Corta Atalaya mine, close to the old British village, is a spectacular sight today, with a few derelict buildings visible round the rim and the track of the old railway winding down the stepped sides of the crater to the base of the mine several hundred metres below and now underwater. Though the mines are no longer worked, the Red River still runs red with the copper and other mineral deposits, and the deer and wild boar which live in these hills know not to drink the toxic water.

However, the water and in particular the sub-surface life of the river are of great interest to the National Aeronautics and Space Administration (NASA) in the United States. Scientists believe that the microbes which live beneath the very acidic waters of the Rio Tinto, using chemical energy to obtain food, may point to the possibility of life below the surface of Mars which, like the Rio Tinto, is rich in iron and sulphur. The Spanish Centro de Astrobiologia and NASA have collaborated on a project, initiated in 2003, which might lead in the future to the discovery of sub-surface life on Mars.

Hugh Matheson was first chairman and co-founder of Rio Tinto, together with a German entrepreneur, Wilhelm (later Guillermo) Sundheim, born in the Grand Duchy of Hesse-Darmstadt, who came to Huelva to participate in its industrial expansion. With German investment a consortium was formed which controlled the Rio Tinto company in its early years, and Sundheim was instrumental in establishing its rail link between the mines and the port of Huelva. He was named *hijo adoptivo* of Huelva and an avenue in the centre of the city, which at one end is opposite the entrance to the Barrio Reina Victoria, was named Alameda Sundheim. The Hotel Colon, built at his instigation, became Rio Tinto's headquarters.

Another German to do the mining company a good turn was Claus, who sold to Rio Tinto the twenty acres which came to form the barrio. This may or may not be the same family as the Claus (or Clauss) whose presence in Huelva during World War II as a well-known agent of the Abwehr persuaded British intelligence that this was where a corpse, carrying false documents intended to deceive the enemy, should be washed ashore. Ludwig Clauss was a rich German industrialist, originally from Leipzig, who came to Huelva at the beginning of the twentieth century and, when Sundheim died, took his place as the richest man in Huelva. He was made Germany's honorary consul in the city and had two sons, the younger of whom, Adolf, joined the Condor Legion fighting for Franco during the Civil War, and then formed a spy ring operating along the coast between the Portuguese frontier and Gibraltar. He was therefore ideally placed to monitor the movements of shipping and report the information, via the German consulate, to his Abwehr superiors in Madrid.

With remarkable ingenuity, British intelligence arranged in 1943 for a body to be dropped from a submarine off the Spanish coast near Huelva, carrying a briefcase which contained high-level documents indicating that the invasion of Europe from North Africa would be made on the coast of Greece and not, as the Germans had hitherto assumed, through Sicily. The body of a Major Martin, Royal Marines (in fact a Welsh alcoholic vagrant who had killed himself with rat poison) was picked up by sardine fishermen, taken ashore at Punta Umbría and, as intended, the corpse carrying 'top-secret' papers came almost at once to the attention of Herr Clauss.* Cooperation between the Spanish and German military was such that the documents were soon being examined by the German embassy in Madrid and photocopies were relayed to Berlin. Operation Mincemeat, as it was called, was swallowed whole. Hitler, convinced that the documents were genuine and that the main thrust of the invasion would be made in Greece, redirected German defensive forces, sending Rommel to Greece and three Panzer divisions with him. When the Allies landed in Sicily, they met hardly any initial resistance, and most of the island's Italian defenders surrendered.

The British vice-consul in Huelva arranged for 'Major William Martin' to be buried with full military honours, and his body now lies in the cemetery of Nuestra Señora de la Soledad on the northern outskirts of the city. Past blocks of modern housing, beyond the Carrefour supermarket and the city morgue, the huge cemetery has a delightful gothic chapel within its boundaries. The grave commemorating Major Martin, shaded by a large cypress tree, records his fictional dates and names of his parents, followed by the inscription 'DULCE ET DECORUM EST PRO PATRIA MORI R.I.P.' But the body that lies buried there belongs to an impoverished Welsh miner's son who was only acknowledged more than fifty years after his death by the addition of a postscript carved on the marble stone: 'GLYNDWR MICHAEL SERVED AS MAJOR WILLIAM MARTIN, RM.' The grave is under the jurisdiction of the Commonwealth War

---

* Punta Umbría is a tourist resort today, though it was originally developed by Rio Tinto as a place of relaxation for its employees.

Graves Commission but, with exquisite irony, it is maintained on behalf of Britain by the German consulate in Huelva, which was presumably responsible for the two bunches of dried flowers which I saw at the foot of the grave. (For some unexplained reason 'Major Martin' is buried within the Catholic cemetery and not in the adjacent British cemetery which contains three Commonwealth war graves.)

Among his many business interests, Guillermo Sundheim was not only involved in the construction of the Hotel Colon, marking the four hundredth anniversary of Christopher Columbus's voyage to discover the new world, but also the restoration of the monastery where Columbus had spent some time before he set forth on his great expedition. The Franciscan Monasterio de Santa Maria de La Rabida was built on the foundations of a Moorish fort in the fifteenth century, standing above the estuary which carries the rivers Tinto and Odiel to the sea. Today it also overlooks the industrial forest of Huelva, but remains peacefully protected by a garden of flowers and trees. Inside the monastery, a church and side chapel give on to a glorious Mudejar cloister which survived the devastating Lisbon earthquake in the mid-eighteenth century. Before Columbus came to Spain he had been living in Portugal and trying to persuade the King to back his idea, which was to sail west across the Atlantic Ocean to India. Having failed in his purpose, and after the death of his wife, he went to Spain with his five-year-old son Diego and presented himself at La Rabida. The monks took charge of the boy while Columbus set off for the royal court, then in Seville, to put his project to Ferdinand and Isabella.

Now aged forty (quite an age in those days), white-haired and an inveterate talker, Columbus could hardly have chosen a worse moment, when los Reyes Catolicos were fully occupied with the task of expelling the Moors from their last redoubt in Granada. His scheme was, however, referred to a royal commission, which took four years to conclude that it was 'vain and worthy of all rejection'. Columbus returned dejected to his son at La Rabida and there confided his disappointment to one of its friars, Fray Juan Perez. He was not only sympathetic to the proposed adventure, but as a former treasurer to the royal household he agreed to take up Columbus's cause and write a letter to his old employers. By an astonishing, and for the future of America world-changing, piece of good fortune Ferdinand and Isabella agreed to receive the friar at court—in spite of the findings of the royal commission and the fact that Christian Spain was engaged in its final struggle with the infidel Moors. (It may have helped that the abbess of the convent at Moguer, only a few miles from La Rabida, was Ferdinand's aunt.) However he may have argued the case, Fray Perez was successful in persuading the King and Queen that such an enterprise should be supported, and Columbus was commanded to attend the court before Granada. Riding a mule, he reached the gates of the city in January 1492, just in time to witness the surrender of the Alhambra and the handing over of the last stronghold of Moorish Spain. Three months later came the royal decree that Columbus should make preparations for a voyage to the Indies, and by the first week of August, with three caravels, he was sailing westward into the Atlantic. He died fourteen years later, still believing that America was Asia.

Columbus's two captains, the brothers Pinzon, were from Palos de la Frontera, the port below the monastery from which he and his crew embarked on their epic voyage. There is no port of Palos today: the waters have receded and the fountain, from which Columbus is said to have filled his water casks as his ships—the *Santa Maria*, *Niña* and *Pinta*—waited at the jetty, now stands in a field close to the main road. Remains of the port were excavated by archaeologists in 2014. Above it is the church of San Jorge Martir, which on one of its exterior walls carries a wonderfully hyperbolic inscription, written in the twentieth century:

> *¡Oh Palos. No puede tu gloria igualar. Ni Menfis, ni Tebas, ni Roma inmortal, ni Atenas, ni Londres. Ninguna ciudad tu historica fama podra disputar!*

HUELVA

(Oh Palos. Your glory cannot be equalled. Neither by Memphis, nor Thebes, nor the immortal Rome, nor Athens, nor London. No city will be able to challenge your historic renown!)

It was apparently in this church, on the night before he set sail, that Columbus and his crew prayed to Nuestra Señora de los Milagros, no doubt well aware that more than one miracle would be needed to bring them safe home. At the monastery of La Rabida they will tell you that Columbus prayed and took Communion there a few hours before he left Palos for the open sea. A similar claim is made at the Sanctuary of La Virgen de la Cinta, Huelva's patron saint, in the Alameda Sundheim in the city. Of course it is highly unlikely that Columbus spent most of his last day in Spain going between three churches some miles apart. However, I like to think that he would have gone back to the monastery to ask for God's blessing on his enterprise. Without the intervention of La Rabida's Fray Perez, Columbus would never have discovered America; in one of the cells upstairs in the monastery he and Martin Alonso Pinzon, together with the friars, discussed and made plans for the voyage. In the next century La Rabida would open its doors to Cortes and Pizarro as they made their way to the new world.

℞

The theatre critic Kenneth Tynan, in his book *Bull Fever* published in 1955, wrote of Huelva:

> The town has four heroes, three of them dead. One is the nameless corpse which floated ashore at Huelva bearing forged information which embarrassingly misled the Germans about the Allied plans for invading southern Europe. Another is Columbus, who sailed westward from the estuary of the red river where his statue towers, staring quizzically at the sea. The third idol, a lean torero christened Manuel Baez and professionally nicknamed 'Litri', was killed in 1926; and the fourth is my Litri, Manuel's half-brother, who outweighs, in local and national esteem, all the other attributes of Huelva put together. I have no doubt that when Columbus crumbles, the street-boys will still be chalking 'VIVA EL LITRI' on the walls of the town-hall.

Fifty years on, Tynan's Litri is still with us, in his eighties and living at Punta Umbría, the beach resort south of Huelva. He was born in October 1930, in unusual family circumstances. Four years earlier, his matador half-brother Manuel, who was said to have *un valor temerario* (foolhardy bravery), was gored by a bull in Málaga; his leg became gangrenous, it was amputated and he died. At the time he was planning to marry a girl from Valencia, but when he brought her back to Huelva his retired matador father Miguel, recently widowed, also fell in love with her. There was clearly a problem which might have developed into a family crisis, but it was solved in the bullring. After a decent period of mourning the father married the girl and a son was born to them. Though he began his life, for a few weeks, in the province of Valencia, this Miguel has spent the rest of his life in and around Huelva, and in 2000 he was formally declared the city's adopted son. (He is therefore an *onubense*, after the originally Phoenician name for the city: Onoba.) Less than two years later, a statue of him was unveiled in what is now called la Plaza Dinastía de los Litri.

An inscription on the plinth records the names of the four taurine members of this illustrious family: the father Miguel Baez Litri, who died in 1932; Manuel Baez Litri, killed in the ring; Miguel Baez Litri, the 'main man'; and his son Miguel Baez Litri, who was born in 1968. They are described as '*la dinastia que tanta gloria y honor a dado a la Huelva taurina*' ('the dynasty which has given so much glory and honour to taurine Huelva') having brought to their profession '*tecnica, estetica y valor*'.

Like most matadors, three of the Litris showed some technique, artistry and bravery in the bullring. But their careers would never have been commemorated in this way were it not for the one sculptured on the statue, Tynan's Litri, who exploded on to the taurine scene in the late 1940s with a style and a contempt for his own safety which mesmerised those who came to watch him.

Having first put on a suit of lights before his seventeenth birthday, he fought a dozen times the following season, but then in 1949 he established a remarkable record, fighting on 114 occasions as a *novillero* (apprentice). In his home town they called him *El Atomico*. These were the days, post-Civil War, when the condition of most roads was appalling and the cars in which the toreros travelled were at best unreliable. Night after night, bumping his way across the country, from Gijon to Granada, from Badajoz to Barcelona, Litri would be driven to yet another town, often reached in the early morning, where he might snatch a few hours' sleep before yet another performance in the bullring. (Nowadays the top *novilleros* will make fewer than forty appearances in the plaza de toros during a season.) According to a *fandanguillo* of the time, advancing Huelva's claims to fame, though with a slightly different emphasis from Tynan's:

Tres cositas tiene Huelva
que le envidia el mundo entero –
La Rabida y Punta Umbría
y El Litri, de novillero,
la flor de la toreria.

Huelva has three little things
which are the envy of all the world –
La Rabida and Punta Umbría
and El Litri, as a *novillero*,
the flower of bullfighting.

There was another flower that year, also a *novillero*, called Julio Aparicio. Followers of the bulls—aficionados, impresarios, breeders, managers, critics—love a contest between two toreros at the top of their game. There was the rivalry between Belmonte and Joselito in the early years of the twentieth century, in the 1950s there would be Ordoñez and Dominguin, and now for a couple of years there was Litri and Aparicio. Both boys—they were still teenagers—were managed by the astute José Flores Camará, who had also handled Manolete's career, and knew when he was on to a good thing. It was a rivalry of opposites: Aparicio the extrovert all-rounder against Litri the inscrutable introvert, moody and aloof, who seemed to know no fear and made the crowds gasp with two highly risky passes which he made his own. For one of them, according to Tynan:

He would skip thirty yards away from the horns and take the charge from that ridiculous distance. Holding the *muleta* behind him with both hands, as if drying his legs after a shower, he would stand stock-still until the bull was almost upon him and moving fast, when he would deflect the horns with a leisurely flourish of the left hand.

The statue of Litri in Huelva depicts him standing with the *muleta* (red cloth) held behind him in his left hand, and the sword in his right. His other trick was to ignore the bull as it passed his body and instead to stare at the spectators or up at the sky.

He and Aparicio became full matadors together in Valencia, then continued their careers independently. By the end of the 1951 season Litri had, in four years, earned something like £250,000 (around £6 million today). But he didn't live or behave ostentatiously, didn't seek out the company of wealthy women or celebrities in other walks of life. He was said to be happy playing cards at home and reading American comics. When, during the winter of 1951-2, he went to fight in Mexico, the expectation and reputation which preceded him were such that the Mexican crowds were bound to be disappointed. More than that, they felt cheated when his performances in the Plaza Mexico (the largest in the world) were less than outstanding. Petrol-soaked cushions were thrown flaming into the ring, Litri cancelled his remaining engagements and returned disconsolately to Spain. He made an erratic start to the 1952 season and some critics were grumbling that, at the age of twenty-one, his future was behind him.

Tynan was following the bulls in Spain that summer: he saw Litri on bad form in Pamplona, when he appeared to have lost his nerve and his will to go on. But everything was different two weeks later in Valencia, when Tynan not only witnessed one of the most memorable *corridas* of the decade, but also wrote a most memorable account of it in *Bull Fever*.

It was the last *corrida* of the Valencia *feria*. Litri had already fought four bulls earlier in the week, and had redeemed himself with one, being awarded both its ears and its tail. Now he was to be on the same bill as Antonio Ordóñez, a prodigy-in-waiting who had begun

14

his career as a full matador the previous year and before the end of the decade would be acclaimed the finest of his generation. Reverting to his persona as theatre critic, Tynan brought Edmund Kean, Laurence Olivier, Marlon Brando and Pope's translation of the *Iliad* into his appreciation of this *corrida*. It was an occasion, he wrote, when 'Reach was confronted with Grasp, Accident with Design, Romantic with Classic, *Sturm und Drang* with Age of Gold'. One knows what he meant; more prosaically it might be said that Litri's style was thrillingly unorthodox, while Ordoñez was the more complete torero, making passes according to the book—graceful, technically correct and no less exciting. The two men were also quite different in physical appearance. Ordoñez was round-faced, with an open expression; Litri by contrast would look haunted, at times resentful, at others mournful, calling to mind the Knight of the Sorrowful Countenance, though without the quixotic idealism of the Don. Photographs give him an El Greco look, not only in the eyes but in his nose, which is at least as prominent as many of El Greco's subjects, including the artist himself.

The *corrida* on that day was the more dramatic, and difficult for those taking part, because of the weather. Heavy rain fell intermittently, thunder was cracking over the city, and the wind was gusting and disturbing the matadors' red serge cloths. Fighting his first bull in a cloudburst, Litri was knocked down by his opponent, killed it with a single sword as lightning forked across the sky and was given the bull's ears. His second bull was, in Kenneth Tynan's words, 'as close as zoology can get to a tank'. According to Tynan, when Litri came to face the animal with his *muleta*,

> Litri embodied all that the human race dislikes about itself—its spite, its wrath, its ineradicable guilt. Ordoñez, by contrast, embodies all that we pride ourselves on—our grace, our intellect, our generosity. Litri's courage is derived from despair; Ordoñez's from hope. Ordoñez is one of the elect, Litri one of the damned, yet out of his purgatory he summoned up a terrible valour which took him to the perihelion of his neurotic powers. He seemed to be willing his own death. Six bleak, still statuaries opened the *faena*, after which he plodded away to the opposite

15

fence, sang out his challenge, and took the full impetus of the charge on his yielding *muleta*, furled in the left hand; the bull was trapped, held, mesmerised, and followed the folded cloth through eight naturals, crowned with a releasing chest-pass. Then—outrageously—three more naturals, with the torero's eyes tightly shut.

The rain fell with doubled force; the sun sulked elsewhere, but Litri was its deputy. Out in the middle of the swamp he completed seven burning *derechazos*, and then as many reckless *manoletinas*. He would not be content with a graze or a mere goring: this was life or death. Now he was on his knees, still waving the muleta and refusing to move, and eight times the bull passed him and granted him life. He was past hearing now, past caring even, though the *olés* must have been heard at the beach, miles away down the dripping streets. When the bull had skimmed under his arm for the eighth time, he threw his sword to the left and his *muleta* to the right and, turning, stroked the brave black muzzle. Still kneeling, he then stretched his hands out to us in supplication. There was a look of inexorable pity in his eyes as he rose, gathered up his tools and killed in a swift, clean thrust.

In a second the ring was white with handkerchiefs. The ears and tail were not enough; the cheers did not subside until a hoof had been cut as well, and Litri had made two triumphant circuits of the ring.

The *corrida* was not over. Ordoñez fought the last bull with consummate grace and fluency in spite of the conditions. The sand was now so wet and slippery that he began the *faena* by removing his shoes and putting his feet into his upturned *montera* (hat). The president awarded him the bull's ears and tail, prompting Tynan to comment that 'it was Litri's day; but for the *aficion* at large, it was Ordoñez's year'. And for most taurine enthusiasts it would be Ordoñez's decade.

I never saw Litri, for by the time I started going to bullfights his career was almost over. In fact he decided it was time to retire in 1952, three months after Valencia and having just passed his twenty-second birthday. He returned to the ring in 1955, fought a respectable number of *corridas* for four more seasons, then once again resolved to call it a day. Six years later he came out of retirement again, and in 1968, after a bad goring in Seville, he announced that he really was hanging up his sword for good. By now he was married and his son Miguel was born in that year. He did occasionally put on a suit of lights again for a *corrida* in Huelva, and made his last appearance in a bullring, in Nimes, when his son became a full matador in September 1987.

It is quite common for matadors to retire and then make a comeback, though it is not clear why Litri changed his mind so often. He kept a shrine to la Virgen de la Cinta (Huelva's guardian) in his house, and was said to have considered joining a monastic order. Every year he would ride across the desolate country of the Coto Doñana to make a pilgrimage to the shrine of the Virgin of Rocio, where he may have received encouragement to return to the bulls. Of course he feared the fatal goring which his half-brother Manuel had suffered, but he was a far better torero. His triumphs often came in the important plazas of Madrid and Valencia, and so every few years, between 1955 and 1968, his reputation among his faithful followers was restored.

No bulls were being fought in Huelva when I was there, but I went along to the plaza in the hope of learning something of the great man's whereabouts, and that he was still flourishing in old age. The multi-coloured façade of the bullring is built in the Mudejar style, and extending from it on to the pavement is the Bar Sol y Sombra. Two old men enjoying their morning glasses of beer told me they thought Litri might be unwell, as he hadn't attended the town's recent annual *feria*. When I mentioned the old maestro's signature passes, one of which was named the *litrazo*, and the unnerving size of many of the bulls he fought, one of them nodded sagely: '*Era un torero*'. In another bar, inside the bullring, a man responded to my mention of Litri's name by taking me into an adjacent room where the walls were covered with old taurine pictures, many of them celebrating the dynasty of Huelva. There is a fine portrait photograph of Litri in profile, awaiting the entrance of his bull from behind the *burladero*, with the sunlight catching his wonderful proboscis. Others show him with Antonio Borrero 'Chamaco', another favourite matador son of Huelva, and with Curro Romero, the old *sevillano* who did his reputation no good by continuing to fight well into his sixties. There is also a family photograph of the wedding of Litri's son Miguel.

I was told that maestro Litri lived in a house overlooking the beach at Punta Umbría and, having got some slightly vague directions, I set off to find him, with a copy of *Bull Fever* in my hand. When I got to the beach road, I looked for a *chiringuito* (beach bar) which was apparently close to his house. I think I found the right *chiringuito*, but one of the houses nearby was shuttered and at another a maid (not Spanish) had never heard of him. It was disappointing: I would like to have shaken his hand, asked him to sign *Bull Fever*, and told him that he was the catalyst for my enthusiasm for bullfighting and, indeed, aspects of Spanish culture. But on reflection it may have been better that I didn't find him. Litri had the reputation, in his youth, of being a man of few words, and he might not have welcomed the intrusion. He might have been entertaining friends, or having a siesta, or unwell. So I returned to Huelva and was delighted to come across the great man's statue. There it stands, twenty feet high, in a square where the Litri family lived for many years. As I read on the plinth the tribute to the dynasty of 'more than a hundred years… of glory, of bravery and much blood', I hoped that the maestro above me was enjoying a *copa* at his beach house while preparing lunch (he is known to be an excellent cook) and watching the sardine boats put to sea.

BADAJOZ

O, Nelly Gray! O, Nelly Gray!
For all your jeering speeches,
At duty's call, I left my legs
In Badajos's breaches!

'Faithless Nelly Gray' is the title of Thomas Hood's 'pathetic ballad' of the plight of Ben Battle who had his legs shot off during the siege of Badajoz in the Peninsular War.

Ben Battle was a soldier bold
And used to war's alarms;
But a cannon-ball took off his legs,
So he laid down his arms.

Now as they bore him off the field,
Said he, 'Let others shoot;
For here I leave my second leg,
And the Forty-second Foot.'

The poem continues in black-humorous vein as it recounts Nelly's refusal to have her legless lover back—'But I will never have a man/ With both legs in the grave'—which drives Ben to hang himself.

One end he tied around a beam,
And then removed his pegs;
And as his legs were off – of course
He soon was off his legs.

And there he hung till he was dead
As any nail in town;
For, though distress had cut him up,
It could not cut him down.

FOOTPRINTS IN SPAIN

The Hispanophile author Gerald Brenan recalled first hearing of Badajoz at school. 'What queer, far-off, schoolboy memories that word calls up! The boring classroom and the smug tone of the history master's voice as he spoke of its sack by Wellington's troops—the pun in Thomas Hood's poem, printed in a little red school edition that cost sixpence—the look of the name itself, so absurd in its English pronunciation!'

The actor-comedian Stanley Holloway wrote a number of monologues between the two world wars which he performed on stage. 'Albert and the Lion' was the most famous, and several related the fortunes and misfortunes of a character he created and called Sam Small, who during those years became part of English folklore. Sam, serving as a private with Wellington in the Peninsular War and at Waterloo, was perhaps best-known for the Christmas pudding which his mother gave him before the Battle of Badajoz. In this story, spoken as a piece of doggerel by Holloway in a northern accent, Sam has his pudding confiscated when a sparrow flies out of the barrel of his musket which he has neglected to clean. Wellington brings Sam his own gun, asking him to reload it, which he does with plenty of powder behind the cannon ball, in order to give them the best chance of smashing the walls of Badajoz. The cannon duly does the job, and Wellington expresses his delight by telling Sam he can have his pudding back. But then...

> Sam bent down to pick up 'is puddin'
> But it weren't there nowhere about.
> In the place where 'e thought 'e 'ad left it
> Were the cannon ball 'e 'ad tipped out!
> Sam saw in a flash what 'ad 'appened –
> By an unprecedented mis'ap
> The puddin' 'is mother 'ad sent 'im
> 'Ad blown Badajoz off the map!

Holloway concludes by remarking that the emblem of a flaming grenade on the cap badge of the Grenadier Guards is in fact a brass representation of Sam's Christmas pudding.

At least Ben Battle and Sam Small survived the bloody siege, which was the third attempt to take the town and in fact claimed the lives of almost five thousand British troops. Badajoz finally fell during the night of 6-7 April 1812. In January of that year Wellington had captured the great frontier fortress of Ciudad Rodrigo to the north; now he had the more daunting task of taking the Extremaduran border stronghold of Badajoz, which would open the way to Madrid. The French first besieged Badajoz at the beginning of the war, but it was not captured, by Marshal Soult, until the first months of 1811. Wellington, in Portugal, was exasperated at the defeat and surrender of the Spanish garrison and ordered General William Beresford to lay siege to the town. This he did in the first week of May, but withdrew a few days later when he heard that Marshal Soult was heading towards him with 24,000 troops.

British forces, supported by a larger number of Spanish troops under Generals Blake and Castaños, engaged the French at Albuera, a few miles south of Badajoz, in a battle which left more than twelve thousand dead in a single day (16 May). 'Oh Albuera, glorious field of grief!' was how Byron put it in *Childe Harold's Pilgrimage*. The tiled memorial tablets on the road approaching the village of Albuera are inscribed (in Spanish, English, French and Portuguese) with the moving words: 'In rows, just like they fought, they lay like the hay in the open countryside when the night falls and the mower falls silent. That is how they were slain.' The allies claimed a tactical victory: Soult had failed to relieve the siege of Badajoz, which was resumed three days later. But when, at the beginning of June, the new French commander, Auguste Marmont, brought his Army of Portugal into Spain to join up with Soult's, Wellington decided it would be wise to take his troops back across the Portuguese border.

After Ciudad Rodrigo, Wellington determined to take Badajoz as soon as possible and before Soult and Marmont, advancing from different directions, could meet up and attack him. The garrison commander, Baron Philippon, had repaired the damage done by the two previous sieges and strengthened the defences. With a new set of iron siege guns, Wellington hurled some twenty thousand cannon balls at the city's near-impregnable walls for two weeks before the assault began.* Breaches were made on the south side, but some walls, up to thirty feet high, would have to be scaled with ladders. Preliminary clashes outside the town walls were mostly inconclusive, though one fort was successfully stormed, using howitzers, in the last week of March. With the help of a large number of *afrancesados* (French sympathisers) among the Spanish inhabitants, Philippon had time to fill the breached walls and the ditches below with horribly ingenious devices—*chevaux-de-frise*, planks studded with spikes and Toledo steel sword blades. At the foot of the walls were not only moats and ditches, made deeper by digging trenches in them, but the Rivillas stream, which had been dammed. Wet weather had added to the hazards, and many British troops were drowned in the flooded ditches before they reached the walls.

The attack began around 10 p.m. on Easter Sunday, 6 April 1812. Those who got as far as the breached curtain wall between the Trinidad and Santa Maria bastions had to scramble over the mountain of rubble covered not only with *chevaux-de-frise* but with exploding mines which, as they neared the top, 'cast up friends and foes together, who in burning torture slashed and shrieked in the air'. The defenders were armed with muskets, guns loaded with grapeshot, barrels of gunpowder and burning bundles of wood which were rolled down on to the hapless 'Forlorn Hopes' leading the uphill climb.† A rifleman in the Light Division wrote afterwards: 'Among the dead and wounded bodies around me I endeavoured to screen myself from the

* Wellington's chief engineer, Lieutenant Colonel Richard Fletcher, having been responsible for the Lines of Torres Vedras, supervised the breaching of the Badajoz walls. Though he was wounded when a bullet forced a silver dollar into his groin—hitting him, it was said, where it hurt most, in his purse—he continued to give invaluable advice to Wellington throughout the siege. He was killed during the assault on San Sebastián the following year.

† As the name suggests, they were the first into a breach, and the ones most likely to be killed by the defenders. They were usually volunteers, many of them wearing a badge with the letters VS, for Valiant Stormer.

enemy's shot… The fire continued to blaze over me in all its horrors, accompanied by screams, groans and shouts, the crashing of stones and the falling of timbers. For the first time in many years I uttered something like a prayer.' Another account carried the comment: 'If a man fell wounded, ten to one he never rose again, for the volleys of musketry and grapeshot that were poured amongst us made our situation too horrid for description. I had seen some fighting, but nothing like this.'

It was the bloodiest night of the Peninsular War: the main assaults on the two bastions were no sooner repulsed than they were renewed, and repulsed again; two thousand of Wellington's men had been lost in an hour. Attacks by escalade were also being made on the San Vicente bastion at the western end of the city, and on the old Moorish castle situated above and behind the walls in the north-east corner. The 3rd Division, commanded by General Picton, advanced on the castle walls with bugles sounding. Ladders had to be brought across the ditches and the sloping ground to the foot of the walls, where the defenders shot the men as they climbed or pushed the ladders away from the walls, causing the British soldiers to fall on the bayonets of their comrades below them. Picton was wounded but continued to direct the assault.

Eventually, around midnight, with the weight of men on the ladders, an officer of Campbell's Brigade was able to lead his fusiliers over the Alcazaba wall and along the ramparts. The castle was soon taken, the French flag torn down from its flagstaff and a red jacket raised in its place. A messenger, sent to find Wellington, galloped up to him with the unforgettable words: 'My Lord, the castle is your own.' At about the same time the 5th Division under General Leith was scaling the walls of the San Vicente bastion, some of whose defenders had been drawn off to man the breaches. Once over a lower section of wall which they had identified, the British assailants fought their way round the ramparts, wielding swords and bayonets, and forced open the town gates to link up with Picton's troops within the fort. The battle was effectively over, General Philippon escaped across the Guadiana river and had surrendered by morning.

There then followed what has been described as one of the worst orgies of indiscipline in British military history. As Elizabeth Longford put it in *Wellington – The Years of the Sword*: 'Sudden release from one hell only plunged them into another. Every door was battered in, old men were shot, women raped, children bayoneted.' Fuelled by liquor, Wellington's soldiers went mad with rage, revenge and relief at having survived. As they plundered and killed and tore rings from the ears and fingers of any women in their path, no distinction was made between the French occupiers and the Spanish inhabitants. The experience of an Irish corporal, Ned Costello, illustrates the hell that the British troops had had to go through. A volunteer with the Light Division's 'Forlorn Hopes', he was carrying a ladder with three others who were shot dead beside him. He was drenched in their blood before falling into a flooded ditch, up to his neck in water. Clambering up the rubble of the Trinidad breach, his face was badly cut by a blade from the *chevaux-de-frise*. He made it into the town, and was on the point of shooting the first Frenchman he encountered when, conscious of what was happening all around him, he restrained himself. 'The shouts and oaths of drunken soldiers in quest of more liquor, the reports of firearms and crashing in of doors, together with the appalling shrieks of hapless women, might have induced anyone to believe himself in the region of the damned.'

They might equally have believed it a couple of hours earlier. Wellington was said to have wept openly when he saw the piles of corpses at the foot of the walls. He may have tacitly acknowledged the general assumption of the victors' right to sack a captured town after such appalling loss of life, although Richard Ford, for whom Wellington was a hero without blemish, wrote that while 'doing everything to prevent excesses [he] was obliged to retire to escape being shot by the infuriate soldiers'. He entered the town the following evening and ordered the looting to cease, under threat of execution, but it continued for another two days without any punishment being meted out. Wellington was to write later, as if he was reluctant, or powerless, to do anything about the disgraceful behaviour of his soldiers (whom he famously described the following year as 'the scum of the earth'):

'Unfortunate Badajoz met with the usual fate of places taken at the point of a bayonet.'

Of those officers and men who refrained from plunder and rape, one in particular stands out. Major Harry Smith was approached in the town by two sisters seeking the protection of a sympathetic officer. Their house had been destroyed by rampaging British troops, they had just had their earrings torn off them, and blood was trickling down their necks. Smith not only took pity on them and gave them shelter: he proposed marriage to the younger one, aged only fourteen, and married her three days later in Wellington's presence. Juana Maria de los Dolores de Leon, now Mrs Smith, followed her husband for the rest of the Peninsular War, and later travelled with him when he served in South Africa and India.* By now General Sir Harry Smith, he returned to South Africa as governor of Cape Colony. His Spanish wife's name, Lady Smith, was given to a town in Natal which would become famous during the Boer War. She died in 1872, sixty years after the taking of Badajoz.

On the day after the battle, Wellington wrote to Lord Liverpool, then Secretary of State for War: 'The capture of Badajoz affords as strong an instance of the gallantry of our troops as has ever been displayed. But I greatly hope that I shall never again be the instrument of putting them to such a test as that to which they were put last night.' It was a victory won at enormous cost, but a significant one, giving Wellington access to the interior of Spain, while the French high command, taking orders from Napoleon in Austria or from his ineffectual brother in Madrid, had lost the initiative. Wellington had now left Portugal behind him and was well on his way to expelling the French from the peninsula. Three months later he was victorious at the Battle of Salamanca, which constituted the turning-point of the war.

One might have thought that in Badajoz today there would be a memorial to the thousands of British troops who sacrificed their lives in liberating the town, and perhaps a statue of Wellington. But I could

* The story is told, vividly and with historical accuracy, in *The Spanish Bride* by Georgette Heyer.

find no mention of Wellington in Badajoz. At the time of the two hundredth anniversary of the battle, an obelisk was erected in a small garden facing the Santa Maria bastion. Its four sides are dedicated to the four principal countries involved in the Badajoz sieges—Spain, Britain, Portugal, France—and inscribed with the same words in their respective languages. The English plaque reads: 'To those who took part in the defence, assaults and occupations during the sieges of Badajoz 1811-12', beneath the royal coat of arms. It is all very even-handed and uninformative: no mention of the resistance to the French invader by the other three countries, nor even of what the Spanish call La Guerra de la Independencia.

For anyone unfamiliar with the history of the Napoleonic war in the peninsula, there is a hint in the park on the other side of the road which crosses the Rivillas stream and is today called Calle del Rivilla. A notice facing what was the Trinidad bastion records 'the most bloody episode' of the war when, on the night of 6 April 1812, 'British troops assaulted the town which was defended by the French'. The number of dead at the foot of the walls is put at 'more than 3,500', and credit for the success of the siege given to 'the troops of General Picton' who were able to scale the walls of the castle 'by means of wobbly wooden ladders, leading to the unconditional surrender of Badajoz to the British army'. A little further along, '1812' is studded into the wall at the site of one of the breaches.

There is no love lost between the people of Badajoz and the British troops who ejected the French occupying forces from their town. The local inhabitants (*pacenses* is the name given to them, a word also suggesting peaceable and patient) have long memories of the sack of Badajoz and the murder and rape of its inhabitants after the end of the siege. Whenever the question has been raised of erecting a memorial on the battle site to honour the British dead, the bad feeling has resurfaced and the idea has been opposed. At the beginning of this century a local resident was quoted as saying: 'We don't want a memorial to a horde of devils and savages who raped our women and profaned our churches.' Another claimed that the British only came to Spain to expand their influence: 'We don't need another monument to British imperialism. We already have Gibraltar.' A commemorative plaque to the British fallen which should have been placed on the Badajoz walls had to be taken over the border to Portugal. There, in the English cemetery within the walled town of Elvas, little more than ten miles from Badajoz, stands a memorial to 'The Storming of Badajoz'. The divisions and brigades involved in the siege are all listed, beneath the words 'In Hell Before Daylight'.

The reputation of Wellington's army for destruction, rape and pillage—the practice started at Ciudad Rodrigo—was confirmed the following year by its behaviour after the battles of Vitoria and San Sebastián. Nor was Wellington himself greatly respected in Spain. Apart from his failure to halt the sack of Badajoz, he was consistently rude about his Spanish allies. In one communication to the war minister, Earl Bathurst, he wrote that, 'they are, in general, the most incapable of useful exertion of all the nations that I have known: the most vain, and at the same time the most ignorant, particularly of military affairs, and above all of military affairs in their own country… I am afraid that the utmost we can hope for is to teach them how to avoid being beat.'

Unsurprisingly, such critical and patronising comments did little for Wellington's popularity in Spain. He defined 'the national disease' as 'boasting of the strength and power of Spain… then sitting down quietly and indulging their national indolence.' He was especially contemptuous of the Spanish officer class—'they oppose or render fruitless every measure to set them right or save them… I cannot say that [they] do anything as it ought to be done, with the exception of running away'—though he did admire the campaign of sabotage conducted by the guerrilla bands, which did much to lower French morale. Wellington also remarked, seeking to explain the poor relationship between the British and Spanish armies, that 'jealousy of the interference of foreigners in their internal concerns is the characteristic of all Spaniards.'

However, not all Spaniards were jealous of the interference of Napoleon in their country. There was a minority of radicals who, having made contact with French intellectuals and absorbed some of their literature, were increasingly hostile to a traditionalist Spain ruled by an absolute, if ineffectual, monarchy and a reactionary Church which still maintained the tribunals of the Inquisition. They looked approvingly at what was happening in revolutionary France, and even welcomed the imposition of Joseph Bonaparte as king in 1808 (he abolished the Inquisition). But these *afrancesado* 'liberals', who four years later would establish a short-lived constitution in Cádiz, were outnumbered by the mass of xenophobic Spaniards who were nevertheless prepared to accept Anglo-Portuguese help in their struggle for independence from France. While that assistance, or interference, was crucial to the expulsion of Napoleon's armies from the peninsula, it is perhaps not too hard to understand why the occupied country did not indulge in too many public expressions of gratitude towards its allies. With one or two exceptions, as H. V. Morton wrote in *A Stranger in Spain*, 'you could travel all over Spain without realising that British armies under the Duke of Wellington fought there during the Peninsular War.' (On the other hand, Wellington's predecessor in Spain, General Sir John Moore, is more fondly remembered for his fighting retreat to La Coruña, and his death in action, which all Spaniards respect, in January 1809.)

Twenty years after the siege of Badajoz, Sir Benjamin Badcock Lovell, on a military mission to Portugal, crossed the border in order to visit the battle site but was not made welcome. After some negotiation with the governor, he was allowed only to walk round the battered walls under escort. However, when George Borrow crossed the Portuguese frontier to Badajoz four years later with his New Testament bibles, he did not encounter—at least he did not mention encountering—any hostility. For most of the three weeks he spent in the town, he was in the company of gypsies, to whom he tried to preach the gospel; he embarked on a translation of St Luke's gospel into the Spanish gypsy tongue. He arrived in Badajoz on a heavily-laden mule, crossing the River Guadiana by the sixteenth-century Puente de Palmas, with its thirty arches. The banks of the river, he wrote in *The Bible in Spain*, 'were white with linen which the washerwomen had spread out to dry in the sun… I heard their singing at a great distance, and the theme seemed to be the praises of the river where they were toiling.'

V. S. Pritchett was here in 1928, setting off on his walk through Extremadura to Vigo in Galicia. He too crossed the same bridge, on which 'the donkeys and mules increased and the songs with them. A gypsy was singing in his shack by the river.' When I walked across the bridge some years ago, there were donkeys grazing near the eucalyptus groves on the riverbank, and an old woman in black was on her knees, gathering what appeared to be grass and stuffing it into a plastic sack, watched by two mongrel dogs. But she wasn't singing. On a more recent visit I noticed that part of the riverbank on the northern side has been reclaimed for development. Featureless modern Badajoz is spreading almost to the river's edge, but the view towards the old town as you walk across the bridge is still impressive, with the walls of the Arab fortress enclosing the remains of the castle, a Moorish tower and a large wooded park. Before I reached the two squat towers of the Puerta de Palmas, once a gate in the walls and giving entrance to the town, I watched a stork paddling in the rushes and an ibis standing on a lily-pad. Beneath one of the bridge's arches a talkative family of geese was swimming upstream.

It is not until you walk up the grassy slope to the foot of the walls that you begin to appreciate how daunting was the task that faced Wellington's troops on that night two hundred years ago. A contemporary painting by Richard Simkin gives some indication of the hell endured by Picton's division as some of them struggled to the tops of their wooden ladders and clambered on to the ramparts of the Alcazaba, brandishing rifles and bayonets. Some Moorish arches remain today, also a Moorish palace converted to a convent and a military hospital which is now the municipal library. I walked up to the castle one evening, when the battlements were silhouetted against a full moon appearing from behind cloud, and looked on the lights of cars flashing by, alongside the river on the road below. It was easy enough to imagine that the lights were exploding shells, and that a distant noise was the beat of regimental drums.

The founding of Badajoz is generally attributed to Ibn Marwan, towards the end of the ninth century; it remained in Moorish hands for more than three hundred years. Muslim influence continued for centuries afterwards, not only in the Mudejar architecture but in the atmosphere of the place. During his visit in the 1920s, Pritchett observed a town 'as oriental as Tunis. It was little more than an Arab Kasbah... Every doorstep had its trade. There were carpenters, smiths, wheelwrights, cart makers, basket makers... and a procession of donkeys carrying cans of milk, or baskets of oranges like red-hot coals, or a struggling sack of chickens tied together in bunches by the legs.' Today one may see Arabic carving in stone on doorway lintels, and a hammam with an Arab inscription over its wooden door.

I found this especially poignant in view of what happened to Badajoz in August 1936, when dreadful atrocities were committed by Moorish troops, in some ways depressingly similar to what had occurred there little more than a century before. During the first weeks of the Civil War, the Army of Africa was moving north through Andalusia under its aggressive field commander, Lieutenant Colonel Juan Yagüe who, with units of the Spanish Foreign Legion and *regulares indigenas* (tribal mercenaries recruited in Morocco), advanced at speed northwards from Seville, took Mérida and then turned west towards Badajoz. When they reached the walled town and encircled it, a Nationalist aeroplane dropped thousands of leaflets warning of the massacre to come.

The defenders of Badajoz numbered about two thousand, of whom one thousand two hundred were poorly armed militiamen, against many more of Yagüe's hardened soldiers and bloodthirsty mercenaries. On the morning of 14 August troops of the fourth *bandera* of the Legion stormed the Puerta de la Trinidad and breached the walls at the same point where the main assault had been made in 1812. Other artillery units forced their way through the southern walls, while Moroccan *regulares* took the Puerta de los Carros which, appropriately enough, gave them access to the fortress built by their countrymen nearly a thousand years before. Now, in chilling repetition of the activities of Wellington's soldiers when they had

30

scaled the walls of Badajoz and entered the town in 1812, Yagüe's troops embarked on an orgy of looting, raping and killing. Even those who had thrown down their arms were shot, as were those who took refuge in the cathedral, where fighting took place on the altar steps. Anyone found with bruises on his or her shoulder from rifle recoil was shot immediately. Corpses were castrated or sexually mutilated by the Moorish mercenaries, while the *legionarios* ripped out any gold-capped teeth, smashing them with their rifle butts.

The retribution of 1936 then turned from victors' plunder and street shooting into a massacre on an altogether different scale. Numbers are impossible to verify, but possibly more than two thousand men and women, many of them non-political civilians and refugees from elsewhere in southern Spain, were herded into the town's bullring over the next two days and machine-gunned to death. There were stories of Yagüe's savage and often drunken troops treating their prisoners as if in a bullfight, stabbing them with blades before cutting off their ears as they died. The Butcher of Badajoz, as Yagüe became known, when asked about the massacre by an American correspondent, was quoted as having said: 'Of course we shot them. Was I supposed to take four thousand Reds with me as my column advanced, racing against time? Was I expected to turn them loose in my rear and let them make Badajoz Red again?' So instead he had them murdered and made the bullring red with their blood. Others were shot at the municipal cemetery, where piles of corpses were dumped, burned and buried in mass graves. When a foreign reporter questioned a priest at the cemetery, he was told: 'They deserved it.' Refugees who managed to escape across the Portuguese border were often arrested and handed back, to be summarily executed in Badajoz.

In view of the atrocities committed or condoned by members of the Spanish Foreign Legion, many of them Africanistas (Spanish officers who had served in and in many cases been brutalised by the colonial war in Morocco), it is extraordinary to find in Badajoz today a park called the Parque de la Legion which, according to a notice, 'owes its name to the combatants of this corps who fell during the taking of the town in the Civil War in 1936'. When the garden and park were established in 1940, a year after the end of the Civil War, at the foot of the walls between the Trinidad bastion and the Alcazaba, it was of course to be expected that it would be named by Franco's victorious Nationalists to commemorate those who had lost their lives in a battle against the Republic. What is so surprising, when all statues of Franco and streets named after him and other Nationalist leaders have been expunged from modern Spain, is that this park's name has never been changed. According to the historian Professor Paul Preston, the best evidence now puts the number of casualties suffered by Yagüe's troops in the attack on Badajoz at one hundred and forty-five, of whom forty-four were killed. Yet the Republican dead totalled several thousand, many of them gunned down by *legionarios* shouting their blood-curdling cry, '¡*Viva la Muerte!*' ('Long Live Death!'). For the oldest residents of Badajoz the *pacto del olvido*—the tacit agreement to forget the horrors and internecine conflicts of the Civil War—still persists; perhaps the young ones are not inquisitive or interested. They have nothing to forget.

When I walked down the narrow Calle Melendez Valdes from the Plaza de España one evening, it was not difficult to imagine the *legionarios* and the Moroccan *regulares* firing indiscriminately at the local residents as they cowered behind the glass-covered balconies of their small houses or ran in desperation towards what they thought would be the safety of the cathedral. I passed a stone doorway with Moorish carving, opposite a greengrocer's shop bearing the name 'Frutas Matamoros'. But it was the Moros who did the killing in August 1936. At the bottom of the street the UGT (General Workers' Union) building, in which Yagüe would certainly have taken no prisoners, today ironically houses a centre for '*personas inmigrantes*'.

The old Badajoz bullring, scene of the massacres, was abandoned, though not until the 1960s. For many years afterwards, it was surrounded by a wire fence barring access, it seemed, to the guilty secret of its past. In its place, at the end of the twentieth century, a Palacio de Congresos was built, following the circular shape of the old plaza de toros, with a high screen of steel strips enclosing the hall and young trees planted in the forecourt. It was opened in 2006 and is used for conferences as well as concerts. In the same year the massacre at Badajoz was declared to have been genocide.

A Nueva Plaza de Toros was opened in 1967, a couple of hundred metres from the Parque de la Legion. One oppressively hot summer's evening, when the temperature registered 42°C and every one of the thirteen thousand seats in the plaza was taken, I watched a fascinating *corrida de figuras* (namely José Tomas and El Juli), when the only blood on the sand was from six brave bulls.

TOLEDO

The naming of the American town of Toledo, in the state of Ohio between Detroit and Cleveland, may or may not have had something to do with Washington Irving. He wrote books of Spanish history, served as US ambassador to Spain in the nineteenth century and had a brother who lived in Ohio. However, Toledo's newspaper, *The Blade*, is unquestionably so called because of the association of the ancient 'imperial city' of Spain with the making of swords—a reputation which it has held for more than two thousand years. The blades, which used to be made of Bilbao steel, were known to Shakespeare: in *The Merry Wives of Windsor* Falstaff speaks of 'a good bilbo', a sword of such temper and elasticity that it could be bent until the point touched the hilt. (Falstaff was comparing it to himself, bent double in a laundry basket.) Shakespeare would also have had the Toledo blade in mind when he has Othello referring to 'a sword of Spain, the icebrook's temper', with which he kills himself. Toledo swords are still evident in the city today, especially in tourist shops which may remind the numerous Japanese visitors of their Samurai warrior past.

Most visitors to Toledo are led to believe that it was formerly the capital of Spain, but that is not quite accurate. When Alfonso VI captured Toledo from the Moors in 1085, it became the principal residence of the royal court, with the King as self-styled Emperor of All Spain. It was not until 1561, when Philip II removed the court to Madrid, that Spain had what was declared to be its capital city. Earlier in his reign the court had moved between Toledo and Valladolid. Ferdinand and Isabella had been married in Valladolid and built a monastery in Toledo where they wished to be buried—though, when the time came, they were buried in Granada. With its narrow streets, hills around the city and space restricted by the bend in the River Tagus, Toledo was not suited to be an expanding commercial and political capital. But for centuries after Philip II left for Madrid, it was argued that Toledo was and should be restored as the cultural capital of Spain, 'the heart of the Spanish spirit'.

More significantly, perhaps, Toledo was known as the City of Three Religions and Cultures, a title bestowed during the time of Alfonso VI. It was a time of tolerance: Jews, Moors and Christians lived in relative harmony, as they did under the Caliphate in Cordoba during the previous century, while keeping their own traditions and administering their communities with a degree of autonomy. Before the Moors arrived in the eighth century, Jews had suffered many restrictions and indignities during the Visigothic period, but their lot improved before the Reconquest. Under Moorish rule they were required to learn Arabic, but were permitted to build their own synagogues. Toledo was a provincial capital of the Cordoba Caliphate until the eleventh century.

When the Archbishop of Toledo started the School of Translators in the cathedral library around 1140, many of its scholars were Jewish, translating texts from Arabic into Latin, sometimes via Castilian. A hundred years later, Alfonso X ('the Wise') expanded the school, while insisting that in future the translated language should be not Latin but Castilian.* He commissioned a number of Jewish translators, including Yehuda ben Moshe (also the King's physician) and Isaac ibn Sid, who collaborated on important astronomical and astrological texts. It was during this century that the number of synagogues in the city reached nine, but thereafter things began to go downhill for the Toledan Jews. A Dominican friar, Vicente Ferrer, who was canonised after his death, is said to have been responsible for encouraging anti-Semitic riots in Toledo at the end of the fourteenth century. Most of the inhabitants of the Juderia, including rabbis, were put to the sword,

---

* His half-sister, Eleanor of Castile, married Edward I in Burgos (before he became king) and was the mother of Edward II. She is not to be confused with Eleanor of England, daughter of Henry II and sister of Richard the Lionheart, who became Queen of Castile in the previous century by marrying Alfonso VIII. Both she and her husband are buried in the convent of Las Huelgas in Burgos, which she founded. The Spanish Eleanor died in Nottinghamshire and is buried in two places: her body in Westminster Abbey and her viscera in Lincoln Cathedral.

and synagogues were demolished. Many of the remaining Jews were persuaded by Fray Vicente to convert to Christianity, but this did not stop the city council of Toledo from banning these *conversos* from holding any public office. Around 1405, following an armed attack on the main synagogue, probably at the saintly friar's instigation, it was converted into a Christian church which, some suggested, should be called San Vicente del Sangre. It was in fact named Santa Maria la Blanca, which is how it remains today, while still being referred to as a *sinagoga*.

What is so remarkable about this 'synagogue' (one of only two remaining in Toledo today) is its fusion of three religions. Santa Maria la Blanca was originally built at the end of the twelfth century, in Mudejar Moorish style by a Jewish councillor to a Christian king. It has a mosaic floor, rows of horseshoe arches on octagonal pillars, surmounted by multifoil arches leading up to a wooden-framed ceiling. On a much smaller scale, the interior puts one in mind of the great mosque in Cordoba. A Star of David is still visible high above the central nave. Below it, on the day I was there, a nun seated at a table was knitting a rug. Close by, the synagogue known as El Transito—dedicated to the Passing of the Virgin—was converted to a church at the time of the expulsion of the Jews from Spain in 1492. Built by Samuel ha-Levi, treasurer to Pedro the Cruel, King of Castile, one of the inner walls is adorned with intricate plasterwork, carvings and Moorish arabesques reminiscent of the Alhambra in Granada. Gerald Brenan wrote that these arabesque patterns had an hypnotic, almost mystical effect on him: 'The surface of the wall had the apparent complexity of nature, yet everything in it—even the Hebrew writing which affirmed its purpose—was under the law of order and eternal recurrence. This gave a deep feeling of satisfaction and reassurance.'

There are both Arabic and Hebrew inscriptions, and an upper gallery where one can imagine the Sephardic women in elaborate head-dresses watching the proceedings below. The Mudejar influence on the architecture of Toledo continued through the centuries, most recently in the hall of the city's railway station—rebuilt in the 1920s—

complete with mosaic flooring and copper lanterns. The aspect of the city, and of the landscape overlooking it on the other side of the Tagus, convinced the twentieth-century philosopher and physician Gregorio Marañon that Toledo was not Castilian but oriental: 'And it's not just the city, but the countryside on the left bank of the river, that so closely resembles the Holy Land. Here the olives seem sacred, the flocks of sheep have a biblical air about them, and the footprints in the earth, smelling of rosemary, could belong to the feet of a prophet.'

There is nothing oriental about the great Gothic cathedral of Toledo, except for the form of the Mass which is held in one of its chapels. The Christians who continued to practise their faith under Moorish rule were known as Mozarabs. As Spain was reconquered by the Christian kings, it was decreed by the Pope, to encourage unity of worship, that in future only the Roman rite of the Mass should be used. But the Mozarabs of Toledo refused to abandon the ancient liturgy which they had used not only throughout three centuries of Arab rule but in the previous Visigothic era. Toledans were allowed to retain the Mozarabic rite in six parishes of the city, until at the beginning of the sixteenth century Cardinal Cisneros, Archbishop of Toledo, published a Mozarabic missal and breviary and, with approval from Rome, established a chapel in the cathedral where celebration of the Mozarabic rite of the Mass continues to this day.*

A few minutes before 9 a.m., I walked past an official at the main door and, mumbling the word *misa*, into the cathedral an hour before any tourists would be admitted. Three circular stained-glass windows in the south aisle, beautifully illuminated by the morning sun behind them, endorsed Richard Ford's comment that at certain times of day the windows would 'brighten up like rubies and emeralds'. The silence and emptiness were awe-inspiring. A priest in red cassock and shoulder-cape hurried from the shadows towards a heavy wooden door protected by an iron grille and surmounted by Cisneros' coat of arms and an image of the Piedad. In the brightly lit interior of the chapel

---

* Cardinal Ximenes de Cisneros was also Grand Inquisitor, twice Regent of Spain, and founder of the country's largest university, at Alcalá de Henares.

seven priests, all cloaked in red, were seated facing a congregation of three. Beneath the tall octagonal dome (a later design by El Greco's son) a wall painting by Juan de Borgoña depicts the siege and capture of the North African town of Oran in 1509, led, and funded, by Cisneros in his role as military leader. I was fortunate to be able to see inside the Mozarabic chapel, which is opened each day only for the hour of the service.

I have to admit that the form of the Mass meant very little to me. According to the ecclesiastical scholar, Christopher Howse, in his book *A Pilgrim in Spain*, the proceedings are mostly in Latin, with occasional interjections of Greek and, most interestingly, when the time came for Communion, the breaking of the consecrated Host into nine pieces. The priest then 'arranged the fragments on circles traced on the paten in the pattern of a cross, each fragment representing an event in the mystery of redemption'. To H. V. Morton, in *A Stranger in Spain*, the prayers and responses of the Mozarabic Mass reminded him of interminable Eastern liturgies; they were followed by a recitation of the Diptychs and the naming of a long list of saints. Morton goes on to say that the most remarkable thing about the Mozarabic rite is that it lives on in the English *Book of Common Prayer*:

> It seems that when our prayer book was being compiled Cardinal Cisneros had just published the Mozarabic liturgy, and a copy is believed to have come into the hands of Cranmer, who was impressed by the beauty of the prayers. Many of these he, or his collaborators, lifted bodily from the Mozarabic rite into the Prayer Book. The exhortations beginning, 'Dearly beloved brethren, the scripture moveth us...' are pure Mozarabic, while innumerable collects are straight translations of the Mozarabic or are adapted from them, notably the collects for Christmas Day, for the first Sunday in Lent and for St Andrew's Day.*

* 'O Lord, who for our sake didst fast forty days and forty nights; Give us grace to use such abstinence, that, our flesh being subdued to the Spirit, we may ever obey...' The line from the Benedicite – 'O Ananias, Azarias and Misael, bless ye the Lord' is included in the blessings recited in the Mozarabic Mass.

So a primitive liturgy having its ancient origins in Spain is incorporated in a Protestant prayer book familiar throughout the Anglican Communion. Elsewhere in Toledo Cathedral another English connection may be found with a bit of diligent research. The Capilla de Los Reyes Nuevos has four tombs: those of Henry II of Castile and his wife, and their grandson Henry III and his wife. The sarcophagus of Henry III's wife has her holding a prayer book, her head resting on three embroidered cushions and wearing a crown. A stone tablet above, held by two putti, has lettering which is hard to make out, but I was just able to read, from a magnified photographic image, that this was the tomb of Reina Doña Catalina de Castilla e Leon, the daughter of the Duque e Duquesa de Alencastre. The Duque de Alencastre (Duke of Lancaster) was John of Gaunt, and the Duquesa (his second wife) Constance, daughter of Peter I of Castile. The inscription credits him with '*paz y concordia prevista para siempre*' ('peace and goodwill expected to last forever')—an ironic description of a man who was more commonly known as Pedro the Cruel. Doña Catalina is named as *nieta* (granddaughter) of Don Pedro, though no mention is made of her paternal grandfather, Edward III, whose son Edward, the Black Prince, went to Spain to fight for Pedro, winning the Battle of Nájera in 1367 against Henry of Trastámara. Pedro surrendered to Edward a ruby which he had taken from a Moorish prince; it was brought to England and is set in the Imperial State Crown. In another link with Spain, Catalina's half-brother Henry IV married Joan of Navarre after the death of his first wife, Henry V's mother. Both the Black Prince and Joan are buried in Canterbury Cathedral.

Catalina, who lies in Toledo Cathedral, was born Catherine of Lancaster in Hertford Castle. H. V. Morton tells us that she knew Geoffrey Chaucer and was living in her father's palace in the Strand at the time of Wat Tyler's rebellion. Then, aged fifteen, a marriage was arranged for her with Prince Henry of Castile, who was nine. He inherited the throne two years later, and Catherine bore him three children before he died in his twenties. She was said to be almost six feet tall, with auburn hair and physically robust, but she ate and drank heavily, became obese and died from a stroke in Valladolid at the age of forty-five. Her son was John II of Castile whose daughter Isabella united the thrones of Castile and Aragon through her marriage to Ferdinand, and expelled the Moors and Jews from Spain in 1492.

The intermingling of Spanish and English royal blood continued from the time of John of Gaunt for at least a hundred and fifty years. Within the space of a year, both Pedro the Cruel's daughters were married to English noblemen: Constance to John of Gaunt, and Isabella to John's brother, Edmund of Langley, who became the ancestors of the Yorkists Edward IV, Edward V, Richard III and, through his marriage to Elizabeth of York, Henry VII. The Spanish link was becoming a bit tenuous by now, but Henry VII did his best to strengthen it by arranging for his elder son, Arthur, to marry the youngest daughter of Ferdinand and Isabella, Catherine of Aragon. Arthur died after a few months, and it was left to his younger brother, when he became Henry VIII, to do his duty and shore up the Spanish connection. By marrying Catherine's daughter Mary in Winchester Cathedral in 1554, Philip II would become King of England and Ireland, a title which he could claim for only four years until Mary's death. But he could also trace a thin English line from Catherine of Lancaster (the Doña Catalina in Toledo Cathedral), via her granddaughter Isabella of Castile, whose daughter Juana ('the Mad') was the mother of Emperor Charles V and Philip's grandmother. (Isabella was also, of course, Mary Tudor's grandmother.)

Seventy years after a Spanish king came to England to marry, a future king of England went to Madrid in the hope of securing himself a wife. The Thirty Years' War had begun, and James I convinced himself, though not Parliament, that the way to avoid war with Spain was by a marriage between his son Charles, Prince of Wales, and the Spanish Habsburg Infanta, Maria Anna, sister of Philip IV. (Ten years earlier, negotiations had begun for Charles's elder brother Henry to marry the Infanta, but he died suddenly of typhoid fever.) Charles and the Duke of Buckingham travelled incognito to Madrid in the winter of 1623, by one account with false beards and calling themselves Smith and Brown, and turned up unannounced at the British Ambassador's residence, the Casa de las Siete Chimeneas ('the House of the Seven

Chimneys') in the appropriately named Calle de las Infantas. It was a serious breach of protocol, but contact was swiftly made with the royal court and with the prime minister, Count-Duke of Olivares, and a lavish state entry into the city was arranged. There were street performances and dancing along the route to the royal palace, and prisoners were released from jail.

When Charles met the eighteen-year-old Spanish king, it was said that 'the greatest matter that passed between them was compliments'. However, the Queen presented him with a gift of table linen and, perhaps surprisingly, underwear. Philip's welcome to his unexpected guest continued with parades, fireworks displays and bullfights in the Plaza Mayor, specially arranged in the Prince of Wales's honour. He was given rooms in the palace but never allowed to speak to the Infanta in private. Though Charles was persuaded to agree that anti-Catholic legislation in his father's kingdoms would be abolished, leading Philip IV to anticipate a Habsburg-Stuart union, he was not going to convert to Catholicism, nor was the Infanta going to marry a heretic. The diplomats Sir Kenelm Digby and Sir Endymion Porter were in Madrid, doing their best to reach a satisfactory outcome, but the Spanish Match, as it was called, never got off the ground. So after a few months of restrained courtesies the Prince of Wales and Buckingham rode north to Santander and set sail for England. The proposed Anglo-Spanish union had failed not only due to religious differences but because of Olivares's determined opposition to the match and his Machiavellian scheming with Rome to ensure that the Pope dictated terms which Charles would find it impossible to accept.

No sooner was Charles back in England than he persuaded his father James I to declare war on Spain. When he became king he immediately authorised, and Buckingham organised, a naval expedition against Cádiz. It was a complete failure. In the same year Charles married Henrietta Maria of France, whom he had met in Paris on his way to Spain. (His intended Spanish bride, Maria Anna, went on to marry Ferdinand III, the future Holy Roman Emperor.) A year after Charles's expedition to Madrid a satirical play, *A Game at Chess* by Thomas Middleton, was staged at the Globe Theatre. The failed negotiations for the proposed Anglo-Spanish marriage take up much of the play, in which the Spanish characters are referred to only as Black (King, Queen, Knight, etc.) and the English as White. The Infanta was the Black Queen and the Prince of Wales the White Knight. The play ran for only nine performances before it was taken off by order of the Privy Council.

Some good did come of Charles's trip across the Pyrenees: he was introduced to the paintings of Titian—in later life he acquired more than thirty of them—and to Velazquez, whom Philip brought to Madrid while Charles was there.* It was in Spain that he was inspired to become perhaps the greatest art collector in English history; as a start, a large number of canvases were bought and shipped back to England. After he became king, Charles received, as a gift from Rubens, his painting *The Escurial*, looking down on the distant royal residence from the Sierra de Guadarrama. (Today it can be seen at Longford Castle in Wiltshire.) A few years later, Charles commissioned the ceiling paintings by Rubens in the Whitehall Banqueting House. Following the example of Philip and Velazquez, he gave his patronage to Van Dyck, who had been Rubens's star pupil.

Since El Greco did not enjoy royal patronage, his work may not have come to the attention of the Prince of Wales during his sojourn in Madrid. The great Cretan made his home in Toledo in 1577, re-maining there until his death in 1614. He was commissioned in 1580 to paint an altarpiece (of the martyrdom of St Maurice) for a chapel in the Escorial, but Philip II rejected it and El Greco returned to his spiritual home in Toledo.

Back in the cathedral, the sacristy is the place to see El Greco's famous *Expolio*, or *The Disrobing of Christ*, and one of his series of portraits of the Apostles. A personal favourite is the affecting *Las Lagrimas de San Pedro* (*The Tears of St Peter*). Some writers and art historians have seen in these paintings evidence of El Greco's mysti-cism and his 'oriental soul'. The faces of the apostles may be open to that interpretation; Hemingway thought they were modelled on the

* Did Velazquez paint Charles's portrait? Laura Cumming explores the mys-tery in her riveting book, *The Vanishing Man*.

painter's homosexual friends. El Greco certainly appeared to capture the soul or spirit of late-sixteenth-century Spain, through the city in which he lived. Jan Morris has written that Toledo even looks like 'one of those El Greco characters who were in fact conceived here— towering, handsome, humourless, sad, a little bloodless'. Laurie Lee, passing through Toledo in 1935, found in the paintings, 'colours I'd never seen before, weeping purple, lime greens, bitter yellows; the long skulls of the saints and their shrunken eyelids, eyes coated with ecstatic denials, limbs and faces drawn upwards like spires ascending, robes flickering like tapered flames…'

At the beginning of the Civil War, when the siege of the Alcázar was raised and the half-starved survivors staggered out into the bombed and rubble-strewn streets, the image reminded one observer of an El Greco painting. Whatever reactions may be prompted by El Greco's work, there is in the cathedral a most unusual statue of the Virgin Mary with child, *La Virgen Blanca*, which shows her smiling as she stands at the entrance to the *coro*. This, I like to think, is in acknowledgment of the genius whose paintings are a few yards away in the sacristy. When the writer and art critic Robert Byron went to Toledo in the 1930s to see the El Grecos, he pronounced it 'the most beautiful town I had ever seen, where the author of those paintings lived'. He once said that he disliked all Western art after El Greco.

While both British and French troops were guilty of rape and pillage during the Peninsular War, the French must be held the more responsible for the indiscriminate ransacking of religious buildings and works of art. Having desecrated Toledo cathedral, Napoleon's troops went on to plunder and set fire to the monastery of San Juan de los Reyes. Built by Ferdinand and Isabella for Franciscan friars, to celebrate a military victory over the King of Portugal, its façade is decorated with chains and manacles said to have been used to fetter Christian prisoners set free at the time of the conquest of Granada by the Catholic monarchs. Three centuries later, Napoleon's soldiers did what they could to destroy this beautiful building overlooking the River Tagus. Richard Ford called San Juan de los Reyes 'one of the finest specimens of Gothic art in the world, all but demolished by the invaders, who entirely gutted and burnt the quarters of the monks. The splendid chapel escaped somewhat better, having been used as a stable for horses.'

The wonderful cloisters are on two levels: upstairs, where the Gothic/Mudejar arches support a coffered larch-wood ceiling, a notice records: 'The Catholic Monarchs equipped the monastery with an excellent library which the friars continued to enrich throughout the centuries until, on New Year's Eve 1808, the cloister together with the monastery was burnt down by Napoleon's army.' Some books and historical archives were saved, but they did not survive the dissolution of the monastic orders by the liberal prime minister Mendizábal in 1835.

The monastery was abandoned and in ruins when Theophile Gautier visited it five years later and bemoaned the actions of his fellow-countrymen: 'The altar, which was undoubtedly a masterpiece of sculpture and painting, has been pitilessly overthrown. These useless ravages sadden one's soul and make one doubt the intelligence of man: how can ancient stones be any obstacle to new ideas? Cannot a revolution take place without demolishing the past?' Restoration of San Juan de los Reyes began in 1883 and took eighty years. A community of Franciscan monks returned there in 1954, and the monastery functions today as a parish church. It is entirely appropriate that the Franciscans should have come back to the monastery where one of their number, Francisco Ximenez de Cisneros, spent some time as a friar in the fifteenth century before his elevation to high ecclesiastical and political office in Toledo.

The British cannot be acquitted of responsibility for some destruction in the city. In the first years of the eighteenth century, during the War of the Spanish Succession, soldiers of the Grand Alliance, which included Great Britain, burnt a large part of the fortress of the Alcázar. A century later French troops occupied it instead of burning it down, and it survived unscathed until 1936. The siege of the Alcázar at the start of the Civil War, and the relieving of it two months later, were well orchestrated as a symbol of Nationalist heroism. But

General Franco's decision to divert his forces (the Army of Africa) to Toledo from their march on Madrid may well have cost him the chance to take the capital before its defences were ready. Having spent three years as a cadet training at the Infantry Academy in the Alcázar, Franco was understandably reluctant to allow the fortress to be taken by the Republican enemy. He gave extravagant praise to the besieged cadets of the Academy, though in fact there were only six of them; the rest were away for the summer holiday. (The majority of the defenders of the Alcázar were members of the Guardia Civil.)

The Nationalist propaganda continued: the besieged commander, Colonel Moscardó, having supposedly greeted his liberators with the words '*Sin novedad en el Alcázar*' ('All quiet in the Alcázar'), had to repeat the performance two days later in front of Franco and a group of cameramen. The Republicans attempted to use Moscardó's son as a hostage, threatening to kill him unless the fortress was surrendered. The story that Moscardó spoke to his son on the telephone, telling him to shout ¡*Viva España!* and die like a hero, is almost certainly apocryphal. But the suffering was real enough: the scores of Republican hostages taken by the defenders into the Alcázar were never heard of again, the streets flowed with the blood of militiamen, and those wounded and taken to hospital were killed in their beds, burned to death by grenades. Many committed suicide to avoid capture by Moorish troops.

The murder of priests and monks in Toledo when the Civil War broke out was witnessed by the South African poet Roy Campbell. Having arrived with his family in Spain in 1933, he stayed in Barcelona, then lived near Altea further down the coast before moving to Toledo two years later. Campbell and his wife were received into the Catholic Church, confirmed in a secret ceremony by Cardinal Goma, primate and archbishop of Toledo. By this time anyone in a religious habit, or seen going to Mass, was in danger of attack by anti-clerical rioters. The Campbells sheltered several Carmelite monks in their house, but when war broke out all seventeen residents of the Carmelite monastery were taken out and shot. However, this was not before the monks had asked the Campbells to look after a trunk containing the Carmelite archives, including the personal papers of St John of the Cross. The Campbells agreed, and when their house was searched by Republican militiamen a few days later, the trunk was left undisturbed. After the war Campbell published a verse translation of St John's letters which was acclaimed both in England and in Spain.

The Campbells spent the next fortnight confined to their house, listening to daily gun battles in the streets. They had no money and little food except for the cucumbers which grew in their garden. When a friend offered money, they bribed some militiamen and left Toledo in the back of a truck. Travelling via Madrid to Valencia, they took ship to Marseilles and from there back to England. But Campbell was back in Toledo the following year, and got himself a Nationalist press pass. It is unclear what he did during the last two years of the war, though his long poem, *Flowering Rifle*, most of it an anti-communist diatribe 'from the battlefield of Spain', has an introductory note written from Toledo in 1939 and refers to his being at the front, where:

> Cooped in a trench, it was my chance to study
> My neighbour for a day or two, a bloody
> Unburied arm, left lying in the snow
> Which melted now its attitude to show…

Unlike almost all his literary contemporaries, Campbell was an ardent supporter of Franco's Catholic crusade—which is what the generalissimo called it and Campbell believed it to be. Perhaps in part because his wife Mary (one of the Garman sisters) had an affair with the predatory Vita Sackville-West, he was contemptuous of the literary elite and in particular the Bloomsbury Group:

> Hither flock all the crowds whom love has wrecked
> Of intellectuals without intellect
> And sexless folk whose sexes intersect.

He respected traditional moral and social values and the Civil War was for him a struggle between God and the Devil. (He denied being a fascist, but did flirt briefly with Nazism in 1939 before agreeing to work for British intelligence in Spain. However, the ambassador in Madrid, Sir Samuel Hoare, decided he was too unreliable.) Having moved to Spain he and Mary found comfort in their conversion to the Catholic faith, and he was inspired by Toledo, which he called 'a sacred city of the mind'. In *Flowering Rifle*, in one of many hyperbolical passages, he seems to confer sanctity on the Alcázar, which was under siege when he left the city, while exaggerating the damage done to it:

> Two towers had fallen of those deathless four
> That steeper into fame than Andes soar
> To dare the loftiest mountaineers of song
> (For all but seraphs else would do them wrong)
> And to that immortality aspire
> Where only the Cabeza holds her spire.

Only a few months earlier, Roy and Mary Campbell would admire the towers of the Alcázar every evening as they sat drinking in the Plaza Zocodover, talking to neighbours and passers-by and watching the swallows darting and swooping above them. On one occasion a young, fair-haired man in the square was playing Schubert songs on a violin, but little could be heard above the chatter of the *paseo*. Mary asked him in French if he was German, and he replied in Spanish that he was English. Thus began a long friendship between Roy Campbell and Laurie Lee, notwithstanding that their political and religious views were poles apart. Lee was more atheist than agnostic, and was already committed to the Republican cause, returning to Spain at the end of 1937 to join the International Brigades. But he enjoyed Campbell's company and his wine and his tales of breaking horses and fighting bulls in the Camargue (his first prose work, *Taurine Provence*, was published in 1932) and in Toledo.

Staying for a week with the Campbells in their rented house under the south wall of Toledo cathedral, Lee read his poems and admired them. The words, he wrote, 'seemed to flare at the nostrils, whinny and thunder, and rise like steam in the air'. Fuelled by cheap red wine (he was allegedly drinking four litres a day), Campbell would talk long into the night, expressing his dislike of England and almost all literary figures except T. E. Lawrence and Edith Sitwell, who admired his poetry. During the day, the two men would tour Toledo's bars, with Campbell, in his wide Cordoban hat, singing, boasting of his exploits—fights with gypsies, getting beaten up by local assault guards—and reciting some of his satirical couplets. Yet Lee found him a gentle, generous companion, and though they would be on opposite sides in the Civil War, he respected Campbell for his romantic idealism. (They may not have shared the same romantic ideals, but Lee had an affair with one of Mary Campbell's sisters before marrying her niece.) He wrote a foreword to Campbell's autobiography, *Light on a Dark Horse*, when it was published in 1951, calling him a big-action poet, a rogue male 'whose poetry was part of a physical engagement with life'.

Among the visitors to Toledo in the previous decade were the Sitwells (Osbert, Sacheverell and Edith) and a travelling trio from Bloomsbury: Lytton Strachey, Ralph Partridge and Dora Carrington. They met briefly during the Holy Week processions, in which some of the *gigantones* (giant wooden and papier-mâché figures) represented unpopular historical personages such as Pontius Pilate. Osbert Sitwell spotted an effigy of Anne Boleyn, commemorating 'the resentment felt by the proud Castilians at the behaviour of King Henry VIII to Catherine of Aragon'. These figures are, or used to be, stored in a room in the cathedral, where H. V. Morton was shown a huge dragon with, on the back of it, a doll with tousled hair, dressed in a wine-red velvet coat. This, he was told, was the wicked Ana Bolena who, in the processions, would dance on top of the devilish dragon to proclaim her sins. In Pedro Calderon de la Barca's seventeenth-century play, *La Cisma de Inglaterra* (*The Schism in England*), Henry VIII is portrayed sympathetically, while Anne Boleyn is held responsible for the schism. In parts of Spain her name was sometimes used as a term of abuse.

In view of this curious survival of historical memory, one might fancifully imagine that the sword used to decapitate Anne Boleyn was the Toledo blade which Catherine of Aragon was said to have presented to Henry VIII. But this is unlikely since she was executed by a French swordsman brought from Calais; she was then buried in an unmarked grave. At least Catherine, who had died four months earlier, rests in peace in Peterborough Cathedral, where respect is still paid to her memory. A Spanish banner and a cross-stitch portrait of her as a young woman hang above her tomb in the north aisle. When I was there it was touching to see two bunches of fresh flowers and seven pomegranates placed on the tomb. The fruit was Catherine's personal emblem—she spent part of her childhood in Granada, which is also the Spanish word for pomegranate. On the four hundred and fiftieth anniversary of her death, in 1986, Peterborough was formally 'twinned' with the university city of Alcalá de Henares, where Catherine was born. She spent all but the first fifteen years of her life in England, where she deserves to be warmly remembered.

VALLADOLID

Philip II was born there; Ferdinand and Isabella married there; Cervantes lived there; Columbus died there. Until 1561, when it was largely destroyed by fire, Valladolid was the principal city of Spain.* The house in which Philip II was born, in 1527, is today a provincial government building, facing the Plaza de San Pablo. On the other side of the square a statue of him rather resembles the young Orson Welles. While the huge, forbidding Escorial palace which the King built outside Madrid is largely responsible for his reputation for austerity, Valladolid, the birthplace of Spain's first Inquisitor General, Tomas de Torquemada, is the city most associated with the autos-da-fé presided over by Philip to garrotte or burn to death those unfortunate so-called heretics who were not in communion with the Holy Roman Church.

When one unfortunate wretch appealed to the King as he was being led to the stake, Philip is supposed to have replied: 'If my son were a heretic like you, I would gladly carry the wood to burn him.' That thought might have been passing through Philip's mind in Verdi's magnificent opera, *Don Carlos*, in which the auto-da-fé scene is usually set outside Valladolid cathedral. Monks are leading heretics to the stake as Philip emerges from the cathedral to witness the proceedings, attended by his queen and the court. Central to this scene are the deputies from Flanders, introduced by the King's son Don Carlos, who prostrate themselves and beg for mercy for their oppressed country. Philip, unmoved, brands them traitors and heretics and orders their arrest. As the scene ends, the people resume rejoicing in praise of their king, the heretics are dragged towards the flames, and a voice is heard from heaven promising the sufferers peace in the next world.

The impression of an auto-da-fé and the power of the Inquisition are chillingly conveyed by Verdi—the scene is described by his

* Philip III removed the court back to Valladolid at the beginning of the seventeenth century, then back again to Madrid five years later.

50

eminent biographer, Francis Toye, as 'an undoubted masterpiece'—
though, on a point of detail, such ceremonies in sixteenth-century
Valladolid were held not in the cathedral square but in the Plaza
Mayor. William H. Prescott, in his nineteenth-century *History of the
Reign of Philip II*, writes of an auto-da-fé held in Valladolid in 1559:
'During the whole time of its duration in the public square, from six
in the morning till two in the afternoon, no symptom of impatience
was exhibited by the spectators, and, as may well be believed, no sign
of sympathy for the sufferers.'

In his novel *El Hereje* (*The Heretic*), Miguel Delibes, one of the
city's favourite sons, gives a detailed description of the day of an auto-
da-fé in the same year.* The prisoners, taken from a secret jail in Calle
de Pedro Barruecos at five o'clock in the morning, walked in pairs
wearing *sanbenitos* (yellow shifts of coarse material), painted with
devils and flames, and conical fools' hats. Round each of their necks
a piece of rope was tied, and they carried green candles. 'Heading the
procession, on horseback, the royal prosecutor carried the billowing
standard of the Inquisition, with the arms of Saint Dominic embroidered on it... [with] two Dominicans carrying the scarlet emblem
of the Pope and the mourning-wrapped cross of the church of the
Saviour.'

The royal entourage processed from another direction towards
the Plaza Mayor, led by a mounted guard with fifes and drums
and followed by the Council of Castile and high dignitaries of the
court. Then came the ladies 'richly attired in rigorous mourning' and
guarded by two dozen mace-bearers and four masters-at-arms. The
King, 'grave, wearing a cape with diamond buttons', and the princes,
applauded by the crowd, were surrounded by archbishops, bishops
and assorted nobles. There was seating for about two thousand in the
square, half of which was converted into an enormous stage, facing
what is today the Casa Consistorial (city hall), which was decorated

* Delibes has been described by Sir Raymond Carr as Spain's greatest novelist.
  This novel was his last, published in 1998, twelve years before the author's
  death. As a Vallisoletano, a resident of Valladolid, Delibes' name has been
  given to a cultural centre in the city.

with 'banners, canopies and brocades glittering with gold and silver'. As the ragged group of prisoners entered the square and filed past the King, the crowd whistled and jeered. After a sermon from the Bishop of Palencia on false prophets and the unity of the Church, the sentences were read out by an officer of the Inquisition. Some were to suffer death by garrotte before being consigned to the flames, others were to be burned at the stake, and others imprisoned for life while perpetually wrapped in their *sanbenitos*.

The prisoners to be put to death were taken on donkeys from the plaza, down the Calle de Santiago which was filled with drunken, sweat-stained men and children blowing whistles and playing between the legs of the animals. Women dressed in their Sunday best watched from windows and balconies. At the end of the street the pathetic procession crossed the square to the Puerta del Campo, the site of the city's most notorious brothel, and entered the Campo Grande, a large field where the final act of the auto-da-fé would take place. Delibes goes on to write:

> A well-to-do lady with a plumed hat and a golden mantilla spurred her donkey to keep pace with the prisoners in order to insult them… Ladies and women of the people, men carrying toddlers on their shoulders, men on horseback, and even carriages took up positions, wondered who everyone was, whiled away the remaining moments at the trinket stands or playing games of chance. Others had taken places right opposite the tall stakes, which had ladders leaning against them, and defended their positions with all their might.

After a couple of garrottings, it was the turn of Cipriano Salcedo, the hero of Delibes' novel. A prosperous wool merchant, he had been born on the very day, in 1517, that Martin Luther nailed his ninety-five theses to a church door in Wittenberg. He became an active member of the Reformation movement in Spain, and he was about to be burned alive at the stake, unless he repented at the last moment, in which case he would be garrotted before his lifeless body was thrown on the fire. Having been tied to an iron ring attached to the stake, Salcedo saw the executioner approach with a smoking torch. Then a Jesuit priest ran forward, climbed the ladder until their two faces were almost touching, and begged Salcedo to confess and declare his faith in the Roman Church. But he would not utter the word Roman, saying instead that he believed in the Holy Church of Christ and the Apostles. The mob was now growing impatient, cursing and demanding that the fire be lit. The priest asked Salcedo again and, having received a no more satisfactory reply, came down the ladder and nodded to the executioner. As soon as his torch touched the pyre, the fire surrounded Salcedo in a roar and overwhelmed him. The mob burst into shouts of joy. Salcedo did not scream, which disappointed some of the people. Instead he whispered, 'Lord, give me shelter' as his body was burned.

Shortly before Delibes' death, a plaque commemorating him and his novel *El Hereje* was fixed to a wall of the church in the Calle de Santiago. It portrays a striking image of the author, behind him an impression of sixteenth-century Valladolid and over his left shoulder three wooden stakes with their iron rings and a ladder leaning against them. Also on this wall a plaque commemorates Dr Agustin Cazalla who, in Delibes' novel, had travelled with Emperor Charles V in Germany and gave sermons every Friday in the Iglesia de Santiago. (He also has a street named after him.) The city council now advertises a Ruta del Hereje, taking in various buildings and streets (some of them now renamed) mentioned in the novel. Cipriano Salcedo was born in the family house in the Corredera de San Pablo (now Calle de las Angustias), ironically very close to Philip II's birthplace in the Palacio de Pimentel. The warehouse for the family's wool business was in the Jewish quarter, in the Plaza de la Trinidad near the Puente Mayor. From here Cipriano's father would walk through the cobbled streets, with open sewer ditches running down the middle, to Garabito's tavern in Calle Orates (today Calle Canovas del Castillo), just off the Plaza de Fuente Dorada. Also in Calle Orates was the Hospital de los Inocentes, to which Cipriano Salcedo's wife Teo was confined when she went mad. Today this short street has a centre of aesthetic medicine and a chiropodist, but no tavern: only a cafeteria called New Orleans and a place selling 'King Doner Kebabs'.

Several convents and churches, already built in the sixteenth century and standing today, play their part in Delibes' story. After the fire in 1561 destroyed the Plaza Mayor, it was rebuilt on Philip II's orders. In the Plaza de Zorrilla, at the head of the Campo Grande, the Academia de Caballeria occupies the area where the heretics were tied to stakes and burnt to death. In the Campo Grande today all is quiet among the plane trees, palms and conifers but for the chatter of children playing and the peacocks giving a passable imitation of the screams which would have been heard as the victims of the Inquisition were consumed by the flames.

Until the nineteenth century bullfights were usually held in the Plaza Mayor. A designated plaza de toros, next to the Juderia (the old Jewish quarter), was built in 1833 and used for almost sixty years until replaced by the present bullring south of the Campo Grande. But the old one was not demolished: it was converted, on an octagonal plan, into houses and flats which today surround an area of grass, paving-stones and gravel. The Coso Viejo (old bullring), as it is still known, incorporates the old wooden balconies of the upper stands. Trees, including a large yew, grow out of what was once the arena of sand.

The patron saint of Valladolid, San Pedro Regalado, who lived in the first half of the fifteenth century, is said to have tamed an enraged fighting bull which had escaped from a fiesta. For this feat he has been appointed also patron saint of toreros, and his memory is honoured here every year, in mid-May, with a *feria* including three bullfights. In this city, which describes itself as *una ciudad taurina*, and has a museum next to the bullring, I attended a *corrida* which was a sell-out ('*no hay billetes*') in a plaza of nearly twelve thousand seats, while the country was in the depths of economic crisis with one in four people unemployed. The previous day, the legendary, if overrated, José Tomas was performing, and the crowds were so dense that—a very rare occurrence in Spain—the bullfight began fifteen minutes late. There is no doubting the strength of the *aficion* in Castile and Leon.

Scenes of blood and suffering, not of the bulls but of Jesus Christ, are commonly found elsewhere in Valladolid. They are disturbingly realistic painted sculptures of Christ before and after his crucifixion. Most striking of all is *Cristo Yacente* (*Dead Christ*), of which there are numerous examples in Valladolid—the best known by Gregorio Fernandez in the Museo Nacional Colegio de San Gregorio and the Convento de Santa Ana. Naked except for a loincloth, Christ's lifeless body has a gash in the ribs from which the coagulating blood has oozed in dark red rivulets towards his groin. There are bloody stigmata on his hands, knees and feet. His recent agony and suffering are evident in the dead eyes and half-open mouth. The sculpture is carved in wood and painted, with the addition of glass for the eyes, and fingernails made from a bull's horn. This striking, indeed shocking image was one of the centrepieces of the exhibition, 'The Sacred Made Real', at the National Gallery in London in 2009.

Also shown there, from the Museo Diocesano y Catedralicio in Valladolid, was Fernandez's *Ecce Homo*, depicting the moment when Christ, having been bound and scourged by Roman soldiers, was presented by Pontius Pilate to the Jewish mob. His arms are crossed over his chest in resignation, and blood from his wounds drips down his back. The bones are pushing against the taut flesh, painted with pink and blue to show the bruises from the beating which he has just suffered. The third sculpture from Valladolid exhibited in London was the *Virgen Dolorosa* sculpted by Pedro de Mena and lent by the Convento de Santa Ana. It is a most affecting image: a bust of the Virgin, with blue headdress and clasped hands, showing her lips parted, tearful eyes and tears on her cheeks. Juan de Juni's famous sixteenth-century sculpture of Nuestra Señora de las Angustias, with her hand over her heart, is in the church of that name. (A number of sculptures and altarpieces by de Juni, Fernandez and others were destroyed during the few days that Napoleon spent in the city on his way back to France in January 1809—while Sir John Moore was retreating to La Coruña.)

In the Iglesia da La Vera Cruz, and elsewhere in the city, the polychrome sculpture, *Cristo Atado a una Columna*, depicts Christ tied to the post where he was beaten. Another portrays his bloody corpse being taken down from the cross. Shocking and unnecessarily gory as these sculptures may appear to some observers, there is no doubting the piety of their creators. In his study of the lives of Spanish painters and sculptors, the eighteenth-century art historian Antonio Palomino wrote of Fernandez that 'he did not undertake to make an effigy of Christ our Lord or His Holy Mother without preparing himself by prayer, fast, penitence and Communion, so that God would confer His grace upon him and make him succeed'.

Some of these sculptures are removed every year during Holy Week for the processions through the streets of the city. H. V. Morton, in his wonderful book, *A Stranger in Spain*, records that his host in Valladolid told him that the Semana Santa processions in this city were the finest in Spain and should not be missed. The *pasos* in Seville during Holy Week he dismissed as no more than tourist attractions. While such a comment from a Vallisoletan is only to be expected, I can confirm that a Holy Week procession at night through the streets of Valladolid is a moving, indeed mesmerising experience.

Good Friday is, of course, the big day. It begins with the *Pregón de las Siete Palabras*, when a man on horseback, together with his mounted followers (all of them dressed in white cassocks and pointed scarlet hats), tours the city centre. At various points he stops and reads from a scroll, in the manner of an ancient town crier, announcing the ceremony to be held in the Plaza Mayor at midday, where many of the windows are draped with black cloth. A *sermón* is held outside the city hall, quoting the seven utterances of Christ on the Cross, each of them illustrated by a sculpture, from 'Father forgive them, for they know not what they do' to 'Into Thy hands I commend my spirit'.

The pity was that the year I was in Valladolid during Semana Santa, a heavy snowstorm on Good Friday morning caused the *Pregón* to be cancelled. The *sermón* was held at midday, but in the cathedral, not the main square. One of the sculptures of Christ on the Cross was carried on a bier by twenty-four men. It swayed gently and very slowly up the aisle, watched in silence by the hundreds of people packed into the cathedral. Then the trumpets sounded, a proclamation was made, and the *sermón* proceeded.

VALLADOLID

The weather had improved enough by the evening for the Procesión General de la Sagrada Pasión del Redentor to take place, though it started well over an hour later than advertised. Thirty-two *pasos*, or sculptures on their platforms, were borne though the streets by the nineteen *cofradías* (brotherhoods) of Valladolid. The men's heads and faces were encased in conical hoods—black, red, purple, olive green, depending on which *cofradía* they belonged to—and they were dressed in cloaks of matching or different colours. Some wore hoods in the manner of medieval executioners, carrying wooden crosses and ladders and walking barefoot along the wet streets. Thoughts of the Inquisition, and of the Ku Klux Klan, came irresistibly to mind. Drums were beaten, brass bands were playing a slow march, but it often sounded more like a banshee wail. The sights and sounds were the more chilling as the route of the processions took it round the Plaza Mayor, where the auto-da-fé rituals used to be held. I was standing on the corner of the square as the procession turned right down the Calle de Santiago to the place where the heretics met their grisly fate.

On this damp, windy evening many of the candle-lit lanterns carried on long poles lost their flame, depriving the children in the procession, who were unsuitably dressed against the weather in thin gowns, of any relief from the cold. The thirty-two *pasos* proceeded chronologically, beginning with the Last Supper. The heavy biers, pushed from behind, had velvet curtains at their base which concealed wheels but occasionally revealed the rubber-soled shoes of men helping to keep the procession moving. On it came, with the huge polychrome sculptures disturbingly illuminated to depict the scourging of Christ, the raising of the cross with Christ nailed to it, then a number of images of the crucifixion, including *las siete palabras*. Towards the end came the Virgin Mary in anguish, the empty cross with a white sheet draped across it, and the tomb with an angel at either end and the sleeping soldiers. By this time the rain had begun again and some of the priceless sculptures were hurriedly covered with plastic sheeting.

The carrying of Gregorio Fernandez's graphic and breathtaking *Cristo Yacente* on the Saturday evening, from the Convento de Santa

Ana, along a few streets and back to the convent, was an absorbing spectacle. The sculpture had been resting at the foot of the altar steps in the convent church, which has three late-eighteenth-century paintings by Goya on its walls, one of them of *Santa Ludgarda*, to whom Christ revealed himself, showing the wound in His side. *Cristo Yacente*, with that open wound bleeding so realistically down His right flank, was borne on the shoulders of members of the Cofradía del Santo Entierro, hooded and dressed in black velvet, with golden girdles round the waist and white gloves. Children were similarly dressed, without hoods, and ladies wore black with black lace mantillas, supposedly representing the weeping women of Jerusalem. Bagpipers accompanied them, and scarlet-hooded figures brought up the rear of the procession. Prayers were said in the small square in front of the convent before *Cristo Yacente* was carried through the doors and received once more into the care of the resident nuns. (In the basement beneath the convent a rather grand restaurant offers a *tarta de las monjas*, which is prepared by the nuns with cream, chocolate and cinnamon. They also wash and iron the restaurant's table linen.)

The Easter Sunday celebration was blessed with fine and almost warm weather. During and after midday Mass in the cathedral, processions seemed to converge from all directions. The colourfully cloaked men were now bareheaded, the mantillas worn by the women were now white, and children of all ages accompanied them. From the cathedral came the sculpture of the tomb (now empty, it had contained Christ's body two days before), a statue of the joyful Virgen de la Alegría, and the risen Christ, with scores of red roses at His feet, raising a cross above His head and still showing the chest wound and stigmata. Over the cathedral square a stork flew, as if in salute, coming to rest on one of the towers. A cacophony of bands played their way, with members of all the *cofradías*, towards the Plaza Mayor, where a huge throng awaited them. Christ and the Virgin faced one another in front of the *ayuntamiento*; the Archbishop of Valladolid gave an Apostolic Benediction; and everyone dispersed for lunch.

On the Monday of Semana Santa each year, the Procesión de la Buena Muerte begins at 11 p.m. when a statue of Christ on the cross

(*Cristo del Olvido*) is taken from the church of Santa Maria de la Antigua. It is borne on a flower-bedecked bier, lit by candles, on the shoulders of members of the Venerable Cofradía of the Most Precious Blood of Our Lord Jesus Christ. The procession passes through the cathedral square, then heads for the Santuario Nacional de la Gran Promesa, where the young Jesuit priest Bernardo de Hoyos promoted devotion to the Sacred Heart of Jesus in the eighteenth century. There is a pause for prayers here, before the statue and its bearers continue, making a wide, gradual circuit back towards the church where the procession began. Along La Merced, a left turn into Calle Don Sancho, and *Cristo del Olvido* (the crucified Christ the Forsaken) approaches the climax of its journey: the meeting with Our Lady the Virgin of the Vulnerata outside the Seminario de los Ingleses, the Royal English College. Her statue, surrounded with banks of white lilies and green foliage, is carried by English trainee priests through the front entrance of the college, turning left into the street to make this famous annual rendezvous. As a choir sings La Salve Popular, the two statues face one another a few feet apart. The two biers halt and sway slightly, while many among the huge crowd of onlookers are visibly moved. Then La Vulnerata retreats slowly, watched by and still facing her son, back through the doors and into the embrace of the college.

This most treasured sculpture is a badly damaged image of the Virgin, with hands and arms severed and nose removed from the horribly disfigured face. Only the tiny feet, no more than stumps, of the infant Jesus remain on his mother's knee. The statue has been in this state for more than four hundred years, when it was picked up in the streets of Cádiz. (It was originally known as *La Virgen del Rosario*, then given the name of *La Vulnerata—The Wounded One—*by the Bishop of Valladolid.) An Anglo-Dutch fleet under the command of Lord Howard of Effingham, together with the Earl of Essex, arrived in the bay of Cádiz at the end of June 1596. After an initial bombardment, in which two Spanish galleons were captured, the Duke of Medina Sidonia ordered the burning of the rest of the treasure fleet, some thirty ships, to prevent it falling into English hands. Anglo-Dutch troops took control of the city, pillaged its churches and houses over the next fortnight, and burned it. One of the many sacred images to be evicted from its church and mutilated before the people was this statue of the Virgin, which was saved from total destruction and—a year or so later—turned up in Madrid, in the house of the Governor of Castile. The priests and seminarians of the English College, wishing to make some reparation, asked that they be allowed to look after the statue in their chapel; and in 1600 it was brought to Valladolid on a litter provided by Queen Margarita, the wife of Philip III, shortly after the royal court had moved back to the city. Having been desecrated by Englishmen in the service of Queen Elizabeth, the statue, now named *La Virgen Vulnerata*, was entrusted to the care of their countrymen, who were intent on returning England to the Catholic fold.

The English Catholic opposition in Europe to their Protestant English queen had begun some years earlier. William Allen, Lancashire-born and the first significant English Catholic exile, founded an English college at Douai, in northern France, then another in Rome, with the encouragement of Pope Gregory XIII. As the spiritual leader of English Catholics in exile, a brilliant polemicist, and the Englishman most feared by Elizabeth's government, Allen wisely kept out of England for the last thirty years of his life (Pope Sixtus V made him a cardinal in 1587 and he died in 1594). Having become a confidant of Robert Persons, a Jesuit priest with whom he had spent time in Rome, Allen arranged for him to accompany Edmund Campion on a Jesuit mission to England. When Campion was arrested and executed in 1581, Persons made his escape and never returned to England.

He was involved in a plot to bring the Duke of Guise, Mary Queen of Scots' first cousin, to England at the head of an army several thousand strong. After her execution in 1587, he urged Philip II to invade England, declaring that all English Catholics 'without a single exception regarded the invasion with approval'. In his *Admonition to the Nobility and People of England and Ireland*, Allen denounced this 'incestuous bastard, begotten and born in sin of an infamous courtesan... this woman, hated of God and man', demanding that she be removed from the throne. But it was a bad mistake to attack

Elizabeth personally. Allen and Persons misjudged the mood of many Roman Catholics in England who, while wishing for their religion to be restored, did not want their queen to be deposed by a foreign invader. In spite or perhaps because of Philip's marriage to the Queen of England thirty years earlier, they preferred to be ruled by a Protestant English queen, remaining 'faithfullest true English subjects'. (Though never crowned King of England, Philip had been given the title while still a Spanish prince, on his marriage to Mary, and now ruled over a large part of Europe.) Seemingly undeterred by the defeat of the Spanish Armada, Persons began infiltrating groups of priests into England to make contact with Catholics and prepare the ground for another attempted invasion by the King of Spain. (Another armada did set sail for England from Lisbon in 1596, but was broken up by storms in the Bay of Biscay.)

In 1589 Persons set about founding an English college for trainee priests in Valladolid. He named it in honour of St Alban, the first English Christian martyr, who was decapitated in the third century at the Roman settlement of Verulamium. It had the royal seal of approval, and Philip paid a visit three years later, in 1592. These English seminary students, not only in Valladolid but in Rheims, Douai and Rome, were branded by Queen Elizabeth as 'depraved and morally corrupt... [they] had escaped from their country, had committed treason, and had fled to the land of the enemy'. Certainly Persons was notorious for his seditious activities: he published a tract on the succession to the English throne in which he nominated Philip's eldest daughter, Isabella Clara Eugenia, through the house of Lancaster a direct descendant of John of Gaunt. Anyone found in possession of this book, which was denounced by many English Catholics, would be judged guilty of treason. Persons spent the last thirty years of his life outside England—having established similar colleges in Seville and Madrid, he ended his days as rector of the English College in Rome.

As part of their training, the students at the English College in Valladolid were required to take an oath that they would return home and celebrate surreptitious Mass for those recusant Catholics living under the Protestant yoke. As soon as they landed on the south coast of England, some of them having journeyed by way of Lisbon and Ireland, the young seminarians were in constant fear of their lives. Queen Elizabeth's spymaster, Sir Francis Walsingham, had set up a network of agents who were relentless in pursuit of these 'heretic' priests. After his death in 1590, these intelligencers continued their secret work under the supervision of Sir Robert Cecil, Lord Burghley's son. They knew of many of the Catholic safe houses which might be sheltering young missionaries, who often had to hide, with their chalices and vestments, in the so-called priest holes constructed for the purpose.* The great majority of missionary priests from Europe during the last two decades of Elizabeth's reign were either imprisoned or executed, some of them hanged, drawn and quartered, with the quarters often distributed as a warning to others.

The training of these young Catholics to infiltrate alien (i.e. Protestant) territory and undermine its government, with the attendant risks of arrest and execution, puts one in mind of the agents of Special Operations Executive who, three and a half centuries later, were dropped secretly into France for the purpose of subverting the occupying power. And their chances of survival were no better than the missionary priests'. The Queen also employed spies in Europe, some of them Catholic double agents, who were adept at infiltrating the English colleges (and even the Spanish court). They numbered about seventy, in France, Spain and Italy. One may have been the dramatist Christopher Marlowe, who was murdered in mysterious circumstances. A century later, Titus Oates, who invented the 'Popish Plot', a supposed conspiracy to assassinate Charles II, was admitted to the English College in Valladolid. When he was suspected of subversion and expelled, he removed his name from the college records.

By the end of the sixteenth century well over a hundred priests had been executed at Tyburn. After Elizabeth's death in 1603, and the

---

* They were the work of Nicholas Owen ('Little John'), who was responsible for hundreds of these hiding-places before he was eventually caught and tortured to death in 1606.

signing at Valladolid of an Anglo-Spanish treaty, the English College, now in the same city as the royal court, lost some of its special favour with the Spanish monarch. And a number of English Catholics, concerned for future relations with their king and their Protestant compatriots, were openly critical of the college for having moved from the spiritual to the political arena. But it continued to train English and Welsh priests to spread the word back home, providing what came to be known as *una escuela de mártires*—a school for martyrs.

Henry Walpole, the first martyr from the English College, had spent some time in Rheims and Rome before he came to Valladolid as a minister, then returned to England and was immediately arrested. He was not born a Catholic but was prompted to convert by the martyrdom of Edmund Campion, who was frequently tortured on the rack before being hanged, drawn and quartered. Walpole suffered the same fate. The appeal of martyrdom in those days may be difficult to comprehend, especially when one reads the words used in sentencing the heretic priests, who were to be 'drawn through the streets upon hurdles to the place of execution, there to be hanged and let down alive, and your privy parts cut off, and your entrails taken out and burnt in your sight; then your head to be cut off and your body divided into four parts, to be disposed of at Her Majesty's pleasure. And may God have mercy on your soul.' It is tempting to detect an echo of this will to embrace martyrdom in the Muslim suicide bombers of today—although, of course, the means to their end not only involve the murder of innocents but have no sanction in the Koran.

George Borrow visited the English College in Valladolid in 1836. He wrote in *The Bible in Spain* of these young priests 'who, like stealthy grimalkins, traversed green England in all directions; crept into old halls beneath umbrageous rookeries, fanning the dying embers of Popery, with either no hope nor perhaps wish than to perish disembowelled by the bloody hands of the executioner, amongst the yells of a rabble as bigoted as themselves.' Inspired by the martyrdom of Henry Walpole in 1595, many students of the English College in Valladolid followed his example in the next century. Not only are their names recorded in a roll of honour, and their portraits hung in the Martyrs' Corridor at the college, but they were all canonised or beatified in the twentieth century. Sainthood was conferred on six by Pope Paul VI in 1970 (he canonised a total of forty martyrs), and sixteen were declared blessed by Pope Paul II in 1987. Though the missionary work of these men in England was entirely pacific, albeit potentially provocative, they were branded as terrorists, dangerous religious extremists owing allegiance to a foreign faith and power. They were, after all, intent on fomenting rebellion and, by celebrating Mass in Elizabeth's England, were guilty of high treason.

John Roberts was one of the Catholic martyrs who travelled in Europe, spent time in Valladolid and returned to England. He was born in Wales, raised as a Protestant, and converted to Catholicism in Paris in the same year that he entered the English College in Valladolid. Having joined the Benedictine monastery in the city, he went back to England and worked in London with the poor who were suffering from the plague. Several times he was arrested, imprisoned and deported. During one period of exile in France, he helped to found a Benedictine monastery at Douai, a community which continues today at Downside Abbey near Bath. Back in London in 1610, Roberts was arrested yet again, this time for celebrating Mass, and condemned to death. At his execution the crowd, remembering the help he had given to those stricken by the plague, refused to cheer and would not allow his body to be drawn and quartered. The life of St John Roberts is commemorated at his birthplace of Trawsfynydd in north Wales.

On the night before Roberts's execution, he was guest of honour at a feast in Newgate prison provided by Doña Luisa de Carvajal, a remarkable Spanish woman of noble blood who had lived next door to the English College in Valladolid and given all her money to the Jesuits. Much affected by the martyrdoms of Henry Walpole and, before him, Edmund Campion, she arrived in London with Walpole's brother Michael and in poor health, a few months before the Gunpowder Plot. She came at the invitation of Henry Garnet, Jesuit Superior in England, who was convicted of treason and executed in 1606, after the Plot. As priests and other recusants continued to be hanged, drawn and quartered, body parts from their corpses were sometimes brought to Doña Luisa for her to wash and anoint them. They were then smuggled to Spain, sometimes hidden in the luggage of the Spanish ambassador, the Count of Gondomar. One of St John Roberts's arms was said to have been taken to the royal court, and a collection of the relics of several English martyrs is still kept in the chapel of the Counts of Gondomar in Galicia. (One of them, John Forest, named Juan del Bosque in the chapel, was in the previous century confessor to Catherine of Aragon.)

When Doña Luisa was arrested and imprisoned in London in 1613, the Archbishop of Canterbury sent fifty armed horsemen to search her house. The Count of Gondomar interceded with James I and, to avoid any further strain on Anglo-Spanish relations, she was released. Not long after, she fell ill and died in London, thereby frustrating her wish to be martyred. Her body was repatriated and her remains, together with her portrait, are now kept in the Monasterio de la Encarnacion in Madrid. Though her name may have been largely forgotten for nearly four hundred years, the national airline Iberia decided, at the end of the twentieth century, to recognise the courage of one of the first female missionaries by naming an Airbus after her.

Some English Catholic exiles went to Spain during Elizabeth's reign and stayed there. Sir Francis Englefield, who had served Philip II as a member of Mary Tudor's Privy Council, left England at the accession of Elizabeth and schemed against her with Allen and Persons. He spent his later years in Valladolid, blind and with a pension from Philip II, and was buried in the old college chapel. So was Lord Cottington, who had been English ambassador to Spain before serving Charles I as Lord Treasurer, and ended his days in a house close to the English College. Jane Dormer, a former lady-in-waiting to Mary Tudor and one of her closest friends, married the Duke of Feria, who had attended Philip II when he married Queen Mary in Winchester cathedral.* He was ambassador in London at the time of Elizabeth's

---

* Following the wedding, Philip brought English elms back to Spain and planted them in Aranjuez, where he began building a summer palace. Only one of the original trees is thought to be still standing today.

coronation, but he and Jane departed soon afterwards to Spain and to his castle in Zafra, Extremadura, where she outlived her husband by forty years.

During this time she corresponded frequently with Mary Queen of Scots, with the Pope (in fact with four Popes) and even occasionally with Elizabeth. She was a benefactor of the English College and gave shelter to countless English exiles, refugees and student priests. Some of them would continue their journeys to Seville, then down the River Guadalquivir to Sanlucar de Barrameda, where they stayed at the English hospice and chapel of St George before sailing back to England and probable martyrdom. When Elizabeth died, Jane's name was put forward as a lady-in-waiting to James I's wife, Anne of Denmark, but she never returned to England. She was buried in the habit, which she always wore, of the third order of St Francis, in a convent in Zafra (the castle is now a parador), but her heart was taken back to England. A portrait of her, showing a fine-looking woman in her twenties with a determined expression, was acquired by the English College in 2008.

Oliver Cromwell once commented that the Papists in England at the end of the sixteenth century were all 'Spaniolized'. This was certainly true of the many hundreds of soldiers who fought for the Duke of Parma in his Army of Flanders and of the Catholic correspondents in England, the Low Countries and Spain. This network was organised by intelligencers such as Hugh Owen, who famously referred to James I as 'this stinking king of ours'. Among his spying duties for Philips II and III, he kept a close eye on former students of the English College, some of whom were turned and became informants for Elizabeth's chief minister, Sir Robert Cecil. Joseph Creswell, having been Robert Persons' assistant, succeeded him as rector of the English College and as superior of the English Jesuits in Spain when Persons went to Rome. Creswell went on occasion to the Escorial to advise Philip II on English Catholic affairs, and was largely responsible for persuading him, and afterwards Philip III, to continue funding the English College. Thanks to Creswell's persistent lobbying at court, Philip III visited the college in 1600.

Among those exiles who had the royal Spanish ear and attended the court, none was more enthusiastic for an invasion of England than Sir William Stanley. Described as an adventurer, he was born a Catholic and fought for Spain as a young man in Flanders, then served his queen in Ireland for fifteen years. Elizabeth was about to appoint him viceroy of Ireland when he changed sides again while in the Netherlands. He advised Philip II that his Armada should invade England by sailing via Ireland to the coast of Wales. Stanley continued to propose military expeditions against England—leading his regiment, which he maintained in Flanders—and he sent one of his junior officers, Guy Fawkes, on Elizabeth's death to warn Philip III against James I. Stanley recommended an invasion which would proclaim as Queen of England either Lady Arabella Stuart (her uncle, Lord Darnley, married Mary Queen of Scots) or Philip's half-sister, Isabella (who was by now joint sovereign of the Netherlands with her husband, Archduke Albert of Austria).

In 1602 a notorious Irish rebel, Red Hugh O'Donnell, who had been fighting the English in his native country, set sail for Spain to seek Philip III's support for an invasion of Ireland. The King was enthusiastic—Spanish forces had landed in Ireland a few years before—but O'Donnell died near Valladolid, only a few months after his arrival in Spain, and the plan was abandoned. A plaque fixed to an appropriately red-painted wall near the Plaza Mayor in Valladolid records his life and death. He is also commemorated in an Irish poem which the novelist Edna O'Brien remembered from her childhood:

And all Valladolid knew
And out to Simancas all knew
Where they buried Red Hugh.

Invasion plans petered out after the Anglo-Spanish treaty of 1604, and relations between the two countries improved for a while when James I attempted to marry off his son, the future Charles I, to Philip III's daughter. During the reign of the Spanish King Charles II, last and most feeble of the Habsburg monarchs, a new chapel dedicated to the mutilated statue of La Vulnerata was built within the college. The Wounded One is placed above the altar, wearing a crown and a gold dress and flanked by St Thomas Becket and St Edward the Confessor. High up on the walls of the chapel, beneath the dome, are eight paintings illustrating the Vulnerata story, from the arrival of the English navy in Cádiz, to the Virgin's desecration, her arrival in Valladolid and the Triumph and Adoration. Kneeling before this image, the young missionary priests took the oath to defend and spread the Catholic faith. Today a reliquary below the altar is said to contain bits taken from the corpses of those priests who were executed for their faith.

La Vulnerata became not only an emblem of English Catholicism but a symbol also of the wounds inflicted on English Catholic recusants when they returned home. Today the iconic status given to this image of the Madonna extends to victims of abuse. In Liverpool and elsewhere, there are young women, many from Africa and Asia, who have been subjected to violence and rape and who have been comforted by being able to relate to this wounded image, and by a prayer written by a woman helping these women on Merseyside.

Vulnerata
Wounded Woman, Wounded Mother
You stay so long in the stillness
I cry for what has been done to you
For the pain in your body
The pain in your soul.
I cry for my own pain
I remember what was done to me
And I know you understand.
You have given your arms
To carry people of sadness.
You have given your child to carry me
In forgiveness and peace
To rescue me
From all I have been through
To make me calm, to give me courage.

VALLADOLID

The prayer has been offered to the inmates of at least one women's prison in England, and has been translated into Spanish.

The English College's library may not be as famous as the image of La Vulnerata, but it is an extraordinary and important archive. There are in fact two libraries, holding something like ten thousand volumes. The one known as the Pigskin Library contains the oldest volumes bound in vellum (in fact usually lambskin). There is a copy of the *Nuremberg Chronicle* of 1493, a history of the world with illustrations of some of the cities of that time, and an edition of the Koran in Latin, promoted by Pope Innocent XI in the seventeenth century. Most fascinating to students of Spanish history, the censorship of the Inquisition can be seen in several books. A history of Great Britain, published in 1632, has words and sentences which have been neatly and entirely successfully obliterated with black ink. The work of the inquisitor is then signed and dated, and in some cases further excisions have been made by a later inquisitor fearful that some phrase might conceivably be thought inconsistent with the Catholic interpretation of history. *Expurgata* is the chilling word used by the ecclesiastical censors to denote that the texts have been purged and purified. During the Napoleonic occupation of the country, some silver was stolen from the college by French soldiers, but the library was untouched.

The archive has a large collection of documents relating to the three English colleges—Valladolid, Seville, Madrid—established under the patronage of the Spanish monarchy, also countless works by Jesuit and other scholars. (When Charles III expelled the Jesuits in 1767, he decided to give his protection to the Valladolid college by granting it the 'Royal' appendage.) One name to catch my eye was Fray Luis Ponce de Leon, the celebrated sixteenth-century theologian who wrote treatises, commentaries and poetry while in prison in Valladolid. It was while teaching at the University of Salamanca that he was arrested by the Inquisition. The charge was that he had expressed heretical opinions in his translation of and commentary on the Song of Songs. As a *converso* his Jewish ancestry also told against him, and he was given a four-year jail sentence in Valladolid. Released in 1576, he returned at once to Salamanca to resume his work at the university and supposedly began his first lecture with the words *Dicebamus hesterna die* ('As we were saying yesterday...').

Fray Luis's statue stands in the courtyard facing the university building's main entrance. The room in which he lectured is on the ground floor, a few doors away from the lecture hall in which another great teacher at the University of Salamanca, the philosopher Miguel de Unamuno, made his most memorable speech, which was to be almost his dying declaration. It was 12 October 1936, Columbus Day, and less than three months after the beginning of the Civil War. Unamuno, rector of the university and initially a supporter of the Nationalist uprising, was presiding over a ceremony attended by Franco's wife Doña Carmen (the generalissimo's headquarters were only a hundred yards away) and the founder of the Foreign Legion, the dangerously excitable and more than slightly manic General Millan Astray, one-eyed and one-armed, who was given to shouting the Legion's motto, *¡Viva la Muerte!* (Long Live Death!) at every opportunity. Hot-tempered speeches were made in praise of fascism and the ruthless rooting out of all 'cancers in the body of the nation'. The seventy-two-year-old Unamuno, who by now was becoming deeply concerned at the character and course of the Civil War, rose to speak. Interrupted by blue-shirted Falangists and, in particular, by General Astray shouting his Legion's motto together with the cry, *'¡Mueran los Intelectuales!'* ('Death to Intellectuals!'), the venerable philosopher concluded with these words:

> *Venceréis, porque tenéis sobrada fuerza bruta. Pero no convenceréis, porque para convencer hay que persuadir. Y para persuadir necesitáis algo que os falta: razón y derecha en la lucha. Me parece inútil pediros que penséis en España.*

(You will win, because you have more than enough brute force. But you will not win over, because to win over you have to persuade. And to persuade you would need what you lack: reason and right in the struggle. I consider it futile to ask you to think of Spain.)

These courageous, devastating words were the last that Unamuno would utter in public. To her credit Doña Carmen gave him her protective arm and ushered him from the hall. He was dismissed from the rectorship and died of a stroke, broken-hearted, ten weeks later, on the last day of 1936.

The Civil War was something of an embarrassment to the English College in Valladolid. The city was the centre of Castilian Catholicism; many of Spain's priests and nuns were drawn from the Castilian peasantry. Valladolid was the birthplace of the proletarian fascist movement known as Juntas de Ofensiva Nacional Sindicalista (JONS), and in Valladolid it formally merged with the Falange. Unsurprisingly, it was one of the cities to fall to the Nationalists on the first day of the war, 19 July 1936, and became known as *la capital del Alzamiento* (the capital of the uprising). During that summer General Mola, commander of Nationalist forces in the north, made his headquarters in Valladolid's *ayuntamiento*. Of course the English College was going to back what Franco called a holy crusade against the largely anti-clerical Republic, some of whose supporters were in the habit of burning churches and murdering priests. However, the rector of the College, Monsignor Edwin Henson, did not appear to have any qualms about the public executions which were regularly taking place in Valladolid, from the very beginning of the war. In the summer of 1937, when the war had been going for a year, the College Old Boys received a telegram from Mgr Henson in Valladolid on the occasion of their annual reunion dinner in London. It offered no prayer for peace in Spain, indeed nothing eirenic at all, but only the bellicose fascist slogan, *España Una—España Grande—España Libre*, followed by *Viva El Generalisimo Franco* and *Arriba España*.

Mgr Henson's rousing call to his English priests would not have been heard sympathetically by one of his former vice-rectors at the college, A. V. Phillips. After ten years at the English College, Phillips returned to England to serve as a curate, then went to Madrid in the late 1920s, where he worked as a journalist, staying on in the Republican capital until it fell to Franco at the end of the Civil War. In addition to writing reports for the *News Chronicle*, he was English

71

announcer for the Republican government's radio station based in Madrid. When the war came to an end in 1939, Phillips remained in the capital but was soon arrested by the Franco government and spent four months in jail. Once back in England he criticised the Church for failing to do enough for the thousands of political prisoners suffering under Franco's brutal regime.

The eminent historian of the Spanish Civil War, Professor Paul Preston, writes of the scale of the repression in Valladolid in *Doves of War*, in which he chronicles the welfare work of Mercedes Sanz-Bachiller, widow of Onésimo Redondo, a co-founder of the JONS. (The organisation which she established in Valladolid, looking after hungry and homeless women and children, spread during the war to the rest of Spain.) There were bloody clashes with left-wing students and workers before 1936; and as soon as Valladolid was in the hands of the military rebels, courts martial were set up and the firing squads began their work. Condemned prisoners were taken in trucks to the Campo de San Isidro, a working-class neighbourhood on the eastern outskirts of the city, in the early morning, and shot in front of large crowds of jeering spectators, who were often accompanied by their wives and children. So popular were these grisly occasions that a stall selling coffee and churros was set up to cater to those who came to watch. The atmosphere at these public executions recalled the burning to death of victims of the Inquisition in previous centuries.

Many deaths were not recorded, but the number of those killed in Valladolid 'behind the lines' in the first months of the war could be counted in thousands. Most of the bodies were thrown into mass graves in the municipal cemetery. Of course there was nothing that the rector of the English College could do about it, but it would be naïve to suggest that he was unaware of the executions and unofficial murders taking place in the city. His support for Franco's Nationalist crusade, albeit one backed by Hitler and Mussolini, may have been understandable; but the enthusiasm with which he expressed it was, at the very least, open to criticism. In 1938 a German SS colonel spent time in Valladolid advising Franco on security and methods of policing; and at the end of the war three thousand people were still being detained in appalling conditions in the city's prisons.

However, Mgr Henson did redeem himself during World War II, reporting on German sympathisers to the British embassy, helping to distribute Allied propaganda and translating Pope Pius XI's letter against Nazism into Spanish. Realising that an understanding between Britain and Spain could be established largely through the Catholic Church, he recommended the appointment of an English Catholic chaplain in Madrid to counter the influence of two German priests suspected of working for the Abwehr. The English College was closed, but Henson stayed on, hanging out the Union Jack every day on the front of the building. He spent most of the time, when not helping British intelligence, painstakingly cataloguing the contents of the library.

In modern democratic Spain, of course, no picture of Franco is to be found in the English College. However, it does accommodate a number of strange bedfellows. The corridors are lined not only with pictures of the English martyrs: here too are the monarchs Henry VIII and Elizabeth I, and even pictures of Elizabeth's spymasters, Sir Francis Walsingham and Sir Robert Cecil, and of Charles Howard, Earl of Nottingham (Lord Howard of Effingham), who commanded the English fleet against the Spanish Armada and again eight years later when Cádiz was sacked. (Sir Thomas More is also among the gallery: apart from his opposition to the English Reformation and strict adherence to the Catholic Church, which cost him his life, he collaborated with a fellow humanist, Juan Luis Vives, who came to England as tutor to Catherine of Aragon's daughter Mary.) Inside the front door of the college the visitor is greeted by a portrait photograph of the Pope, flanked by King Felipe VI and Queen Letizia on one side and the head of the Church of England, Queen Elizabeth II, on the other.

If this is intended to represent a healing of old wounds, so perhaps does the appointment in 2011 as rector of the college of a Gibraltarian, Father John Pardo. His name was put forward by the Archbishop of Westminster, then approved, after lengthy inquiries as to his suitability for the position, by the Vatican, and finally endorsed by the then king, Juan Carlos. The king was not expected to veto the appointment, and the nomination might be said to have been provocative, but his acceptance of it was conciliatory. While Father Pardo has encountered no hostility from fellow Catholic priests or local politicians since moving to Valladolid, no one would suggest that his appointment may lead to a resolution of the Gibraltar question between Britain and Spain. However, as the only British Catholic college in Spain—the Scottish college in Salamanca remains open as a pilgrimage centre, though not for the training of seminarians—the fact that it is run by a Gibraltarian does have a certain irony, and perhaps significance.

LA CORUÑA

When William Wey, a fellow of Eton College, sailed from Plymouth to La Coruña in 1456, to make his pilgrimage to St James at Santiago de Compostela, he counted eighty-four ships lying at anchor in the bay of La Coruña, of which thirty-two were English, all conveying pilgrims to St James's shrine. Seventy years earlier, John of Gaunt sailed into La Coruña with a fleet comprising several thousand archers and lancers, together with a retinue of knights and ladies, to claim for himself the kingdom of Castile. (It was exactly three hundred years since William the Conqueror was offered the kingdom of Galicia following Alfonso VI's defeat by the Moors, but his death a few months later put an end to any prospective transfer of sovereignty.)

John of Gaunt took with him to Spain his Spanish second wife, Constance of Castile, daughter of Pedro the Cruel, and their daughter Catherine of Lancaster. He had assumed the title of King of Castile and Leon in right of his wife, and even signed papers 'Yo El Rey'. But once a marriage had been arranged between Catherine and an eight-year-old boy who subsequently became King Henry III of Castile, together with a handsome annual income for her parents, John of Gaunt decided that Castile could get along without him and so retired to France. Although self-styled, this was the only kingdom that John of Gaunt could claim, whereas in England he had to be content with being the son and father of monarchs (respectively, Edward III and Henry IV) and, for a time, effective head of state after the death of his brother the Black Prince.

Little more than a century later, Catherine, the youngest child of Ferdinand and Isabella, who had united the kingdoms of Aragon and Castile, sailed from La Coruña to England to marry the Prince of Wales and, after his death aged fifteen, to be the first wife of Henry VIII. (The link with John of Gaunt continued: Catherine was descended from his first two wives, while Henry VII and his heirs were descended from John of Gaunt's third wife.) La Coruña was also the point of departure for Philip II when he took ship for England to marry Catherine's daughter Mary; and for the ill-fated Spanish Armada (the fleet had started its voyage of invasion from Lisbon) in 1588.

Following this misfortune, and the previous unhappy relationships with England in which La Coruña had played a transitory part, the city could be said to have got its revenge the year after the Armada defeat when Sir Francis Drake was driven out of La Coruña harbour by the action of a courageous woman. Drake had already raided La Coruña and Vigo during his voyage down the coast of Portugal in 1587 to 'singe the King of Spain's beard' at Cádiz, where a number of the Armada ships were destroyed. Now, two years later, Drake took an Anglo-Dutch fleet and an expeditionary force of some twenty thousand to Spain's north coast in order to attack the galleons of the Spanish Armada which had survived the voyage back to their home ports. Delays due to bad weather and other circumstances persuaded Drake to bypass Santander, where most of the ships were being refitted, and attack La Coruña instead. Merchant ships in the harbour were destroyed, and soldiers under the command of General Sir John Norreys laid siege to the city, plundering their way through the streets, houses and wine cellars.

As they attempted to breach the walls of the old city, they met fierce resistance from the defenders, who included a number of women fighting alongside their men. When one of them, Maria Pita, saw her husband killed by a shot from a crossbow, she grabbed his spear and felled a young British officer who was climbing over the wall. Then, according to legend, she stood on the wall, cried, 'You who have honour, follow me!' and roused the defenders to drive the English soldiers back to the harbour. The assault on the city was abandoned, the raiders regained their ships and the fleet withdrew. It is a good story, no doubt with some truth to it; and it is enjoyable to compare Maria Pita with Joan of Arc when she forced the English army to withdraw from the siege of Orleans. (One point of difference: while Joan was generally acknowledged to be a virgin, Maria was married four times.) At any rate Maria Pita is honoured in La Coruña, with the city's principal square named after her. Facing the city hall is a large statue of Maria: she stands on a plinth, brandishing her spear above her head, with a dead English soldier at her feet. Las Fiestas de Maria Pita are held in La Coruña every summer during August; and her name is celebrated in a large modern hotel, the Melia Maria Pita.

When a large British force was next in La Coruña, more than two hundred years later, its commander was greatly honoured, not only because Spain and Britain were on the same side, but because he was killed in battle. Wellington (then Arthur Wellesley) was conducting a successful campaign against the French in Portugal in the summer of 1808. Recalled to London in October with two generals senior to him—to face a court of inquiry for having agreed unnecessarily generous terms with their defeated enemy—command of the army in the peninsula was given to General Sir John Moore, the 'Father of the Light Brigade', a Scotsman who had seen action in America, Ireland, Corsica and Egypt. It was while in Corsica that he witnessed the effectiveness of a fort which he used as a model for the Martello towers built and placed along the south and east coasts of Britain against an invasion from France.

The idea was that Moore, coming from Portugal, would meet up with a second force under General Sir David Baird, which had disembarked at La Coruña and was making its way over the mountains towards Valladolid. By now (the beginning of December) the Spanish armies had suffered a series of defeats in Aragon and Navarre, and the French had reoccupied Madrid. Napoleon himself was paying his one visit to Spain in order to direct the expulsion of British forces from the peninsula. Having arrived in Spain on 6 November, Napoleon opined that 'Moore is the only general now fit to contend with me. I shall advance against him in person.' Moore was in Salamanca, Napoleon in Burgos before advancing to Madrid and reinstating his brother Joseph on the throne at the beginning of December.

Napoleon intended to invade Portugal and deal with the British Army, and he continued to believe for another fortnight that Moore was falling back to Lisbon. Moore was encouraged to learn that Marshal Soult, with twenty thousand men, was isolated north of Valladolid, enabling the British cavalry to inflict a defeat on their French counterparts at Sahagun. But the bad news was that eighty thousand French soldiers, led by Napoleon, were advancing north from Madrid, and Moore's lines of communication, both with Portugal and with the north coast, would now be dangerously exposed. Against overwhelming odds (Napoleon's armies in the peninsula numbered ten times as many men as Moore's), and knowing that Napoleon was determined to cut him off and destroy the British Army, Moore had no alternative but to order what has become famously known as 'the retreat to Corunna'. However, Napoleon would later concede that it was Moore's decision to withdraw his army through northern Spain which distracted him from his mission to take southern Spain and Portugal.

Moore and Baird finally joined up at Mayorga, south of Leon, on 22 December, and the retreat began on Christmas Eve. Baird's soldiers had just marched about two hundred and fifty miles, over the steep hills and through the wooded valleys of Galicia and Leon. Now they would have to tramp the same route back to the coast. Mayorga today is an unmemorable town, except for its Museo de Pan (bread museum), in flat country growing wheat and wine. Not far away the town of Valderas, with a fortified castle, sits on the only hill for miles around. Napoleon had made this his temporary headquarters, but in spite of its commanding position Moore gave him the slip by crossing the flooded River Esla at Castrogonzalo, blowing the bridge and marching to the nearby town of Benavente.*

The weather in the north-west, traditionally the wettest in Spain in midwinter, had been miserable throughout most of December. As the year ended, it got wetter and colder. Constantly pursued by the French, Moore's rearguard division engaged in 'fighting withdrawals',

---

* Having forded the river in pursuit, General Lefebvre-Desnouettes, one of Napoleon's favourite officers, was wounded and taken prisoner. He was given hospitality by Moore before being transported to England and permitted to enjoy relative freedom in Cheltenham, on his assurance that he would not try to escape. But after almost three years he broke his parole and returned to France in time for the Russian campaign. He also joined Napoleon for the Battle of Waterloo.

successfully holding off the French cavalry. They remained a disciplined fighting unit, but in other divisions morale and discipline broke down. Many soldiers went on the rampage in Benavente, where they stole wine from a monastery; looting and drunkenness were commonplace, as were rape and violent assaults on the local inhabitants who refused them food or shelter. Things only got worse as the army struggled on through rain and snow towards Astorga.

This is Maragatos country, inhabited by people supposedly descended from the Berbers of North Africa or, according to George Borrow, from the Goths who sided with the Moors when they invaded Spain. In these parts they had prospered for centuries as muleteers and married only among themselves. The poet Robert Southey, who had travelled along Moore's route a decade earlier but in the opposite direction, wrote of the Maragatos that they were 'never known to defraud'. They drove the transport mules and ox-carts for Moore's retreating army, but when their villages were ransacked for food and wine, they left their charges and disappeared. A large part of the baggage train had to be abandoned on the mountain slopes, and the wagon carrying the army's supply of cash—£25,000 in silver dollars—was rolled in barrels into a ravine so it would not fall into French hands.

'If our army were in enemy country,' Moore wrote, 'it could not be more completely left to itself... The people run away, the villages are deserted.' It was hardly surprising: in every village doors and windows were broken as the soldiers foraged for food, firewood and, most of all, wine to fuel their drunken rampages. Morale had fallen so low that officers admitted there was little they could do to stop their men running riot. One noted:

> This is no longer a campaign we are conducting; it is rather a devastation by bandits in uniform...The towns and villages half-burned, the farm animals and mules killed or stolen, all the tools and instruments of the peasantry and artisans used as fuel because it is easier to throw them on the fire than to cut down trees, all the churches sacked and profaned...

Some British stragglers, barefoot and resembling beggars, fell by the wayside, or by wayside taverns, and drank themselves literally to death, their bodies frozen in the snow. In *The Recollections of Rifleman Harris*, the author Benjamin Harris described how a group of soldiers, exhausted and starving, threw away their weapons and packs and 'linked arm in arm to support each other, like a party of drunkards'. Women, and even children, accompanied the retreating army. There was no question of their being allowed to ride on the baggage carts, though they might collapse from exhaustion. They had to stagger along with the rest, and if they fell too far behind they risked being captured and raped by the pursuing French soldiers.

It was not unknown for a woman to give birth during the retreat, though the baby's chances of living more than a few hours in the freezing conditions were slim. However, Rifleman Harris recounted one remarkable story of survival:

> One of the men's wives, being very large in the family way, towards evening stepped from among the crowd and lay herself down amidst the snow, a little out of the main road. Her husband remained with her; and I heard one or two observations amongst our men that they had taken possession of their last resting-place. The enemy were indeed not far behind at this time, the night was coming down, and their chance seemed in truth a bad one. To remain behind the column of march in such weather was to perish.
>
> To my surprise, however, some little time afterwards I again saw the woman. She was hurrying with her husband after us, and in her arms she was carrying the babe she had just given birth to. Her husband and herself, between them, managed to carry that infant to the end of the retreat, where we embarked. Many years afterwards I saw that boy, a strong and healthy lad.

On one occasion Harris entered a peasant dwelling and managed to persuade the family to give him bread and wine, but he was not going to mistake this for an offer of hospitality, and was wary of falling asleep. 'Knowing the treachery of the Spanish character, I refused to relinquish possession of my rifle, and my right hand was ready in an instant to unsheathe my bayonet.' Harris cannot be blamed for mistrusting the impoverished villagers he came across during this harsh winter. A few years later, in 1832, Richard Ford travelled along this same mountainous route where 'squalid natives, tattered and half-clad, almost starve in ill-constructed hovels'.

When Moore arrived in Spain, he ordered his troops to treat the people with respect, and 'not shock by their intemperance a people worthy of their attachment'. But in his last dispatch to the Secretary of State for War, Lord Castlereagh, the local people had clearly lost Moore's respect. He wrote of their 'apathy and indifference... beaten, making no efforts for themselves', and wished he had withdrawn his army from Salamanca in early December, after the several defeats suffered by Spanish forces the previous month. Had he done so, the route from Salamanca through northern Portugal to Vigo would have been easier and shorter than the hard slog to La Coruña.

The predominant impression today, when crossing the flat plains between Benavente and Astorga, is of the distant snow-covered mountains. To the retreating British Army at the end of December 1808, they would have presented a most depressing and threatening prospect. The outrages committed in Benavente were resumed in Astorga; the town was effectively sacked and marauding bands of drunken soldiers roamed the streets. A statue of a lion and an eagle in the centre of town pays tribute to its 'heroicos defensores', not against the British Army's excesses but against the armies of Napoleon which besieged Astorga twice, in 1809-10. The Maragatos are also still celebrated here, in the dish offered in almost every restaurant. Cocido maragato consists of a casserole of different products of the pig, together with chick peas, cabbage and peppers—a sustaining rustic meal which British troops would have forcibly grabbed from the local residents at every opportunity.

In Astorga, Moore was joined by some six thousand Spanish troops commanded by the Marquis de la Romana, and on the following day, the last day of the year, he ordered two brigades, led by Brigadier-General 'Black Bob' Craufurd, to head due west to Vigo, which they reached on 12 January and there embarked for home. Napoleon, himself in Astorga only a day after Moore left, received despatches persuading him that he had more important business to attend to in

Austria. He left Soult with orders to continue the pursuit and departed for Valladolid and thence back to France. He was still confident that his army would cut off Moore's before it reached the sea—though by the time he was back in France the British expeditionary force was preparing to embark in La Coruña harbour. The Emperor of the French had been in Spain for barely two months, and he never returned.

Once Moore left Astorga the going got really tough and the army began to fall apart. His men had to struggle uphill and at night through the steeply rocky and oak-wooded country of the Montes de Leon, then over the pass at twelve hundred metres. Even on a warm spring day and driving up a modern road, there is a bleakness and isolation to the landscape which in midwinter and on snow-covered tracks must have been daunting. The march was made more arduous by the transports, field artillery and howitzers they had to drag with them. Captain Bogue of the Royal Greenjackets wrote in his diary: 'One mountain that we had to pass was seven leagues [eighteen miles] over, covered with frost and a deep snow on top of which we found sticking a great many sick carts with men and women dead and dying in all directions.'

Observing the harshness of the landscape, one can understand why the more numerous French Army, suffering the same conditions, failed to surround Moore's soldiers or cut them off. When the two sides did skirmish, the British were often able to hold up the French until night fell, then escape under cover of darkness. Some lost their way and were captured the next day by French cavalry, but during the whole retreat the French did not capture one British standard or gun.

Descending into the valley after the uphill slog over the mountains, Moore's army passed through Bembibre, described then as 'a disgusting collection of hovels' and today a featureless modern town with roofs of local slate. It was here, according to the pursuing Marshal Soult's account, that the British troops 'marched in great disorder and committed many excesses'. While food became scarcer, some soldiers were able occasionally to bring down a deer, providing welcome fresh meat and protein. Frequent signs on the road today indicate the wealth of deer living in these hills; in the valley poplars, alders and vines grow in the brick-red soil around Bembibre. When George Borrow rode this way in the 1830s, his description of the country verged on the ecstatic:

> Perhaps the whole world might be searched in vain for a spot whose natural charms could rival those of this plain or valley of Bembibre... for it exhibits all the peaceful beauties of an English landscape blended with something wild and grand... At the time I would have desired no better fate than that of a shepherd on the prairies, or a hunter in the hills of Bembibre.

After leaving Astorga, Borrow covered sixty miles on his horse in a day over these inhospitable hills, but he still found time to lecture some resting ox-cart drivers on the virtues of the New Testament. They listened bemused as he read them the parable of the Sower, then sold them a copy of the Bible from his saddle-bag. Climbing out of the Bembibre valley, Borrow noted that 'the aspect of heaven had blackened, clouds were rolling rapidly from the west over the mountains, and a cold wind was moaning dismally'. The weather was now beginning to resemble that experienced by Moore's soldiers, whose thoughts would have been far removed from contemplation of 'the peaceful beauties of an English landscape'.

Past Ponferrada, where a castle of the Knights Templar rises above the town, elements of the two armies engaged briefly at Cacabelos, while Sir Edward Paget's rearguard division was withdrawing across the River Cua. The encounter became famous for the killing, with a rifleman's single shot, of the thirty-one-year-old General de Colbert.

Moore went ahead to Villafranca del Bierzo, where he stayed the night at the sixteenth-century castle, which was later sacked and partially burnt by the French. (Today it is the home of the classical composer and conductor, Cristobal Halffter.) Here he addressed his army, exhorting them to be disciplined and resolute for the remainder of their march to the coast, then rode back to Cacabelos, where he threatened the miscreants among his troops with condign punishment. Paget ordered some to be flogged and two to death by hanging from a tree. (They were saved by news of French forces approaching the town.) Most of the foreigners seen walking the road today between Cacabelos and Villafranca are making their pilgrimage to Santiago de Compostela. In autumn the local population is swelled by east Europeans hired for the harvest: the countryside is covered not only in vines but in apple and pear trees.

From Villafranca a second steep and extended climb began to the pass, Puerto de Piedrafita, which divides Leon from Galicia. Had he been able to appreciate it, Moore was now passing through charming villages with Romanesque chapels, grazing cattle and poplars and walnut trees growing along the riverbanks. One such is Vega de Valcarce, where pigs and sheep share pasture alongside lichen-covered copses leading up to heather moorland in the hills. Approaching the pass, as the hills become steeper and bleaker, huge viaducts have been built to carry the EU-funded highway, often almost free of traffic, from Leon to Galicia. In the nineteenth century, as Borrow records, the path was narrow and precipitous:

> A car, drawn by oxen, is creeping around yon airy eminence; the nearer wheel is actually hanging over the horrid descent; giddiness seizes the brain and the eye is rapidly withdrawn… Still more narrow becomes the path along which you yourself are toiling, and its turns more frequent… Shortly before we reached the summit of the pass thick mists began to envelop the tops of the hills, and a drizzling rain descended.

As I neared the summit, low cloud descended and a thick fog soon reduced visibility to a few yards. How many of Moore's army stragglers, I wondered, would have lost their bearings in such conditions and either been captured by the enemy or fallen to their deaths? One officer recorded that, apart from the hundreds left to die in the snow, the roadside was 'strewn with carcasses of horses, mules and oxen… the troops without shoes, marching barefoot and the horses without forage'. Reading such accounts, and travelling these mountainous roads, the landscape harsh and forbidding even in summer, one wonders how Moore's army ever got to La Coruña.

LA CORUÑA

Following a steep descent into Galicia and gentler slopes through birch trees, broom and gorse, Moore called a halt at Lugo, realising that many of his men were at the end of their tether. Here was one of the only depots left by Baird the previous month which had not been plundered. Food, ammunition, clothes and equipment were distributed to the more fortunate, while the army rested for two days in anticipation of an attack by Soult's troops. Many of the British soldiers were anxious to turn and fight, but the French too were exhausted and short of supplies, and Soult decided to wait for reinforcements under Marshal Ney. Having adopted a strong defensive position outside Lugo, along the banks of the River Miño, and waited a day for Soult to attack, Moore resumed his march to La Coruña. For many, however, it could hardly be described as a march. A diary entry recorded: 'They were all in tatters, hollow-eyed and covered with blood and filth. They looked so terrible that the people made a sign of the cross as they passed.'

While more than a thousand British stragglers were captured by the French during this last leg of the retreat, and British attempts to blow up the bridges they had crossed met with limited success, the main body reached the outskirts of La Coruña during the night of 11-12 January. Two days earlier they had crested a hill between Guitiriz and Betanzos and had their first view of the sea. The prospect of getting home now seemed attainable at last. The crossing of the estuary at El Burgo was completed without incident and, for once, several piers of the bridge were successfully blown up. Moore watched his men pass him on the far bank; for many of them it would be the last sight of their commander. The rebuilt bridge still stands alongside a road bridge, and a plaque records its crossing and demolition on 11 January 1809 as 'la ultima mision' of Sir John Moore's army. When he looked over the harbour of La Coruña the following morning, the transport ships that would take his men home were nowhere to be seen. They had been kept at sea by unfavourable winds, and arrived three days later. The wounded and sick were embarked, also the cavalry—having killed most of their horses—which would be of no use on the rocky, broken slopes of the hills where Moore was determined to fight and defeat the French before he left for home.

The battle began in earnest on 16 January. Much of the fighting took place in and around the village of Elviña (the name by which the battle is sometimes known), on the southern perimeter of the city. Moore held the ridge of Monte Mero, but was exposed to artillery fire from the higher ground occupied by the French. During the course of the day Elviña was captured by French infantry, then retaken by two Scottish regiments, to the evident delight of the Glaswegian Moore, who was directing the battle from the slopes above the village.

However, in mid-afternoon, while seated on his horse, a cannon-ball hit the ground in front of him, bounced up and struck him in the left shoulder, smashing his arm, ribs and lungs. He was mortally wounded, but he was still conscious as dusk fell and news was brought to him that his army had bought enough time to complete their embarkation during that night and the following morning. A correspondent for *The Times* reported some days later that it was a bayonet charge by the redcoats that was 'conclusive of the fate of the day, the enemy absolutely flying with the greatest precipitation'.

The wounded general would not allow his sword to be unbuckled while he was borne in a blanket by soldiers of the 42nd Regiment of Foot (the Black Watch) to the centre of the city two miles away, to a house overlooking the port. Here, in great pain and close to death, he was attended by several of his officers, whom he asked: 'Are the French beaten?' On being assured that they were, he said: 'I hope the people of England will be satisfied. I hope my country will do me justice.' He died around midnight, aged forty-seven.* Towards dawn his corpse was hurried to the rampart—remembering the Irish priest Charles Wolfe's poem—above the harbour, to 'the grave where our hero we buried'.

---

* He was said to have died with the name of his friend Lady Hester Stanhope on his lips; he had written to her during the campaign. She was the niece of William Pitt the Younger, and acted as hostess at 10 Downing Street when he was prime minister. She began her travels in the Middle East the year after Moore's death, in 1810.

Slowly and sadly we laid him down,
From the field of his fame fresh and gory;
We carved not a line and we raised not a stone,
But we left him alone with his glory.

It was a moving tribute, reflecting the high regard in which he
was held by his officers and soldiers. Many who went on to fight
with Wellington through the Peninsular War and even to Waterloo
remained proud to call themselves 'Sir John Moore's men'.

Before the British Army departed, two magazines of some twelve
thousand barrels of gunpowder were destroyed in an explosion which
was said to have broken every glass window in the city. The residents
could cope with that, but when it was discovered that a postern
gate, through which the British soldiers passed before boarding their
ships, had been locked and its keys taken (by an officer of the Royal
Welch Fusiliers, who were the last to leave), there was understandable
annoyance. Ever since, in a miniature version of the dispute over the
Elgin Marbles, La Coruña has been asking for the keys to be returned.
Replica keys have been sent from Wales, but the originals remain in
Caernarvon Castle.

The Spanish garrison successfully held off the French until the
British ships had all made their escape, but soon capitulated to Soult,
who also captured a large quantity of British muskets and the neighbouring naval base of Ferrol. (A British force had tried unsuccessfully
to take Ferrol in 1800.) The *Encyclopaedia Britannica* refers to 'the
glorious battle of Corunna', but it was not so considered in England.
When the army of about twenty-six thousand landed at Portsmouth
there was no parade through the streets, no talk of a victory against
Napoleon. In London the government did little to counter the widespread criticism of Moore's campaign. He was accused of indecision
and of failing to defeat and turn back the French during the retreat. A
letter to *The Times* stated: 'The fact must not be disguised... we have
suffered a shameful disaster.' Nevertheless Parliament lost no time in
commissioning a memorial to Moore which was placed in St Paul's
Cathedral.

The historian Sir Charles Oman contends that the Battle of La Coruña enabled Moore's men to redeem their honour through a defensive victory. But the fact remains that at the end of the battle the city was occupied by the French and the British were lucky to escape. Comparisons can be made with Dunkirk in 1940, also recalling Winston Churchill's words that 'wars are not won by evacuations'. However, within three months of the army's humiliating return to England, Wellington (he was still Sir Arthur Wellesley) was back in Lisbon at the head of a larger force, and by mid-May he had clashed with Soult, who had come south to Oporto from La Coruña, and expelled him from Portugal. He then advanced into Spain to inflict defeat on the French at the end of July at Talavera de la Reina, less than eighty miles from Madrid. Wellington later paid tribute to Moore when he said, 'We'd not have won, I think, without him'—referring to his predecessor's achievement in diverting Napoleon's superior forces to the north, thereby frustrating his plan to conquer Lisbon and the rest of Spain south of Madrid.

Following the retreat and evacuation of the army from Spain, public opinion in England was generally directed against Moore's leadership and any future British involvement in the peninsula. But there was no denying the almost unanimous respect and affection in which he was held by those who served under him. No less impressive was the honour bestowed on his memory by both the French and the Spanish. Napoleon said of him: 'His talents and firmness alone saved the British Army from destruction,' and Soult praised his enemy for having 'skilfully taken [the] advantage given him by the terrain to demonstrate his talents and valour, offering an energetic and calculated resistance to me'. Soult went further and had a monument erected to Moore at the place where he fell, with an inscription in Latin. The words had become almost illegible by the end of the twentieth century, when a memorial plaque was fixed to the restored monolith, repeating the Latin words in Spanish and French. It is recorded that this was unveiled on the one hundred and eighty-ninth anniversary of the battle, in the presence of the French ambassador, the mayor of La Coruña, the rector of the university of La Coruña, the Historical

LEFT Goya's portrait of Wellington was painted in 1812, shortly after his victory at Salamanca

RIGHT Major Harry Smith married a 14-year-old local girl, Juana, three days after the Battle of Badajoz, 1812. As Lady Smith, her name was given to the town which became famous in the Boer War

LEFT General Sir John Moore (portrait by Sir Thomas Lawrence) died at La Coruña in January 1809

RIGHT The writer Richard Ford was the best-known English traveller in Spain in the 19th century

British-built houses at the Rio Tinto mines (Huelva)

Thanks to the British consul in Málaga, an English cemetery was provided in the city in 1830

LEFT The Duke of Berwick, bastard son of James II, commanded a Bourbon army to capture Barcelona in 1714

RIGHT Robert Persons, a Jesuit priest, founded the English College in Valladolid in 1589

Queen Victoria's youngest granddaughter Ena married Alfonso XIII in 1906

A statue of the Virgin, mutilated by Anglo-Dutch troops in
Cádiz in 1596, is revered as *La Vulnerata* at the English College
in Valladolid

Clement Attlee, with the Republican General José Miaja, before the Battle of Teruel, December 1937

mbers of the POUM militia – George Orwell is the tall one at the back – outside the Lenin racks in Barcelona, January 1937

The Carlist General Ramon Cabrera retired to Wentworth, Surrey in 1850

El Palacio de Miramar in San Sebastián was built by an English architect in the 1890s

LEFT The theatre critic Kenneth Tynan was a passionate follower of the bullfight

RIGHT Sir Peter Chalmers-Mitchell, Secretary of the Zoological Society for more than 30 years, lived in Málaga during the first months of the Civil War

The poet Roy Campbell (ABOVE) and Laurie Lee became friends in Toledo in 1935 but were on opposite sides in the Civil War

Both Disraeli (LEFT) and Byron (RIGHT) enjoyed the delights of Cádiz in their twenties

LEFT Prince Edward, Duke of Kent, father of Queen Victoria, kept his French mistress at a farmhouse in Andalusia while he was Governor of Gibraltar

RIGHT George Borrow published *The Bible in Spain* in 1842

Cultural Association 'The Royal Green Jackets' and the Order of Knights of Maria Pita. The monolith stands on a piece of grass beside a road running through the university campus.

Half a mile down the hill, the church of San Vicente still stands in the village of Elviña, the site of the fiercest fighting on 16 January 1809. Today Elviña is almost next to the main highway from La Coruña south towards Santiago de Compostela. Only a few yards behind a service station the church and village remain largely undisturbed by modern development. On the slopes up to the main French positions there are allotments and open fields. Outside the church marble plaques record the deaths during the battle of Brigadier-General Robert Anstruther of the Scots Guards and Lieutenant Colonel John Mackenzie, and of a French Brigadier-General, Joseph-Yves Manigault-Gaulois, who 'died on the field of honour' aged thirty-eight. On the other side of the main road, and overlooking the mouth of the Rio de Burgo, is the ridge of Monte Mero chosen by Moore as his defensive position. One can easily see today how unsuitable this sloping, broken ground would have been for the British cavalry. Pylons and blocks of industrial buildings now stand on the hill, and in 2015 bulldozers were witness to further development.

Despite the fact that both Moore and Wellington had uncomplimentary things to say about their Spanish allies, to them Moore, by dying in action, had shown courage and nobility of the highest order. According to George Borrow, writing twenty-five years later, Spaniards spoke of his death and his grave 'with a strange kind of awe'. In the romantic Spanish imagination, comparison might be made with the death of a matador. Borrow also wrote that Moore's 'very misfortunes were the means which secured him immortal fame: his disastrous route, bloody death, and finally his tomb on a foreign strand, far from kin and friends'. An analogy could be drawn with the death of Captain Scott of the Antarctic. Both had great qualities of leadership, but both met their deaths as heroic failures. 'One sound, romantic defeat goes twice as far as three vulgar victories' was the comment of Philip Guedalla, the twentieth-century writer noted for his *bons mots*. In Britain Scott was acknowledged as a hero rather sooner after his death than was Moore, while in Spain the fallen general was accepted almost at once as a son of Galicia.

The Marquis de la Romana, who had fought a number of minor rearguard actions with his troops during the retreat to La Coruña, was the first to raise a memorial over Moore's grave in 1809. It took the form of a wooden column inscribed in chalk by Romana: '*A la Gloria del Excelentisimo Señor Don Juan Moore… La España Agradecida* [grateful]'. The permanent memorial was erected later, on the instructions of the prime minister, Lord Liverpool, and a garden laid out around the grave. Two marble plaques are affixed to a wall overlooking the harbour of La Coruña. On one are written the words of Wolfe's famous poem; on the other an extract from an elegy to Moore composed by the Galician poet Rosalia de Castro in 1871. This poem reads, in part and in translation from the Galician language:

> Please God, noble foreigner, that this be not an alien place for you. There is no poet or spirit of imagination that cannot but contemplate in autumn the sea of yellowing leaves which covers your tomb with love, or the fresh buddings of May… and say, 'How I wish that when I die, I could sleep in this garden of flowers by the sea, far from a graveyard'…
>
> Oh Moore, may you rest in peace. And you who love him, zealous for your honour, sons of Albion, rest at ease. Our land, as chivalrous as it is beautiful, well knows how to honour those who deserve it; and thus honoured, as he deserved, was Moore. He does not lie forsaken in his sepulchre; with compassionate respect a people watches over this foreigner, by death kept far from his own.
>
> When you cross over the waves of the sea, and you go to visit your brother, press your ear to the tomb tenderly. Should you feel the ashes stirring—should you hear unfamiliar voices and understand what they are saying—your soul will be comforted. He will tell you that nowhere in the world could he have found a better resting place, save among his own in their loving embrace.

The garden is named Jardin de San Carlos, and its flowers are suitably English: blue hebes, white begonias, pink hydrangeas. There are clipped low hedges, some taller topiary and—most appropriately of all—four elm trees standing sentinel round Moore's tomb. It is an oblong burial-urn, standing on a plinth and surrounded by two sets of railings. There are cannons below the tomb, and on the outer railings four flaming grenades, the emblem of the Royal Artillery. An inscription reads: 'In memory of General Sir John Moore who fell at the Battle of Elviña while covering the embarkation of the British troops—16 January 1809.'

A bust of Moore is placed against a backdrop of the harbour and the old fort at its entrance, where so many of the British troops waited to embark. The remains of the ramparts are visible below the garden, while the main road round the harbour runs alongside a municipal swimming pool and tennis courts, from which enthusiastic shouts can be heard. A siren sounds from a huge cruise ship about to depart for the Canary Islands. Above the modern port city, in Moore's garden, there is an atmosphere of perpetuity, unchanging and eternally peaceful. This is the finest British memorial in all of Spain.

Such is the enthusiasm in La Coruña for commemorating the 1809 battle and the death of Sir John Moore that a body was founded in the city in 1996 calling itself Asociacion Historico Cultural 'The Royal Green Jackets'. (They took the name of the English regiment, albeit without permission, to honour the memory of Moore as founder and trainer of the Light Infantry, using rifles instead of muskets. The Rifle Brigade was raised in 1800 and became part of the Green Jackets in the mid-twentieth century.) Re-enactments are staged both in the Jardin de San Carlos and elsewhere, and in the Palacio de Capitania (military headquarters). Thanks to this association, a street below the memorial garden and next to the military hospital was renamed Paseo del General Sir John Moore, and the plaques and memorials to Moore and the battle are well looked after. When a group of Peninsular War enthusiasts from the Royal Green Jackets in England walked the route of the retreat in 1984, they were lavishly feted in La Coruña by civil and military dignitaries, and presented by the mayor with a statuette of Moore. Annual ceremonies in Moore's garden include the laying of a wreath by the mayor, cannon shots, uniformed participants and even a Scots piper playing 'Scotland the Brave'.

Walk down Moore's Paseo, turn right along the harbour front and within a few minutes the house where he died is readily identifiable by a plaque on the wall at 5 Canton Grande. It now houses the Banco Popular and a medical library on the first floor. The plaque, placed there in 1909, records that the general died while *'luchando heroicamente en defensa de la independencia española'*. Wellington fought no less heroically for Spanish independence from France, and over a much longer period—more than four years compared with Moore's two months—but he did not die. One is bound to conclude that it was because of his survival, as much as for his arrogance towards his Spanish allies, that no statues of Wellington have been erected in Spain to mark his expulsion of Napoleon's armies from the country. In contrast to his customary dismissal of Spain's supporting role in the war, Wellington did, however, pay fulsome tribute to the Galician soldiers who, in the Battle of San Marcial at the end of August 1813, drove the forces of Marshal Soult back into France across the Bidassoa river. On a plaque in Sir John Moore's memorial garden Wellington decided to indulge in a bit of hyperbole when he referred to *'los inimitables Gallegos'* who showed *'un valor desconocido hasta ahora'* ('bravery hitherto unknown'). 'Every soldier,' he wrote, 'is more deserving than I of the baton which I carry.'

Galicia did not suffer greatly or for long from French occupation; the invaders were expelled from Vigo and the province of Pontevedra after barely two months. The city had had more of a problem with Sir Francis Drake, who ransacked Vigo twice, before and after the defeat of the Spanish Armada. The walled fortress on a promontory at Baiona, south of Vigo (it is now a parador), is still known locally as the Parador de Drake, from the time that the walls were breached by English forces. It is said that the blond Spaniards whom you may see in Vigo today are descended from Drake's sailors. Brigadier-General Robert Craufurd, having taken a brigade of light infantry across country from Astorga to Vigo in the first days of 1809, gave his troops no time to impregnate the local girls and they set sail for home shortly before the French occupied the city. But having lost Vigo by the end of March, Marshal Ney withdrew his forces from Galicia little more than three months later.

Due mainly to the weather—gales and fog are frequent hazards—there was little communication along the seaboard of Galicia in the early nineteenth century. Craufurd had no idea that Moore had been killed until he reached Portsmouth. Some of the ships which rescued Moore's army from La Coruña and Vigo were so delayed by storms that they took two weeks to get home. (Submarine communication between England and Galicia was established in 1873 with the laying of a cable from Cornwall to Vigo by a telegraph company known locally as El Cable Inglés.) In October 1949 my uncle, August Courtauld, decided to sail his yacht, with three friends, across the Atlantic to the West Indies. With winter approaching, it was a somewhat foolhardy idea, and thanks to dreadful weather the boat's engine was put out of action and the topsail yard broke in the Bay of Biscay. August put into La Coruña for repairs, then returned to sea; the mizzen boom was smashed by an even stronger gale, and he had to turn for home. Little wonder that the headland west of La Coruña is called Cape Finisterre—the end of the earth, matched by Finistère in Brittany at the other end of the Bay of Biscay.

The elements in Galicia make for a tough, resilient, self-reliant people. Much of the countryside, when it is not wooded, consists of grass and granite, and smallholdings separated by stone walls. This *minifundia* system worked to the advantage of Galicians during the economic recession of the early twenty-first century. Almost everyone had enough space to subsist on the potatoes, maize and kale which they grew on their 'handkerchief plots' and the few chickens or house cow which they kept. Outside remote villages cows may still be seen grazing the roadside verges, tethered by a long rope held by an old woman who may be dressed in black, wearing *zuecos* (clogs) and carrying an umbrella to protect her from the persistent rain. Most of the thatched cottages with granite walls, which families used to share with their cattle, may have been abandoned; but there is a strong feeling of the west of Ireland in some isolated parts of Galicia. In this Celtic country bagpipes are played in city and village fiestas, and *café irlandes* is widely available in restaurants.

In the nineteenth and early twentieth centuries, as the Irish emigrated to the United States to escape the misery and deprivation of life at home, so did the Galicians take ship from Vigo and La Coruña to South America. (In Argentina and Uruguay, where most of them went to settle, all Spaniards are called *gallegos*.) During the Franco era, many went to other parts of Europe and, if they returned with money, built themselves chalet-style bungalows, without any apparent planning restrictions or thought for the landscape. Here is another similarity with Ireland, where new houses are often constructed in hacienda style, with garishly coloured stucco walls. The number of emigrants increased again after 2008, as the effects of the recession led to the closure of shipyards in Vigo and a rise in official unemployment to more than 25 per cent in 2013 (a lower figure than in the country south of Madrid). Per capita incomes may be among the lowest in Spain, but things are seldom quite as they appear. The *economia sumergida*, or black economy, flourishes in the north-west, with agriculture responsible for the largest share. The growing, marketing and export of the little green peppers, *pimientos de Padron*, named after the town south of Santiago de Compostela, became a hugely successful industry in the first decade of the twenty-first century. And then there are the drugs. Much of the heroin and cocaine imported into Spain through the Colombian network is brought by boat up the narrow estuarial inlets (*rias*) of the coastline around La Coruña and Pontevedra. The former tobacco mafias have been replaced by the drug dealers, but smuggling has always been a way of life to many in Galicia. I was told that a schoolgirl in the coastal town of Cambados, asked by her teacher what was her father's occupation, replied without a hint of embarrassment, '*contrabandista*'.

A shining example of legitimate business success is provided by Zara, the chain of retail clothing shops founded in La Coruña by Amancio Ortega, who is listed as the richest man in Spain, and fifth richest in the world. He is much better known, at least among young people, than Galicia's most famous, if not favourite, son: General Francisco Franco. Born in Ferrol, which he renamed proprietorially El Ferrol del Caudillo, he was given a country property between

Ferrol and La Coruña in 1938, where for the rest of his life he would shoot (only game) and fish and ensure that Galicia remained an isolated rural backwater. His legacy continued in Galicia after his death in the person of Manuel Fraga, the last of Franco's ministers still in public life at the turn of the century. He did not relinquish the presidency of the Galician regional government until 2005, and died in 2012.

While La Coruña is proud to remember and honour the death of Sir John Moore in the Peninsular War, it still keeps alive the memory of Spain's Civil War through two Nationalist figures whose names have been almost completely erased elsewhere. In all Spanish cities, statues of Franco have been removed and streets commemorating him renamed, yet in the centre of La Coruña a square still carries the name of one of the most ruthless and hated generals of the war. José Millan Astray, who was born in La Coruña, fought in the Philippines at the end of the nineteenth century, then went on to found the Spanish Foreign Legion, urging on its recruits with the cry, '¡*Viva la Muerte!*' ('Long Live Death!') His legionaries were known as *Los Novios de la Muerte*, and he earned a reputation for brutality during the colonial wars in Morocco in the 1920s, where he encouraged the mutilation and killing of prisoners. He lost an arm and an eye in battle, and his appearance, with eye patch and several gaps in his front teeth, and his only arm raised in a fascist salute, confirmed his aggressive fanaticism. His famous confrontation with Miguel de Unamuno, at the University of Salamanca shortly after the outbreak of the Civil War, persuaded Franco that this volatile character could harm the Nationalist cause, and he gradually fell from favour. When the maverick general died in 1954, Franco did not attend his funeral.

Until 2011 a statue of Millan Astray stood in the square which bears his name. It had not been daubed or defaced, but to some it was an embarrassment. When a court ordered its removal the mayor of La Coruña, representing the right-wing Popular Party, reluctantly agreed it would have to go. The founder of La Legión was taken down during the night without alerting the public, except for those in apartments overlooking the square whose sleep was unavoidably disturbed, and re-erected in a military museum. But his name lives on in the square almost adjoining the city hall where the heroism of Maria Pita is celebrated. She is La Coruña's favourite daughter, and José Millan Astray was once La Coruña's favourite son.

I thought I had found one street, in Santiago de Compostela, still carrying the name of General Franco, but it was pointed out to me that the 'Franco' referred not to the Galician generalissimo but to the early Frankish pilgrims to Santiago. However, I did come across the name of José Antonio Primo de Rivera inscribed on the wall of the Monasterio de San Payo (which houses the Museum of Sacred Art) in a square behind the cathedral in Santiago. After this son of the dictator General Primo de Rivera, and founder of the fascist Falange, was executed in 1936, his name was incised on the façade of countless church walls in Spain. Despite an order at the beginning of the twenty-first century that these inscriptions should all be erased, a few remain in Galicia (I saw another in Pontevedra).

But the *caudillo*, the dictator of Spain for more than a third of the twentieth century, has been rubbed out of his native Galicia. One name that is still mentioned among *gallegos*, however, almost fondly and with a measure of pride, is that of Fidel Castro. The communist dictator of Cuba he may have been throughout the last thirty years of the Soviet era but, they will tell you in La Coruña and in Vigo, Fidel is one of us. His father was born in Galicia, went to Cuba to fight in the war of independence (against the Cuban revolutionaries), then settled on the island and took up with a peasant woman with whom he had seven children, the third of them Fidel. Castro and Franco always admired one another: they shared a hostility to the United States, a guerrilla mentality and, with roots in the same region of Spain, the characteristic *galleguismo* or Galician guile. When Franco died in 1975, Castro ordered a week's official mourning in Cuba which, though a surprise to many foreign observers, was to fellow *gallegos* entirely understandable.

Though the name Castro is common enough in Galicia, its association with the Cuban dictator may not long outlive him. And almost forty years after Franco's death, his name will mean little or nothing to Galicians born at the end of the century. In La Coruña, however, it may be that the name still best remembered in history is that of a nineteenth-century British general.

SAN SEBASTIÁN

Three queens put their stamp on San Sebastián. Isabella II was the first, going to the north coast to take the cold Atlantic waters in 1845, on the advice of her doctors, to alleviate a skin ailment. She was then aged fourteen and continued every year to spend the summer months in San Sebastián. She survived two Carlist wars in support of her uncle, but was unable to halt the revolution instigated by the navy and army in Andalusia in September 1868. As other parts of the country joined the revolutionary coalition, Isabella realised that her summer, and probably all her future summers, in San Sebastián had come to an end. In the words of Raymond Carr, in his magisterial book, *Spain 1808-1975*, 'With peculiar delicacy San Sebastián waited till the queen was in the train for exile and France before it pronounced against her'—having been the first city to recognise her as queen at the age of three. She would spend the last thirty-five years of her life in Paris. After a messy five-year interlude, Isabella's Sandhurst-trained son succeeded to the throne as Alfonso XII, taking as his second wife Maria Cristina of Austria, who really put San Sebastián on the fashionable European map.

After six years of marriage and three children, Alfonso died aged twenty-seven. A couple of years earlier, Maria Cristina had spent a few hours in San Sebastián with her husband before he sailed to Germany to visit Kaiser Wilhelm I. But it was enough for her to decide, within months of Alfonso's death, to take her family to San Sebastián for the summer, which she so enjoyed that the city became her summer residence as queen regent and the diplomatic and political capital of Spain for two months every year. With her encouragement San Sebastián became a desirable place both for wealthy Spanish and French visitors. A Gran Casino was opened, and Maria Cristina built a palace overlooking the bay (of which more later). Having nominally become king at his birth, Alfonso XIII took over from his mother on his sixteenth birthday and three years later paid an official visit to England, where he met Queen Victoria's granddaughter, Princess Victoria Eugenie (Ena) of Battenberg and married her the following year. Before the wedding, however, she was obliged to convert to the Catholic faith, in a ceremony which took place at Maria Cristina's Miramar Palace in San Sebastián.

Ena was born at Balmoral and spent her early years at Windsor and at Osborne House on the Isle of Wight. She took easily to summer life in San Sebastián, playing tennis, riding and participating in the *thés dansants* which were popular at the time. Ena's Habsburg mother-in-law, who insisted on rigid protocol, did not welcome the more informal atmosphere of the court: the young queen smoked cigarettes, bathed off the beach and strolled along the Paseo de la Concha, past the tamarisk trees and the Gran Casino. Building continued along the seafront, in the Belle Epoque and an eclectic mix of other styles. Two large hotels were opened, named Maria Cristina and de Londres y de Inglaterra, and the Victoria Eugenia theatre (all of them still going strong a hundred years later).

During World War I, in which Spain remained neutral (in spite of Maria Cristina's enthusiastic support for the Central Powers), San Sebastián's casino flourished while gambling in France was prohibited. Things began to change, however, with General Primo de Rivera's coup in 1923, which Ena had warned against but Alfonso did not oppose. Casino gambling was made illegal, and the royal family decided to spend their summers in future along the coast in Santander. However, the marriage was no longer happy, Alfonso was conducting numerous affairs and had fathered five illegitimate children, in addition to six with Ena, by the time of his abdication in 1931.

In their carefree pre-war days young Alfonso and Ena were in the habit of driving with their entourage across the border to Biarritz for polo matches. A Russian grand duchess commented that 'the majority of the San Sebastián colony spent their days, and especially their nights, in their automobiles, tearing madly backwards and forwards between San Sebastián and Biarritz, making the roads a menace to the rest of humanity'. One wonders if it ever occurred to any of these young hedonists, as they sped between two countries, from one fashionable watering hole to the other, that they were all the time in the country of the Basques.

Seven provinces make up the Basque country: in Spain Vizcaya, Guipuzcoa, Alava and Navarre, and in France (the names are little used nowadays) Labourd, Basse Navarre and Soule. The origins of the Basque people are unclear. Turkish, Magyar or Berber descent has been suggested, and their language (Euskera) has been said to have Sanskrit roots. According to legend, it can be traced back to Babel, and survived the Flood because Noah spoke it. More credibly, Euskera—the Basques traditionally refer to all other languages by the name Erdera—is thought to be descended from Aquitanian, an ancient language spoken in Gascony and on both sides of the western Pyrenees until about the ninth century. Several English kings were also dukes of Aquitaine; one of them, Edward III, made his eldest son Edward Prince of Aquitaine. This was the Black Prince who, with his brother John of Gaunt helped to restore Pedro the Cruel to the throne of Castile by engaging and defeating the forces of Enrique of Trastámara at the Battle of Najera in 1367—no more than a temporary victory, as Enrique killed Pedro two years later. (Najera lies west of Logroño, which is just outside the Basque country, though Basque witch trials were held there by the Inquisition in the seventeenth century.) For his efforts on Pedro's behalf the Black Prince was offered the lordship of Biscay.

Basque fishermen were among the first to go after cod and whales off the Newfoundland coast, possibly as early as the fourteenth century. One of Columbus's captains was a Basque, and after the death of Magellan in 1521 it was Juan Sebastian de Elcano, from Getaria a few miles west of San Sebastián, who assumed command of the expedition and became the first man to circumnavigate the globe. In the same century the Society of Jesus was founded by two Basques, Ignatius Loyola and Francis Xavier, who were both canonised as saints. One of San Sebastián's most distinguished sons was the novelist Pío Baroja, who with his fellow Basque Miguel de Unamuno and other literary figures formed the Generation of '98—those who, affected

100

by the loss of Spain's remaining colonies at the end of the nineteenth century, were looking for a way forward in the cultural development of their country.

Less well-known but deserving of a niche in the history of San Sebastián is Catalina de Erauso, known as La Monja Alférez (The Nun Lieutenant). Born in 1592, she entered a Dominican convent at a very young age, escaped from it when she was fifteen and disguised herself as a man. She took ship for the New World, joined the Spanish Army in fighting the Araucanian Indians in Chile, and distinguished herself by her bellicose qualities both in battle and in duels and argument. She was said to have fought alongside her brother, who did not recognise her, and then to have killed her brother in a duel, without any recognition on either side. But whether these stories relate to two brothers or to the same one is not clear. Catalina then rode alone across the Andes, a considerable feat, and apparently promised marriage to two women.

In one of the many fights in which she became embroiled, she was so seriously wounded that, believing she was about to die, she confessed to a bishop that she was a transvestite. He induced her to enter a convent in Peru, from where she returned to Europe and was granted an audience with the Pope, who gave his permission for her to resume her life as a man. She then sailed once more across the Atlantic and died in Mexico aged fifty-eight. One portrait of this remarkable woman, who was said to have no discernible breasts, gives her an androgynous face and bearing; she is dressed in scarlet and carries gloves and a broad-brimmed hat. Another painting shows a more masculine face and a distinctly hostile expression. In the two films of her life made in the twentieth century, there is no mistaking La Monja Alférez for a man.

A memorial plaque recording brief details of her life stands in the grounds of what was the Dominican convent in San Sebastián and since the 1890s has been the site of the more than slightly grotesque Miramar Palace, overlooking the beautiful crescent bay of La Concha. Commissioned by an Austrian daughter of an archduke and designed by an English architect, Ralph Selden Wornum, it is hardly surprising that the building should look so out of place on the north coast of Spain. In a style variously described as 'American Queen Anne' and 'English mock-Tudor', this 'palace' is built of red brick and sandstone blocks, with painted, dark-brown timbered gables, dormers and shutters. There are battlements, a tower at one end, above a *porte cochère*, and Austrian coats of arms on the outside walls. Altogether the impression is of a Victorian prep school in the south of England. The garden in summer is laid out with pink begonias, orange marigolds, striped petunias, multi-coloured busy lizzies—a clash of colours appropriate to the building's lack of taste and style—redeemed only by an orange tree growing up one side of the building. King Juan Carlos attended a school there in the 1950s, and his father was permitted to use the palace during the Franco years. It became the property of the city council in the 1970s.

A mile up the hill, the Aiete Palace, built by a French architect for a Spanish duke in the 1870s and used by Queen Maria Cristina until the construction of the Miramar was complete, has an attractive mansard roof, a white façade and a restrained neo-classical elegance which her palace so conspicuously lacks. It was to the Aiete Palace that Queen Victoria came to lunch, on 27 March 1889, marking the first time that a reigning British monarch had set foot on Spanish soil. Her schedule—spending little more than three hours in San Sebastián—was reported in some detail in *The Times*. Queen Victoria left Biarritz by train at 12.10 p.m., accompanied by Prince Henry and Princess Beatrice of Battenberg (her son-in-law and daughter), seven courtiers, two footmen, 'her Highland attendant in a kilt and two Indian servants in their native dress'. At the border town of Irun she changed to a Spanish royal train and arrived at San Sebastián at 1.05 p.m., where she was met by the Queen of Spain. Together they proceeded to the Aiete Palace, past cheering crowds along the route and various bands playing the National Anthem—'not on every occasion quite perfectly rendered, it must be admitted'. After lunch—disappointingly, the menu was not disclosed—the two queens attended an exhibition of national dance at the town hall and heard 'God Save the Queen' sung in Basque. Then it was back to the station, where the train departed at 4.30 p.m. Maria Cristina made a last-minute decision to accompany her royal guest as far as the border, and Queen Victoria was back in Biarritz in good time for dinner.

Two days later *The Times* reported from Madrid that 'the doyenne of female sovereigns of Europe [aged sixty-nine] has given to the youngest Queen [aged thirty] a remarkable proof of the sympathies which Queen Cristina has inspired'. The visit of 'Victoria Alexandra, Queen of the United Kingdom of Great Britain and Ireland, Empress of India' is recorded on a plaque fixed to a stone column surmounted by a crown in the Aiete garden. In view of the friendly relations apparently established between the two monarchs over lunch in San Sebastián, it was a pity that Queen Victoria did not live long enough to give her blessing to the marriage, five years after her death, of her granddaughter Ena, Princess Beatrice's only daughter, to Maria Cristina's son Alfonso XIII.* (After his abdication, followed by the Republic and the Civil War, Franco had the good taste to choose the Aiete Palace rather than the Miramar Palace as his summer residence. It was from here that he travelled to the French border in 1940 for his only meeting with Hitler; and he spent part of every summer at Aiete until 1975, the year of his death.)

The expansion and conversion of San Sebastián from its role as the principal fortress facing France took place in the years following the destruction of the city by British troops in 1813. After a siege lasting seven weeks, San Sebastián fell to Wellington's army on 31 August. 'The horrors... which attended its capture were never surpassed during the Peninsular War,' Elizabeth Longford wrote in *Wellington: The Years of the Sword*. There was 'slaughter in the breaches so ghastly that there were not enough officers left alive when the town was entered to control their maddened troops; a sack more murderous than Badajoz'. A seventeen-year-old Scots lieutenant, George Gleig, described what happened:

* In the 1920s, Princess Beatrice used to visit Ena and the royal family during the winter in Málaga, where she gave her patronage to a new golf course. Both she and Ena had their portraits painted by the fashionable artist Joaquin Sorolla.

As soon as the fighting began to wax faint, the horrors of plunder and rapine succeeded. Fortunately there were few females in the place; but of the fate of the few which were there, I cannot even now think without a shudder. The houses were eventually ransacked, the furniture wantonly broken, the churches profaned, the images dashed to pieces; wine and spirit cellars were broken open, and the troops, heated already with angry passions, became absolutely mad by intoxication. All order and discipline were abandoned.

Then came the fires, which took hold and spread, destroying almost all the city's buildings. As the flames spread in the high wind, streets were blocked by the stones which fell from collapsing walls. The local population could scarcely believe what their 'allies' had done. Wellington, who had already described his men as the scum of the earth, also blamed the French for having been responsible for some of the destruction. Every year, on the anniversary, the battle and the burning are commemorated in a procession along the street named 31 de Agosto in the Parte Vieja, the old quarter of the city. This is said to be the only street to survive the fire. A little more than twenty years later, volunteers of the British Auxiliary Legion (BAL) went some way to atone for this shameful episode in the Peninsular War by helping to defend San Sebastián from attack by Carlist rebels in the First Carlist War. Several thousand British officers and men volunteered for service under General de Lacy Evans. As no previous experience was required of the soldiers, the legion was, according to the Annual Register, largely made up of 'the wasters of London, Manchester and Glasgow'. Some of those killed were buried, and the names of officers recorded, in a cemetery on the slopes of Monte Urgull, where the French had finally surrendered in 1813. It was given official recognition by Queen Ena of Spain in 1924.

The so-called Cementerio de los Ingleses is a sorry sight today. On a steeply wooded bank, surrounded by pink hydrangeas, tamarisk and very English brambles growing out of euonymus bushes, the monuments and memorials have been neglected, and some desecrated, over the years, while inscriptions have become illegible. Dotted between the stone slabs, a few clusters of thrift and oxeye daisies do their best to brighten the scene. It is ironic that the largest memorial still standing and undamaged in this 'English' cemetery is to a Scotsman, Colonel Whiliam [sic] Tupper 'who at the head of his reg° at the taking of Ayete on the 5 of May 1836 fell mortally wounded at 32 years of age'. When I first visited the cemetery in the 1990s I found a memorial to 'John Callender Esq, lately inspector-general of hospitals', and to his wife Sara and infant daughter Maria Mathilde who had died shortly afterwards. But fifteen years later the inscription was no longer legible. A plan of the cemetery marks the graves of several British officers whose headstones have gone. The name of F. C. Ebswort is barely legible on a stone no longer upright.* And there was no trace of a memorial to four engineer officers who were buried there, among them Lieutenant Colonel Sir Richard Fletcher, Wellington's chief engineer, who had designed the lines of Torres Vedras and died in the final phase of the 1813 siege of San Sebastián. He has a memorial tablet in Westminster Abbey.

An inscription on a stone slab, in Spanish and in English, pays proper tribute to the officers and soldiers of the BAL: 'England has confided to us their honoured remains. Our gratitude will watch over their eternal repose—and to the gallant British soldiers [of the Peninsular War] who gave their lives for the greatness of their own country and for the independence and liberty of Spain'. Below it is inscribed: 'Honour to the Heroes known only to God 1808-14 / 1836-38'. In view of the wanton destruction of the city in 1813, it is perhaps not surprising that this sad little cemetery remains uncared for. When Elizabeth Longford was there in the 1960s, she noted that of the six English gunners sculpted on the principal monument, four had lost their heads. By the beginning of the twenty-first century, the other two were headless, and one soldier, standing next to a cannon partially hidden by ferns and weeds, had been cut off at the waist,

---

* According to the history of the British Auxiliary Legion, Lieutenant Colonel F. C. Ebsworth was 'killed at Hernani by the Spanish soldiers of Santa Cruz when interposing his own body to save that general from assassination in July 1837'.

suggesting more than natural decay. Honour may once have been accorded to the heroes in their 'eternal repose', but as the condition of the cemetery continues to deteriorate they get no respect from the city council, which has consistently ignored proposals to restore and maintain the site.

The bus which runs two or three times a day from opposite the Victoria Eugenia theatre up the Monte Urgull to the Castillo de la Mota was crammed with parents, grandparents and children as we wound our way up the steep hill and round the tight bends, with the driver maintaining his speed as if afraid that the bus might start going backwards if he slowed down. It was a hazardous journey for standing passengers, until we came to a level parking area below the castle and the huge statue of Christ. Everyone got out to admire the view over the city below us and the grand sweep of La Concha bay, while the children ran off to play among the pine trees. No one else walked the few yards downhill to the cemetery, half-hidden on the slope among boulders and tree trunks. The cemetery faces north, out across the Bay of Biscay and towards Britain. But the local visitors prefer the more interesting views in the other direction.

A month before the start of the siege of San Sebastián, Wellington had won the critical Battle of Vitoria, in the southern Basque country, forcing Joseph Bonaparte to abdicate and flee back to France. Exhibitions held in both cities in the summer of 2013 to mark the bicentenaries of the battles appeared to give little credit to Wellington for the victory at Vitoria, preferring instead to celebrate the brilliant achievement of one General Miguel de Alava in effectively bringing to an end the French occupation of Spain. This may have had something to do with the fact that Alava was born in Vitoria and bears the same name as the province in which what is now the capital of the Basque country is situated. At the Museo de Armeria in Vitoria engravings showed Alava entering and liberating the town at the head of his troops, an image which also appears on a monument in Vitoria's main square. Maquettes of the battle gave equal prominence to the Spanish and British forces.

Beside a portrait of Alava, his swagger stick and a cast of his hand were exhibited. Wellington, referred to as a 'noble veteran', was hardly given a look in. No military paraphernalia accompanied a small print of him, but instead his china tea service, complete with an egg-cup and a silver teapot. Neither Elizabeth Longford's account of the battle, nor Peter Snow's in his book *To War with Wellington*, makes any mention of the Basque general, who was in fact Wellington's Spanish liaison officer, and that was all. Perhaps the most interesting fact about Alava's career is that he enjoyed the—possibly unique—distinction of having fought with the French at Trafalgar, then ten years later with Wellington at Waterloo. Wellington gave him a house on his estate at Stratfield Saye in Hampshire, and Alava was ambassador in London in 1834 when Wellington was acting prime minister.

Like Salamanca, Vitoria has two cathedrals: one twentieth-century nco-Gothic, the other of medieval origin which had been undergoing restoration since the 1990s. Outside this building is a statue which, from a distance, I assumed would be of the Virgin Mary or General Alava. But no: it is a curious representation, with one hand on his chin, of the author Ken Follett, who wrote a novel apparently inspired by the cathedral.

For centuries the Basque country south of the Pyrenees was recognised as *una tierra apartada*: it was self-governing, subject to an absolute monarchy, and it had its own code of laws and rights (*fueros*). It was not until 1876 that the Basque country was assimilated into the rest of Spain. The jealously guarded *fueros* were taken away, ostensibly to punish those Basques who had supported Carlism, and before the end of the century a nationalist party had been founded. The father of Basque nationalism, Sabino Arana, was a xenophobe and has been described as an 'unpleasant zealot'. He insisted that to be Basque a person's four grandparents must all have been born in the Basque country and have Euskera names—a qualification which would be much modified when the terrorist organisation ETA admitted to its membership people whose families came from elsewhere in Spain. Both Arana's party and ETA were officially founded on the saint's day, 31 July, of the Basques' most famous son, Ignatius Loyola. (The first Basque underground movement in the 1950s, formed by a handful of Guipuzcoans, initially called itself by the acronym ATA, unaware that in the dialect of the neighbouring province, Viscaya, *ata* means 'duck'.)

ETA's 'armed struggle' began in 1968. One of the most notorious breeding-grounds for terrorists was the town of Renteria, between San Sebastián and the French border. Until the 1960s Renteria was known for its biscuits and for little else. When King Alfonso and Queen Ena used to drive through Renteria on their way to enjoy themselves in Biarritz, it was not much more than a village. Half a century later, factories had been built and a major housing pro-gramme was initiated by the Franco government. As elsewhere in Europe at the time, featureless blocks of low-cost apartments were built, often of poor construction, with corrupt profiteering and a lack of planning. With consequent overcrowding and poverty, Ren-teria became one of the grimmest examples of what in Spain was called *urbanizacion*. Lured by the prospect of jobs in the industri-alised Basque country, migrants came from Castile and Leon, the town's population doubled in two decades and became a seed-bed of crime, vice and terrorism.

The ideology of ETA (Euskadi Ta Askatasuna: Basque Homeland and Liberty) initially followed the tenets of Arana's Basque Nation-alist Party. But it was soon attracting support from non-Basques who identified with the aspirations of the people whose land they had come to share. When the violence began, Franco was still alive, though suffering from Parkinson's disease and losing his grip. He real-ly had no idea how to handle ETA: he couldn't bomb them from the air, as he had done to the Basques of Guernica in the Civil War. Nor could he send a battalion of Moroccan troops to put them down, a tactic he carried out with ruthless success in Asturias in 1934. So he had a number of suspects arrested, tried by a military court and shot. (After protests within and outside Spain, some sentences were com-muted to long terms of imprisonment.) Then, at the end of 1973, in the first major operation by ETA outside the Basque country, Franco's prime minister, Admiral Carrero Blanco, was assassinated in Madrid in his car after attending Mass.

Idoia Lopez was born in San Sebastián (Donostia in Basque) in 1964 and brought up in Renteria. Under the conditions prescribed by Arana for acceptance as a Basque, she would never have qualified, as her parents came from Salamanca. In Renteria in the years after Franco's death, as elsewhere in the Basque country, economic recessions led to the closure of factories and more unemployed young turned to violence. Lopez was ripe for recruitment, and by the age of twenty she was committed to the cause of Basque independence and to ETA. She became a ruthless killer, mostly of policemen, and acquired the nickname of *La Tigresa*, or sometimes *La Muelle* (The Bedspring), because of her rumoured sexual appetite and her habit of seducing policemen before murdering their colleagues. Photographs of her on 'Wanted' posters showed a striking-looking woman with large green eyes and thick, tousled black hair. She was finally arrested in France in 1994, extradited to Spain seven years later and sentenced to a maximum prison term for the murder of twenty-three people.

Following her second marriage in jail (both to ETA prisoners), she was moved to within a hundred kilometres of San Sebastián, where her family was living. In 2011 ETA announced the ending of the armed struggle, but when in the same year Lopez and other prisoners issued a statement renouncing violence and asking for forgiveness from the murdered men's families, they were expelled from the Basque separatist organisation.

While the killings may have stopped, the weapons had not been given up by the end of 2013. There was speculation that this would not happen until the government gave an assurance that all ETA prisoners would be brought back to the Basque country to serve the rest of their sentences. ETA's political party, Batasuna, was declared illegal in 2003 and disbanded a few years later after an unsuccessful appeal to the European Court of Human Rights. Another Basque nationalist party was formed, condemning violence but still with aspirations towards independence for the 'homeland'. It made a strong showing in local elections in 2013; but no one talked of ETA, which probably had a rump of fewer than fifty members.

Back in the 1990s, San Sebastián's main square, the Plaza de la Constitucion, carried posters of all the ETA terrorists in jail, many of them arrested in France and sent back to Spain; and a city councillor was assassinated in the Calle 31 de Agosto, the historic street in the Parte Vieja where other killings took place. Three miles south of San Sebastián, the town of Hernani was known to be one of the centres of ETA activity. (Guipuzcoa, the province in which San Sebastián, Renteria and Hernani are situated, has the highest proportion of regular Basque speakers in the region.) In 1994 I went there on midsummer's eve to attend the traditional fiesta for San Juan. Coming out of the main church, I was confronted by the faces of ETA terrorists hung on cloth banners over the street. Red and green flags bore a sinister black logo, graffiti daubed on the walls announced a '*Marcha de Solidaridad*' and threatened '*Arrepentimiento o Muerte*' ('Repent or Die'). There were posters promoting homosexuality and drugs. As dusk fell, bonfires were being lit, which seemed more menacing than celebratory.

An Irish acquaintance who lived in Hernani told me that the town used to remind him of Crossmaglen during the Irish Troubles. But by the time I went there again in 2013, there was no sign of any ETA presence. Collections may still be taken to support families of the prisoners, but the only visible reference to the organisation was a banner on a public building: 'ETA EZ', adding in Spanish 'ETA NO'. Visitors to Hernani today would not feel intimidated as they made their way to the park on the outskirts of town to admire the abstract sculptures of the internationally famous Eduardo Chillida, who began his professional life as goalkeeper for San Sebastián's football team.

When Queen Victoria travelled by rail from Biarritz to San Sebastián in 1889, she was obliged to change trains at the border. But who would have thought that, more than a century later, it would still be impossible to make this journey without changing trains? The train from San Sebastián (Euskotren, on a one-metre narrow-gauge track) goes as far as Irun, and over the bridge to Hendaye on the French side of the border, but you then have to get out and wait for a French train (SNCF). Trains operated by the Spanish national railway, Renfe, either stop at the border or—such as the Madrid-Paris overnight train—cross the border on the broad-gauge track without a change of train but do not stop at San Sebastián or Biarritz. When the railway lines were first laid in the 1860s, Spain adopted a broader gauge than that used in France in order, it was said, to prevent a French invasion by rail. After all, it was only a few decades since Napoleon had crossed the Pyrenees and deposed the Spanish king.

The narrow gauge operates in much of northern Spain. Given time, it is possible to travel along the length of the coast, from Galicia to the Basque country, by trains which stop about every six minutes. (Some stations are listed as *discrecional*—request stops.) The journey from Ferrol to Oviedo takes approximately six and a half hours, and from Bilbao to San Sebastián two and a half hours. The bus will do the journey in half the time. When Augustus Hare took to the railways for his *Wanderings in Spain* in the late nineteenth century, he commented that the Spaniards 'bring the trains as nearly as possible to the speed of the old mule traffic'. V. S. Pritchett, on his journey through western Spain in the 1920s, observed in his book *Marching Spain* that the railway was 'a thing treated no better than a mule or donkey that everyone can ride on, kick and beat as he wishes. The trains are as slow as oxen and as rare as eagles.' Those who travel today on the narrow-gauge railway along the north coast might think that little has changed. The two-and-a-half hour journey from Bilbao to San Sebastián, a distance of about sixty miles, should be compared with the AVE train service, which takes the same amount of time to cover the 330 miles from Madrid to Seville.

British engineers played a large part in the construction of the Spanish railway network in the second half of the nineteenth century, and British-built locomotives were commonly used. This led to a minor tourist boom, though the adventurous railway passengers ran the risk of falling prey to bandits or Carlist guerrillas. To Hans

Christian Andersen, however, travelling through Spain by train in the early 1860s was entirely pleasurable: 'We now fly on wings of steam past what is dull, get out and linger with what is beautiful—is that not magic?'

One hundred and fifty years later, I would willingly endorse Andersen's feelings. Spain does not have the largest rail network in Europe, but it may well have the largest number of stations. On a train journey which I took some years ago from Oviedo to Santander (four and a half hours, more than forty stops), the scenery was often beautiful and always varied. We crossed fast-running rivers, passed villagers haymaking with pitchforks and horse-drawn carts and watched birds of prey circling over the mountains of the Cordillera Cantabrica which were often dramatically close to the railway line. Most of the other passengers were elderly, travelling short distances between villages; one of them carried a fishing-rod. We stopped at one station called Poo, another called Boo. Every station records its height above sea level or, more precisely, *sobre el nivel medio del Mediterraneo en Alicante*, on an oval plaque carrying the impressive authority of the General Direction of the Geographical and Statistical Institute.

Returning to the Basque country, there are two stations in San Sebastián, one for the narrow-gauge railway, the other for the trains which travel on the broad gauge with Renfe. The efficiency, comfort and, above all, cheapness of Spanish cross-country trains put the British equivalents to shame. In 2013 a journey to San Sebastián from Vitoria, with an allocated seat, taking a little under two hours, and with a discount for those of a certain age, cost eight euros.

Once there, the culinary capital of Spain tempted with its nine Michelin-starred restaurants, though not with its prices. Better to wander through the streets of the Parte Vieja, where numerous bars beckon with their displays of tapas (here called *pintxos*)—most memorably a little dish of octopus with a *membrillo* sauce (made with quince) and a mouthful of spider crab tart. It is no surprise that San Sebastián is also the home of gastronomic societies (*txokos*), most of them still all-male, which a hundred years ago refused to admit Queen

Maria Cristina as a member. Although she had a new hotel and a new bridge named after her in the first years of the century, and was made honorary mayoress, no similar honour was conferred on her by any of the city's gastronomic societies.

BARCELONA

St George's Day, 23 April, is celebrated in many countries, including Spain. The old kingdoms of the Crown of Aragon, which also embraced Catalonia and Valencia, all have the dragon-slayer as their patron saint. In Barcelona La Diada de Sant Jordi (in Catalan) is also known as Lovers' Day (the Catalan equivalent of St Valentine's Day): it is the day when a rose is given to a woman by her husband or lover in exchange for a book. The tradition of the rose goes back many hundreds of years, while the gift of a book is a more recent custom, probably introduced by some bright Barcelona bookseller promoting the fact that both Cervantes and Shakespeare died on 23 April 1616 (though not in fact on the same day, as the calendars then were different). There are statues and reliefs of Sant Jordi, and a chapel in his name, in the Generalidad, seat of the Catalan regional government in Barcelona and a St George's Anglican church in the city's northern district of Sant Gervasi.

The books and roses are mostly sold along that great promenade known as Las Ramblas, named after the Arabic word for river bed, which used to flow past the walls of the old city and down to the sea. It is said that by the end of St George's Day three million roses, many of them accompanied by an ear of corn, and half a million books may have been sold in what is the publishing capital not only of Spain but the Spanish-speaking world. Many authors turn up to sign their books from stalls decked with the scarlet and yellow striped colours of Catalonia, while groups of students participate in marathon readings of Spain's most famous book, *Don Quixote*. (Cervantes's hero had his first sight of the sea in Barcelona.)

The street stalls and kiosks in the Ramblas have been thriving since the plane trees were planted in the mid-nineteenth century, and probably for many decades before that. In his delightful book, *A Stranger in Spain*, published in 1955, H. V. Morton comments on the variety of pets for sale in the Ramblas. 'You can buy a marmoset, if you want one, or a tortoise, a kitten, or goldfish.' When I was there ten years later I remember particularly the caged birds—linnets, canaries, parakeets, quail—the number of foreign newspapers, the shoe-blacks, and that the stalls were open, and crowds of people were walking by, or sitting at café tables, until the early hours of the morning. When she was there in the late 1940s, Rose Macaulay described the crowds in the Ramblas as 'bewitched into perpetual nocturnal animation'.

Returning to Barcelona and the Ramblas, soon after the death of Franco, I was immediately struck by the wealth of reading material which becomes available when a country is freed from a generation of censorship in a totalitarian state. On one bookstall in the Ramblas a pamphlet entitled 'Para la Anarquia' was next to another proclaiming 'Practicas de Amor en Grupo'. There were numerous volumes of memoirs relating to the Civil War, almost all of them from the republican side and I was amused to see George Orwell's *Animal Farm* with the rather less ambiguous title, in translation, of *Revolucion en la Granja*. Those with long memories would recall a similar literary atmosphere in the early 1930s, after the end of dictatorship and the abdication of the king. Albert Weisbord, an American visitor to Barcelona, recorded what he saw shortly before the Civil War began:

In Las Ramblas, adjacent to the flower stalls, large numbers of bookstalls had opened up selling revolutionary literature of all sorts. But it must be admitted that among the serious pamphlets and books, 'literature' of a quite different sort was common: pornographic novels and magazines that purported to speak of physical culture, of nudism and the emancipation of women but in reality were cheap commercial ventures calculated only to stir up the sexual passions of the 'liberated' readers.

At night the avenues were filled with prostitutes and in the old quarters of the town vice did a flaming business. From lurid dives in narrow streets men painted like women leered openly at the passer-by. In the dance halls women dancers with big, firm breasts, writhing to the torrid music of Andalucia or the Levante, exposed their lithe bodies to the gaze of the male public sipping coffee or liqueur and fondling themselves in ecstasy.

115

East of the Ramblas towards the cathedral, you enter the district known as the Barrio Gotico (Barri Gotic), which in some of its dark and narrow streets still evokes the atmosphere of the medieval city which arose from its Roman and Moorish foundations. In the 1960s the gas lamps in the street were lit by hand, at the end of a long pole, each evening, and those of us staying in modest lodgings in the barrio had to find the man with the key to be admitted at night. He would emerge from a dimly lit alley, with a limp which I imagined had resulted from a wound sustained in the Civil War, and he would be jangling his great bunch of keys, putting me in mind of one of Shakespeare's gaolers. Chattering prostitutes of a certain age, protruding fore and aft in their tight, cheap dresses, added some colour and a frisson of excitement to the scene.

When I was last in Barcelona, prostitutes were no longer to be seen in the streets around the Ramblas. They appear to have been replaced by living statues—less appealing though more popular with tourists of both sexes and all ages. However, towards the bottom end of the Ramblas, near the port, one old 1960s favourite remains: Panams, still advertising its 'Showgirls' in neon lights and now calling itself a 'puticlub', which means, in fairly literal translation, a whorehouse. The adjoining district, El Raval, behind the Liceu opera house, used to be associated with drugs and crime and may be again, now that so many immigrants, particularly from Asia and eastern Europe, have moved there.* This was where Carlos Ruiz Zafon placed the 'Cemetery of Forgotten Books' in his novel *The Shadow of the Wind* and its sequels. Across the Ramblas, past the Plaza Real where one of the principal characters in the book lives, and down the Calle Escudellers, I was glad to see the restaurant Los Caracoles still doing business every day *'ininterrumpidamente'* from lunchtime to midnight. First opened in 1835, it has remained continuously in the hands of the same Bofarull family. Towards the Plaza de Cataluña, the walls of the café/restaurant Els 4 Gats, designed by Puig i Cadafalch, one of the leaders of the *modernista* architectural school, feature reproductions of portraits by the young Picasso. He

---

* Also known as the Barrio Chino, this was where the poet Roy Campbell stayed with his family in 1933 and bumped into Aldous Huxley.

used to spend time there at the turn of the twentieth century, and had his first exhibition there while still a teenager.

At the centre of the Barrio Gotico are the cathedral, the Palacio de la Generalidad, with its impressive Renaissance façade, and the city hall. One of the most remarkable things about the cathedral, apart from its Catalan Gothic architecture, is that the cloister is inhabited by a flock of geese. No one seems to know quite how long they have been there, splashing in the cloister's pond and waddling about on the ancient stones, nor why they are there at all. They have been called Capitoline geese, after the geese which are said to have saved Rome from the Gauls when they disturbed the invaders with their squawking one night in the Temple of Juno on Capitoline Hill. Perhaps the Catalans suppose that the geese will protect them from any further encroachment on their liberties and independence from Madrid. Another oddity in the cathedral is a Moor's head, which lies beneath the organ. One might think that this commemorates the expulsion of the Muslims from Catalonia after centuries of Islamification, but in fact Barcelona was occupied by Muslims for fewer than a hundred years. (Subsequently the Knights Templar helped the rulers of Catalonia regain land from the Moors.)

Walking away from the Plaza Real, one of Barcelona's finest squares, laid out in the mid-nineteenth century after Nash and fringed with lamps designed by Gaudí, I came upon a smaller square of undistinguished buildings with a surrealist sculpture of uncertain meaning in its centre. It was not marked on my street map, but it should have been, as it had been renamed Plaza de George Orwell, in recognition of the time he spent here during the first year of the Civil War and of *Homage to Catalonia*, the book he wrote about his experiences.

It is undoubtedly his most honest book of reportage. He had spent years seeking his proletarian dream, and in Barcelona at the end of 1936 he found it. 'It was the first time that I had ever been in a town where the working class was in the saddle.' Orwell was never really at ease with the *plongeurs* of Paris and the tramps in London (*Down and Out in Paris and London*), nor with the poor families with whom he

117

stayed in the industrial north of England (*The Road to Wigan Pier*), and in these books one feels that some of the incidents he relates are at least partly fictitious. But in Barcelona there was no need for elaboration or invention; the city had been taken over by anarchist workers and—possibly for the first time in his life—he didn't feel out of place. Everyone addressed each other as *camarada* or *tu*; the shops and cafés had been collectivised; tipping was forbidden; anyone wearing a tie risked arrest as a bourgeois; and even the Russian foreign minister, Litvinov, was denounced for wearing a hat.

Orwell was not the first British volunteer to go to Barcelona at the beginning of the Civil War. Among the first arrivals were women, one of whom, Felicia Browne, joined a communist militia and was killed on the Aragon front in August 1936. Sylvia Townsend Warner, author and poet, went to Barcelona with her friend and fellow communist, (Mary) Valentine Ackland, working for a British medical aid unit. She found the city to be 'the nearest thing I shall ever see to the early days of the USSR', and, in an article in the *Left Review* in December 1936, described the street stalls in the Ramblas:

> Mixed with the old wares, the flowers, the shaving-brushes, the canaries and love-birds, the watermelons, are new wares: militia caps, pistols (toy pistols to our shame be it spoken), rings and badges and brooches carrying the initials of the anarchist FAI and CNT, the Trotskyist POUM, the communist PSUC and UGT, the inter-party clenched fist with its motto No Pasaran and the hammer and sickle. The bookstalls show new wares, too. Books on political theory, the classics of Marx and Bukharin, Proudhon and Ferrer, the novels of Zola and Rolland and Barbusse.

Orwell knew nothing of the various factions and parties opposed to Franco when he arrived in Barcelona. He didn't join the International Brigades because one of their recruiting officers in Britain, Harry Pollitt, general secretary of the British Communist Party, judged him to be politically unreliable and refused to help. So he contacted the Independent Labour Party which passed him on to the militia calling itself the Partido Obrero de Unificacion

Marxista (POUM). After a few days' training at the Lenin Barracks in Barcelona, Orwell spent the next four months in Aragon, where he saw very little fighting. He commented that, 'In trench warfare five things are important: firewood, food, tobacco, candles and the enemy. In winter on the Saragossa front they were important in that order, with the enemy a bad last.' On one occasion he refrained from shooting a man on a parapet who was half-dressed and holding up his trousers.

But he was joined in the common purpose, to fight against fascism and 'for common decency', and he no longer felt himself to be an outsider. Back in Barcelona, however, at the end of April 1937, he found that the war in Catalonia had become more complicated. The anarchist revolutionary fervour of the previous year had been replaced by the increasingly Soviet-controlled republican government which was not inclined to tolerate any loose cannons likely to upset their strategy. Put perhaps too simply, the communists and the Catalan Socialists (PSUC) were intent on winning the war and postponing the revolution, which was a condition of the aid they received from Stalin. For the anti-Stalinist POUM and the alliance of anarchists and the CNT union (Confederacion Nacional del Trabajo) 'war and revolution are inseparable'. Orwell was now leaning towards the communist view—he wanted to get on with the war—and was considering a transfer to the International Brigades. But no sooner had he got back to Barcelona than he found himself embroiled in five extraordinary days of street fighting in the Ramblas—in which the enemy were not the forces of Franco but of the communist government.

The shooting began when civil guards of the Generalidad attempted to take over the telephone exchange in the Plaza de Cataluña from the CNT, which had controlled it since the outbreak of Civil War the previous summer. The barricades went up, rifle fire was exchanged across the Ramblas, a posse of civil guards took refuge in the Café Moka, and Orwell tried to reach his wife Eileen in the Hotel Continental at the top of the Ramblas. He was ordered to man the roof of the nearby Poliorama cinema where for the next three days, by his account, he read a number of Penguin library books. He was fired at several times and fired only one shot, at an unexploded grenade, which he missed.

Like many of the citizens of Barcelona, Orwell didn't really know what was going on. The historian Raymond Carr has written that 'both sides blazed away at buildings held by their opponents without plan, without any other logic than that your enemies were those who fired against you'. The May Days came to an end when food ran out and government reinforcements arrived from Valencia. Orwell returned to the front near Huesca, but not before he learnt that the POUM was to be suppressed, branded as a disguised fascist organisation, not only by the communists in Spain but by the *Daily Worker* in England. He had come face to face with the Totalitarian Lie, with Newspeak; the seeds of *Animal Farm* and *1984* were sown.

He stayed in Spain only for another six weeks. Wounded by a bullet in the neck, he got his discharge from the militia and was lucky to escape across the French frontier. The POUM had by now been declared illegal, several of his comrades were arrested, imprisoned without trial and shot, and the POUM's former Trotskyist leader, Andres Nin, was tortured to death by agents of the Russian NKVD. Having witnessed, and been a victim of, communist tactics and propaganda in Barcelona, and the suppression of the truth about the war in the English left-wing press, Orwell knew where he stood. 'Every line of serious work that I have written since 1936,' he stated some years later, 'has been written, directly or indirectly, against totalitarianism and for democratic socialism as I understand it.' *1984* began in 1937, in Barcelona, and the course of the remainder of his life was set.

Most of the buildings which feature in accounts of the May Days were hotels along the Ramblas. The Hotel Continental, where Eileen Orwell stayed, and the Hotel Oriente, which was taken over by anarcho-syndicalists, remain today, the Continental still run by the same family that owned it in the 1930s. The Hotel Falcon, further down the Ramblas, was used by POUM militiamen on leave from the front. It was still open in the 1970s, sharing the building with Radio España, but today it houses a library named after the murdered POUM leader, Andres Nin. One of the grandest hotels in those revolutionary years, the Colon, was requisitioned by the PSUC and had a huge picture of Stalin, three storeys high, on its front façade. Today there is another Hotel Colon, built in the 1950s and overlooking the cathedral.

The Café Moka is doing business today under the same name, though now unappealingly modernised and calling itself a restaurant, selling paella, pasta and pizza. Next door is the Hotel Rivoli Ramblas, which in 1937 was the POUM headquarters. The Poliorama, where Orwell spent three uneventful days on the roof, is now a theatre offering musical shows, flamenco and the Catalan *sardana* dances. The building, opened in 1899 as a six-hundred seat cinema, still sports the twin domes which Orwell described and the rooftop observatory where he sat 'marvelling at the folly of it all'. Opposite what was the Hotel Falcon stands the Teatro Principal, with three fine pillared arches and a balustrade above its entrance. During the 1937 May Days it housed what Orwell called the POUM's Comité Local, where he was given a rifle and a few clips of cartridges. There he spent the night wrapped in a stage curtain and woke to the building of cobblestone barricades outside the theatre. A few minutes' walk away is the plaza which now bears Orwell's name, also his real name, Eric Arthur Blair, his dates (Motihari, Bengal 1903—London 1950) and his description: *Escriptor*. By a delicious irony, a notice warns that this square named after the author of *1984* is a *zona vigilada*, continuously watched over by a Big Brother surveillance camera.

That extraordinary firebrand from the Basque country, Dolores Ibarruri, better known as La Pasionaria, followed the Soviet line in ascribing the events of May 1937 in Barcelona to an 'anarcho-trotskyist' plot to shut down the Catalan government on orders from General Franco. She wrote disingenuously of the 'unconditional' aid given by Stalin to the Spanish republic, and of the Russian 'volunteers' who supported it; and she remained an unreconstructed Stalinist during her years of exile in Moscow. Yet, however stubbornly and fanatically pro-communist she may have been, it is impossible not to admire her demagogic power to inspire people through the rousing speeches she gave throughout the Civil War, at mass rallies and on the wireless. Among her most memorable exhortations to Republican troops were her rallying cries to 'die on your feet rather than live on your knees' and, echoing Petain at Verdun, '*¡No pasaran!*' No less remarkable, and moving to read today, was her speech of farewell to the International Brigades in Barcelona when they were withdrawn in November 1938. She first addressed the women of Spain:

> When the years pass by and the wounds of war are staunched… then speak to your children. Tell them of the International Brigades. Tell them how, coming over sea and mountains, crossing frontiers bristling with bayonets and watched by ravening dogs wanting to tear at their flesh, these men reached our country as crusaders for freedom… Today they are going away. Many of them, thousands of them, are staying here with the Spanish earth for their shroud, and all Spaniards remember them with the deepest feeling.

La Pasionaria then spoke directly to the foreigners of the International Brigades:

> You can go proudly. You are history. You are legend. You are the heroic example of democracy's solidarity and universality. We shall not forget you, and when the olive tree of peace puts forth its leaves again, mingled with the laurels of the Spanish republic's victory—come back!

After the death of Franco, she was honoured by the surviving British Brigaders with a memorial statue in Glasgow.

There can be few underground railway stations which lead almost immediately, from their exits, to two such wondrous experiences. From Liceu, beneath the Ramblas, you climb the steps on one side to Barcelona's famous opera house (rebuilt since the fire in the 1990s), and on the other side to La Boquería, the huge covered food market where every imaginable fresh produce is sold. It is one of the great treasures of Barcelona.

While not ignoring the colourful displays of fruit and vegetables, far more attractively presented than in an average British market, I head for the meat stalls to inspect the offal and the parts of animals not normally sold by a British butcher. The pig is, of course, Spain's most popular food animal (trotters and ears are much in demand in the market), but I was intrigued to see lambs' feet, tongues, tripe and heads—with disturbingly bright eyes—plus cakes of unidentified blood for sale. Apart from calves' liver and kidneys—fairly standard fare in London, if not in the rest of England—the animals' feet and tripe (raw and cooked) were also displayed. The white, leathery, flannel-like, honeycombed stomach lining that is tripe can have little appeal on a butcher's counter. I have only tried it once, and then by mistake. In a tapas bar in Madrid one evening I ordered *callos*, believing them to be quail, for which the French word, *cailles*, is very similar. But no: *callos* are tripe, and quail in Spanish are *codornices*.

To make life more confusing, what we call langoustines or Dublin Bay prawns (the ones with little claws) are *cigalas* in Spanish. *Langostinos* are just large prawns. In the Boqueria market the langoustines/*cigalas* were much larger than those available in Britain, which is particularly galling when most of those sold in Spain come from Scotland. Also bigger than we can buy were the John Dory and the hake. The latter fish were either ten-pounders or tiny. Quantities of baby hake were attractively displayed on the slab in the shape of a fan; they were probably below the size permitted by EU regulations, but since they are the national fish of Spain, no one seems to be concerned. We went on to admire the prawns with bright red shells called *carabineros* and the *percebes*, or goose barnacles, gathered from the rocks of the north-west coast known as the *costa de muerte*, where the fishermen do put their lives at risk and consequently the *percebes* are prohibitively expensive. A bar within the market provided delicious, simply cooked dishes of sliced octopus tentacles in olive oil with paprika, razor-clams with garlic and parsley, and the freshest, sweetest grilled prawns ever tasted.

In various restaurants and tapas bars—Barcelona has more than a hundred listed in the Michelin guide—more modern Catalan cooking is to be found. Among memorable dishes were raviolis stuffed with spider-crab meat, carpaccio of veal with a truffle paste, and baked turbot with red piquillo peppers and pieces of *morcilla* (black pudding). On other restaurant menus I spotted a sea-urchin quiche, and *espardenyes* (translated as sea cucumber but they are a variety of marine slug) with a hamburger made from Catalan sausage and pig's trotters. More basic Catalan fare includes salt cod, a beef stew called *escudella* with *romesco* sauce (tomatoes, red peppers, garlic and almonds) and *crema catalana*, similar to crème brulée. While most Spaniards seem to prefer red wine to white, even with fish, the Catalans make some excellent white wines, and not far west of Barcelona is Cava country.

When Richard Ford was travelling through Spain in the 1830s, he accused the Catalans, quite unreasonably in one of his ill-tempered outbursts, of being 'the curse and weakness of Spain'. But he did pay Catalan innkeepers the compliment of being the best in Spain, 'and among the least bad cooks'. Their cooking consisted principally of *garbanzos* (chickpeas) and some part of the pig, stewed in an *olla*, or pot, which was found in every Spanish kitchen. Ford commented on the soup he was given in Barcelona as 'made of bread and garlic in equal portions fried in oil and diluted with hot water. This mess is called *sopa de gato*, probably from making cats, not Catalans, sick.'

In 2010 one Michelin-starred restaurant, Gaig, was offering steak tartare on its menu made from an animal which had been fought and killed in the Barcelona bullring. This was the year that a decision was taken in the Catalan parliament to ban bullfighting in the region. A good deal of hot air was expended on both sides: those in favour of the ban spoke of animal welfare and morality, those against protested that it was a denial of freedom and showed a contempt for culture and art. In fact, the ban was mostly about the Catalans' wish to distance themselves still further from Spain and Spanish traditions. Bullfights had been declining in popularity for some years in Catalonia, most town councils had already banned them, and the Plaza Monumental in Barcelona was the last place in the region which continued to hold *corridas*. 'Catalans deliver a mortal blow to ancient and bloody Spanish "art"' was the headline in *The Times* after the vote. What nonsense: the ancient and bloody Spanish 'art' was largely unaffected in the rest of Spain. The vote had to do with separatist politics rather than any concern for 'animal rights'.

The overwhelming majority of the parliamentary votes to ban the bulls came from the Catalan nationalist parties (*Convergencia i Unio* and *Esquerra Republicana de Catalunya*). The president of the Generalidad, by birth an Andalusian from Cordoba, voted against the ban, declaring that 'I believe in freedom'. The government in Madrid confirmed that it had no intention of putting the bullfight on its legislative agenda, and the Ministry of Culture, reiterating its support, agreed in future to take over from the Interior Ministry the administration and regulation of *corridas* in Spain.

After the Catalan decision in 2010 most ministers in the Madrid government made clear that they would have voted against the abolition of bullfighting and had no intention of debating the issue in parliament. A poll showed that two thirds of Spaniards, while they were not necessarily aficionados, considered that it was rooted in the popular culture of their country. The end of bullfighting has been predicted several times in the past. At the turn of the twentieth century, after the retirement of the two great matador rivals, and national heroes, Frascuelo and Lagartijo, who had been appearing together for nearly twenty-five years, the editors of the two principal taurine magazines, *La Lidia* and *Sol y Sombra*, both wrote that there was no future for the *corrida*. A few years later the so-called Golden Age of bullfighting was ushered in by Belmonte and Joselito. Decades later the distinguished critic Antonio Diaz-Cañabate said the same thing, just before the arrival on the scene of El Cordobes, when the annual number of *corridas* almost doubled. Like it or not, *la fiesta brava* will continue in some regions of Spain for the foreseeable future.

When I attended a bullfight in Barcelona a few weeks before the vote to ban the spectacle, the few placards held by noisy protesters and brandished outside the bullring were, rather surprisingly, written only in English: 'Stop Animal Cruelty—No More Blood'. Within the Plaza

Monumental, the second largest in the country and surmounted by Moorish-style mosaic domes which have been compared to dinosaurs' eggs, we watched a *corrida* which included a Catalan torero and the famous *figura* Enrique Ponce. But the plaza was less than half full, and no report of the proceedings was published the next day in the city's principal newspaper, *La Vanguardia*.

Until the 1970s, Barcelona had three bullrings, with *corridas* every Sunday during the season. Then the weekend social life of Catalans began to change, the beach and the bars were more attractive options, tickets for the bullfights were too expensive and, especially among the young, demand fell to an unsustainable level. One ring was closed, then another (Las Arenas), which was redesigned as a shopping centre by Richard Rogers and opened in 2011. Still retaining its Moorish façade, it sits oddly with the modern buildings in the Plaza de España—though in the architecture of Barcelona anything goes. Other legacies of bullfighting in the city remain. There is a restaurant called Los Toreros, with old, faded posters of *corridas* on its walls. And, more significantly, two public places, a street and a square, are named after Alexander Fleming. The Jardines del Doctor Fleming, behind the Boqueria market, display a bust of the great man and a plaque: 'Barcelona A Sir Alexander Fleming'. He is remembered with gratitude by all toreros for having discovered penicillin, successfully fighting infections caused by horn wounds that in the past had often proved deadly.

The perversity, or hypocrisy, of the Catalans' position, professing concern for animal welfare, was underlined by their determination to continue with their tradition of bull-baiting in village fiestas. In these *correbous*, as they are called, fireworks or flaming torches are attached to the bulls' horns, ropes are used to pull them round the village square, and in some instances they are driven into the sea. This taunting and maltreatment of the animals is justified on the grounds that the bull is not—or not intentionally—killed. The more realistic explanation is that the mayors of many towns and villages, particularly in the province of Tarragona, would lose their jobs if they attempted to abolish the *correbous*.

Where there is opposition to bullfighting in Spain, things are unlikely to be as straightforward as they may appear. Animal rights groups were quick to applaud the mayor of Tossa de Mar as a hero when he banned bullfights from his town on the Costa Brava in 1989. But they looked rather foolish when the circumstances became known. It was not so much a principled stand against a barbarous practice as a cautionary tale of the Spanish character. The mayor was a tough old fisherman who did not always get on with the councillor responsible for developing tourism in this popular coastal resort. At meetings the councillor kept on insisting that Tossa needed to hold more bullfights, but the mayor thought there were quite enough already. The argument continued until one day he became so exasperated by the councillor raising the matter yet again that, in order to shut him up, the mayor got to his feet and announced that he would ban all bullfights in Tossa. He was later happy to admit that his concern for the welfare of the bulls was not uppermost in his mind at the time. But, as he said when he became famous in animal protection circles, a man can change his views—especially when he is getting such good publicity for his town.

Those who fondly imagine that Brussels will exert its influence against a member state which continues to indulge in the savage torture and killing of innocent animals overlook the fact that one of the areas in which the *corrida* is most popular is south-west France. Bullrings are to be found along the Mediterranean coast as far east as Arles, and all over the Basque country on the Atlantic side, to within forty miles of Bordeaux. In fact the bullfight has been increasing in popularity in France. A blanket ban imposed some years ago on the mistreatment of animals was held not to apply to those areas of southern France where there was an 'unbroken local tradition' of bullfighting spectacles. There is a widely held, and entirely mistaken, belief among most people in Britain that 'they don't kill the bull in France'. The *corrida* in France is conducted precisely as it is in Spain— usually with Spanish matadors and Spanish-bred bulls.

'Without the bulls,' the philosopher José Ortega y Gasset said, 'Spain cannot be understood.' Spanish Catalans might dispute or dismiss such a statement, but their siblings in French Catalonia, across the Pyrenees in Roussillon, remain passionate aficionados. The town of Ceret holds a two-day *feria* in mid-July—two *corridas*, two *novilladas*—which has grown in popularity in recent years. The French Catalans are not only contemptuous of the decision taken in Barcelona; they boast proudly of their Catalan heritage, singing folk songs and anthems in the bullring, wearing Catalan costume and waving the red-and-gold barred Catalan flag. When Barcelona banned under-fourteen-year-olds from attending bullfights, Ceret responded by decreeing that in future those under fourteen would be admitted free. It is ironic that while French Catalans celebrate what they like to think of as their distinctive nationality, far removed from central government in Paris, by supporting bullfighting, the Catalans in Spain do the opposite, abolishing it to underline their independence from Madrid and the rest of Spain.

The 2010 football World Cup provided an illustration of Catalonian attitudes to Spain. Little enthusiasm for the national team was shown in Barcelona during the early rounds, except when a Catalan scored a goal. But the fact that FC Barcelona (Barça) provided seven members of the Spanish side in the final ensured at least a temporary stirring of national pride among Catalans. One hundred thousand people gathered in Barcelona's appropriately named Plaza de España to watch Spain's victory on giant screens. In the same month Spain's constitutional court rejected a Catalan statute which would have given the region greater autonomy.

Hans Christian Andersen made a perceptive comment when he called Barcelona the Paris of Spain. Its inhabitants are said to turn their backs on the rest of Spain, to which they consider themselves superior, looking rather to the Mediterranean world and Europe north of the Pyrenees. Their psychological problem, if it can be so described, began with the marriage of Ferdinand and Isabella and the union of Aragon and Castile. Catalonia and Aragon were united in the twelfth century and flourished through commercial expansion round the islands of the Mediterranean. By the mid-fifteenth century, however, Aragon had declined while Castile prospered, so that when the two came together Aragon was very much the junior partner. During Spain's 'golden age' the court moved from Toledo to Valladolid and then Madrid. The new colonies across the Atlantic Ocean were administered from Castile. Barcelona felt isolated, ignored; its resentment of Madrid, and indeed the awakening of Catalan nationalism, can reasonably be traced from that time. Catalonia was and remains loyal to the Hispanic tradition, but not to a uniform Spain ruled from Castile.

In the seventeenth century Philip IV's prime minister, Count-Duke of Olivares, provoked a peasants' revolt among Catalans against his regime of taxation and military levies, leading to a political war against Castilian domination. The Catalan nobility turned to Cardinal Richelieu, the Catalan government (Generalidad) proclaimed Louis XIII king of Barcelona and tried to secure its future under French protection and independent of Madrid.

Sixty years later, the Habsburg dynasty came to an end, leading to the War of the Spanish Succession. Having been, for a time, in effect a French colony, Catalonia initially accepted the Bourbon claimant, Philip V, as king, then changed sides in 1705 when Barcelona fell to an Allied army supporting the Habsburg Archduke Charles and led by the Earl of Peterborough, described by Richard Ford as 'that chivalrous commander, the Don Quixote of history'.* The Catalans, deciding they would be better off under Austrian than French Bourbon rule, were once again at odds with Castile.

When their so-called ally England made peace in 1713 with Louis XIV and with his grandson, Philip V, Catalonia was left in the lurch. Philip had already taken his revenge on the perfidy of the Catalans by abolishing their constitution and the rights and privileges which he had promised them a few years before. Catalonia fought on but, after a siege lasting several months, Barcelona had the misfortune to fall in 1714 to another Englishman, the Duke of Berwick, bastard son

---

* Peterborough went on to take Valencia and remained there for several months, 'enjoying its gaieties' and giving rise to the suspicion that he was less than enthusiastic in support of the Habsburg cause.

of James II.* Berwick was commanding the Bourbon army having defeated an Anglo-Portuguese force at the decisive Battle of Almansa, south of Valencia, in 1707, which effectively secured the Bourbon monarchy in Spain (Cayetana Fitz-James Stuart, Duchess of Alba, who died in 2014, also held the title, among many others, of Duchess of Berwick.) The date of Barcelona's defeat and final surrender to the Bourbons, 11 September, is, perversely, still commemorated as Catalonia's national day.

However, Barcelona soon recovered, both industrially and commercially. In the nineteenth century much of the city's wealth came from the textile industry; French and English fashions in clothes were adopted by the bourgeoisie; and the more expensive restaurants served French food and had their menus printed in French. The cultural centre of Barcelona was the Liceu opera house, built in 1844 and the largest of its time after La Scala. The cosmopolitanism of Catalan opera-goers was such that they would spend much of the time arguing the respective merits of their favourite composers, Verdi and Wagner.

Is it too fanciful to imagine that Catalan intellectuals of the late nineteenth century might have drawn an analogy between the work of Wagner, in whose operas time, as generally understood, has no meaning, and of Gaudí, for whom conventional architectural form had no relevance? Perhaps it is, but his most famous building, La Pedrera (Casa Milà) in the Paseo de Gracia, which is without any straight lines, does seem to possess volcanic qualities which might put one in mind of *The Ring of the Nibelung*. The Casa Milà, and his other celebrated building in the same street, Casa Batlló, can be equally well appreciated as gloriously futuristic, slightly loony, works of art. Miguel de Unamuno characterised them as 'drunken art'.

Having had anti-clerical leanings in his youth, Antoni Gaudí became devoted to the church, and to Catholic ritual, and he refused to speak anything but Catalan. His great ambition, to build a church for Barcelona which would accommodate 13,000 worshippers, was

* In this battle an English general (Berwick) at the head of a French army was opposed by an English army commanded by a Frenchman (Marquis de Rouvigny, aka the Earl of Galway).

deemed eccentric at a time (the 1880s) when Catholicism was losing its hold on the Spanish people and the vast majority did not attend Mass after leaving school. But he was not to be deterred, and for the rest of his life he devoted all his remaining energies to his church, La Sagrada Familia, which has been described as the pride of Barcelona's simpler citizens, and the jest of the more cultivated. Gaudí lived in the crypt during his last years when, according to caricatures of the time, he was an ascetic figure looking rather like a bearded, lugubrious Mister Magoo. In 1926, his church unfinished after forty years, he became perhaps the most famous person to be killed by being run over by a bus—to be precise, a tram—and was buried in his crypt. Had he lived another ten years he would have been torn by his devotion to the Catholic Church, which would have claimed his support for the Nationalists in the Civil War, and to the Catalan culture and language which Franco so ruthlessly suppressed.

When Orwell was in Barcelona, he called the Sagrada Familia 'one of the most hideous buildings in the world… I think the anarchists showed bad taste in not blowing it up when they had the chance.' But they did destroy Gaudí's drawings and models, which makes one wonder whose plan is being followed in the building work which has continued for the best part of a hundred years. When I last saw the church, the smaller of the sculpted fun-fair towers, having been recently repointed and repainted, were surmounted by what looked like fruit, tomatoes and sweetcorn. During Gaudí's lifetime, when construction was proceeding very slowly, he was said to have commented: 'My client is not in a hurry.' In 2010 the Sagrada Familia was consecrated by the Pope and officially declared a basilica, suggesting perhaps that God had intimated to his representative on earth that the time had come for completion. This may or may not take place in 2026, marking the centenary of Gaudí's death; but there are many of Barcelona's citizens who think that it will never, and indeed should never, be finished.

The park which Gaudí designed for his wealthy patron, Count Eusebi Guell, and a Gothic fairytale castle which was the work of Puig i Cadafalch, were Disney-like examples of *modernisme*, which flourished in Barcelona at the turn of the twentieth century. The movement was exclusively Catalan, both culturally and politically, and its principal exponent was Domenech i Montaner, whose Palau de la Musica Catalana is thought by some to be more important than any of Gaudí's work. Its exterior has been described as looking 'as if a Mudejar palace, a number of vaguely classical pillars and St Pancras Station had been stirred in the same pot and then reassembled and turned upside down'. Inside, there are fantastical stone carvings (Wagner's Valkyries are represented here), glazed ceramic mouldings, a huge inverted stained-glass skylight—and wonderful acoustics.

This iconic concert hall was completed shortly before the 'Tragic Week' of 1909, when a general strike degenerated into an orgy of killings and destruction, with churches burned and nuns raped. Graves were dug up and anarchist workers dressed themselves in stolen vestments. Barcelona had had more than its share of violence in the nineteenth century, when the soldier-politician General Espartero, regent of Spain in the 1840s, crushed revolutionary uprisings in the city. 'Barcelona needs to be bombarded at least once every fifty years,' he commented. Anarchism, directed especially against the Church, persisted in Barcelona in the twentieth century until the outbreak of Civil War. Bomb-throwing became commonplace—twenty-one people were killed at the Liceu opera house—as did police brutality and systematic torture in the prison fortress of Montjuich, exhuming memories of the Inquisition.

During all this time, Catalan artistic creativity continued, albeit in a reaction to *modernisme* and a return to a sort of neo-classicism. (Others followed Le Corbusier, wishing to demolish areas of Barcelona and replace them with tower blocks.) But Catalan nationalism was no longer secure. It was suppressed in the 1920s by the dictator, General Primo de Rivera, then revived in the 1930s before being stamped out by Franco at the end of the Civil War. The language was made illegal, and the only chair of Catalan literature was to be found at the University of Madrid. The people of Barcelona, however, have always been resilient, and were publishing books again in Catalan before the death of Franco in 1975. Their resistance has continued, whether to cultural norms or to Spanish influences and traditions.

Perhaps it was this slightly perverse trait in the Catalan character which led to the construction, in the late nineteenth century, of a statue of Christopher Columbus, two hundred feet high, which dominates the square at the far end of the Ramblas adjacent to the old harbour. Presumably Columbus qualified for such a monument by not being a Spaniard. He may have been born in Genoa, or Portugal, or eastern Europe; but in Barcelona you are likely to be told that he was a Catalan, and that is why he returned to Barcelona from his first transatlantic voyage, where he was welcomed by Los Reyes Catolicos, Ferdinand and Isabella. The evidence for this is, at best, insubstantial. When Columbus and his three ships came back across the Atlantic a storm forced them to put into Lisbon. One of the ships, the *Pinta*, was then blown north to Baiona in Galicia, while the other two made it back to their home port of Palos, on the south-west coast. There would be no reason for him almost to circumnavigate the Spanish coast to the Mediterranean port of Barcelona.

Another question arises over the fact that Columbus, on his statue, is pointing not towards the new world but east—perhaps towards his birthplace of Genoa, or towards the ancient world and the Asia which he believed he had discovered. Had he been pointing towards America, and therefore also towards Madrid, that could have given quite the wrong message. The monument was erected for the Universal Exhibition of 1888, a century before the Olympic Games were held in the city. Barcelona likes to think of itself in global terms—too big, too cosmopolitan, too modern to be associated with the ancient Spanish ritual of the bullfight, or indeed the rest of Spain.

TERUEL

Teruel is one of the neglected cities of Spain. It is perhaps the least populated provincial capital in the country, and the only one without a direct rail link with Madrid. At a height of almost one thousand metres, in barren hills some eighty miles north-west of Valencia, Teruel has the reputation of being, in winter, one of the coldest places not only in Aragon but in all of Spain. Even the award of world heritage status by UNESCO in 1986—for its four magnificent Mudejar church towers—did little for Teruel's popularity or its investment prospects. In an effort to put their city more securely on the map, local *turolenses* ran a campaign at the turn of the century with the slogan: '*Teruel existe*'. Both Spaniards and foreigners may have needed the reminder. But they were not reminded—indeed no memorial is to be found in Teruel today— that sixty years earlier the city had literally almost ceased to exist. Over a period of two months in 1937-38, during the coldest recorded winter of the century, Teruel suffered continuous air and artillery bombardment and endured a protracted battle between Nationalist and Republican forces in which casualties exceeded 100,000. It constituted the turning-point of the Civil War, after which the victory of Franco's forces was assured.

Knowing that the city was poorly defended by the Nationalists, the Republican command encountered little opposition when, on 15 December, with snow falling, troops under Enrique Lister encircled the city and occupied the ridge overlooking it known as La Muela de Teruel (Teruel's Tooth). This pre-emptive attack so surprised and annoyed Franco, who was planning a major offensive against Madrid via Guadalajara, that he decided to turn his forces on Teruel. Had he gone ahead with his original plan, as he was urged to do by his military commanders and by Mussolini, the war would almost certainly have ended in 1938, with many thousands of lives saved. But that was not Franco's way: this minor provincial capital must be retaken, at whatever cost, and the enemy driven back towards the Mediterranean.

No one had reckoned with the severity of the weather. In the last week of the year the lowest temperatures of the century, down to minus 18°C, were recorded. Blizzards made troop movements virtually impossible; aircraft were unable to fly; tank engines froze; roads were impassable and supply depots cut off; frostbite casualties were widespread, and those who tried to keep warm by drinking *aguardiente* died in their sleep when the alcohol wore off.

Franco broadcast a confident New Year message, announcing that 'the chain of victories of the year now ended has been clasped with the Teruel brooch'. But his statement was somewhat premature, no more than wishful thinking: the bloody brooch would not become his for another seven weeks. In the first few days of January the cold and the fighting, on La Muela and within the city, became more intense. *The Times* reported on 5 January: 'The snow-swept plateau and the embattled city offer a scene of great desolation. The fighting during the last fortnight probably brought the worst suffering to Spain which she has yet experienced in this war.'* The Nationalists' massive artillery bombardments delivered even more explosive than the Junker bombers of the Condor Legion.

When the Republicans entered the city, much of the civilian population suffered death by grenade and bayonet in brutal house-to-house fighting. The besieged Nationalist garrison surrendered on 8 January, by which time their counter-attack on the outskirts of Teruel was making slow headway. The Republicans within the city now became the besieged. Supplies of food, fuel and ammunition had been unable to get through, and there were reports of soldiers being executed for refusing to attack with empty rifles. In mid-January La Muela was retaken by the Nationalists, who soon afterwards began

---

* On the same day, in the midst of all this darkness and suffering, there was a flicker of light elsewhere in Europe which would have great significance for the future of Spain. In Rome Doña Maria de las Mercedes de Borbon-Dos Sicilias y Orléans gave birth to a son. He was christened Juan Carlos and, on the death of Franco in 1975, he would become king.

their advance on Teruel from the north, across the Sierra Palomera. The International Brigades were brought into the battle to defend part of this sector: the British Battalion, under the command of Bill Alexander, lost about one third of its strength over the coming weeks. Teruel itself was recaptured on 22 February; the Republican forces withdrew in disorder, and the Nationalists went on to reach the Mediterranean two months later.

From below, the trees on the hillside of La Muela give the impression today of several teeth. With their commanding view of the city, the houses on La Muela also command relatively high prices and are partly hidden behind conifer hedges and pine trees. A field of young vines is planted nearby. I was there during the annual July *feria*, when an impressive firework display over the city, seen and heard from La Muela at midnight, put me in mind of the Civil War battle. To any Teruel resident over eighty years of age, the explosions of the rockets, and the cloud of smoke hanging over the city, illuminated by the flash of the fireworks, must have jolted terrible memories. Thoughts of the battle were still present the following morning when I walked into the city centre, to find shop doors and windows barricaded with wooden planks and sheets of iron, and even the great entrance to the cathedral blocked by a wall of steel. Was another attack expected? Yes, but this time it was not by men carrying rifles with fixed bayonets but by bulls with horns not much less deadly.

One of the highlights of Teruel's annual *feria*, called Las Fiestas del Angel, is the running of bulls through the streets of the city centre. This is not like the *encierro* of Pamplona; Teruel's *ensogado*, as it is called (*soga* is a rope) involves one bull at a time, restrained, up to a point, by a long rope tied round its head under the horns. The other end of the rope is held by several young men as the bull, incited by the crowd, charges hither and thither round the Plaza de la Catedral, down the street and into the Plaza del Torico. In its centre is the emblem of the city, a tall column with stars round its rim, surmounted by a square block on which stands a rather diminutive bull. (This acknowledges the name Teruel, derived from two Aragonese words: *tor—toro*, bull and *uel—estrella*, star. The bull was knocked off its pedestal by a bomb during the Civil War battle and kept safely in the city hall until the end of hostilities.) Several hundred people may congregate in this square during an *ensogado*, some of whom will attempt drunkenly to pass the confused and angry bull, usually with some sort of makeshift black cape, and get tossed or even gored for their demonstration of doubtful machismo.

In the Calle Muñoz Degrain, close to the square, the open door of what appeared to be a garage revealed a wealth of framed photographs on the walls, of past *ensogados* and of famous toreros at the Teruel bullring, always standing with the same man. That man, who was sitting at a workbench, introduced himself as the president of one of the local *peñas* (bullfighting supporters' clubs) and offered me a swig of fire-water from his wineskin. This *bota* was made from a bull's hoof, with its cork fashioned as a bull's head and an open mouth through which the liquid was expelled. Having visited an exhibition of bulls' heads and bull paintings in the seventeenth-century Iglesia San Martin, it was time to go to the plaza de toros where, in a *corrida* described afterwards as *regular*, only the French matador, Sebastian Castella, distinguished himself and was awarded two ears. A plaque records the construction of the bullring in 1935, but does not mention that it had to be substantially rebuilt after it was shelled and bombed less than three years later, at the end of the Battle of Teruel. The bullring was the Republicans' last stronghold before they were finally evicted from the city.

One of the most important survivals in the city centre is the mausoleum of two young lovers, Isabel de Segura and Diego de Marcilla. They are Los Amantes de Teruel who, according to the thirteenth-century folk story, died for love because they could not marry. Since Diego's family had little money, Isabel's father, who was the wealthiest man in Teruel, would not allow them to marry, though they had loved one another since childhood. However, Diego undertook to leave the city for five years to make his fortune; and if he were successful within that time, Isabel's father agreed to let him marry his daughter. Nothing was heard of Diego during those five years. Isabel's father arranged a suitable husband for her, but she refused to marry him until the five-year period had expired. On that very day, the wedding took place, and Diego turned up during the nuptial celebrations, having become a wealthy man, to claim his bride. But he was a day too late. Diego was distraught, and he went to Isabel's bedroom that night and said to her: '*Besame, que me muero*' ('Kiss me for I am dying'). She refused to deceive her husband by kissing Diego, and he fell dead. The next day, at Diego's funeral, Isabel came to the church in her wedding dress, placed a kiss on his lips and, falling prostrate over his body, died.

In the mausoleum next to the church and Mudejar tower of San Pedro, and adjoining the Plaza de Los Amantes, the sarcophagi of the two lovers are set side by side, with Diego's hand reaching out to Isabel and almost touching it. (They were removed to a convent during the Battle of Teruel.) Paintings illustrating their deaths hang in the foyer of the *ayuntamiento* (city hall). It is a melancholy tale, the stuff of operatic tragedy, which the people of Teruel are proud to commemorate. But the dreadful story, still within living memory, of the Battle of Teruel, they have decided to forget. In the decades since the Civil War there has been, across Spain, a tacit agreement, known as the *pacto del olvido*, to forget the horrors and internecine conflicts of those years. During this century, however, as few veterans of the war are still alive, there has been a move towards 'truth and reconciliation' in some parts of the country, and an organisation has been established 'for recovering historical memory'. There is evidence of a greater willingness now to talk about and dig up the past— sometimes literally, as mass graves have been uncovered. But not, it seems, in Teruel, where artillery shells and human bones, occasionally turned up by the plough or on building sites, are quickly and quietly removed. Unlike, for instance, at Arromanches or Hiroshima, there is no museum in Teruel exhibiting artefacts or explaining the circumstances of the battle and the war; no memorial, no inscriptions on the walls of the cathedral, no reference to the battle in the city's tourist brochure.

TERUEL

Further north in Aragon, on the featureless plain south of Saragossa, the ruined town of Belchite, besieged and bombed twice during the Civil War, remains as a chilling and affecting memorial to the futility of war. It looks eerily and in miniature rather like Caen in 1944 or Dresden in 1945. Yet there is nothing to tell the visitor that this is what was left of the town after it had been destroyed by Republicans in 1937, then retaken by Nationalists after another battle six months later. The one sign at the entrance to the site carries only the words: '*Pueblo Viejo, Ruinas Historicas*'. There are, or were, two churches in Belchite. At one end of the town the tower of the church of San Martin still stands, its spire holed by mortar shells. At the other end is the crumbled façade of the church of San Agustin, with bishops sculpted in stone and traces of frescoes still visible in the interior, now invaded by swallows and the branches of fig trees. Unusually for Spain, no storks nest in these dead church towers. In the old town's centre, surrounded by smashed tiles and airbricks, an ugly modern cross has been erected, on a plinth scarred with graffiti. But it carries no inscription, no explanatory words.

A mile away, a new Belchite was built after the war. The church is dated 1940 but without any reference to its predecessors. When I first visited Belchite, in 1977, two years after Franco's death, a plaque in the square facing the church recorded the construction of the new town in memory of its '*heroismo sin par*' ('unequalled heroism'). Another plaque, on a wall in the old town, referred to 'one of the most glorious episodes of the crusade'. (Glorious it may have been—the town had held out for ten days against superior Republican forces—but the Nationalists lost the battle.) On a subsequent visit in 2008 there was no trace of either plaque; the one in new Belchite had been replaced in the square by a sculpture resembling a broken length of lead piping.

Teruel has been rebuilt and its ancient monuments—the Mudejar towers, the sixteenth-century aqueduct—restored. But in the surrounding villages the legacy of the Civil War is still apparent. The crumbled stone walls of houses and collapsed tiled roofs remain today in and around Celadas, a village north of Teruel in the

Sierra Palomera, which was just beyond the positions held by the Republicans at the beginning of 1938. It was bombed by them from the air and effectively destroyed. On a hot summer's afternoon in 2011 the village was not only completely quiet but had an air of sadness and decay and lack of life. The only inhabitants to be seen were elderly and stooped. The same impression was conveyed in Concud, close to the Saragossa road, where not only were the village streets deserted, but so was the café opposite the church. During the war Concud was raked by artillery fire from both sides. Once the Nationalists had expelled the Republican forces and the villagers from the ruins, they set up headquarters here as they advanced towards the city. On the wide, undulating plateau outside the village General Monasterio's cavalry division made the one great mounted charge of the war (and one of the last cavalry actions in the history of war). The Mac Paps (a Canadian contingent of the International Brigades) were on the receiving end of this onslaught, which reminded the British commander Bill Alexander, who witnessed it, of *Beau Geste*.

In the third week of January 1938, Alexander and his Brigaders occupied a hill looking down on the Alfambra river valley. Their advance necessitated a climb down two hundred feet of cliff, bravely undertaken also by Charlotte Haldane, secretary of the Dependants' Aid Committee, who visited the men at night in their trenches by the river, near the village of Villalba Baja.* The British battalion made some progress beyond the river, but was driven back, with heavy loss of life, and withdrew from the line at the beginning of February. Villalba Baja today has a memorial cross by the roadside, again without inscription, and looks on to groves of poplar, willow and walnut in the river valley. The ground beyond rises steeply to the cliff—a hill of rock, small scrub oaks and juniper—where the British had manned machine-guns and anti-tank guns as their rifle companies scrambled down the rocks to the river.

---

* Before the British battalion entered the battle, it was visited, in December, by the leader of the Labour Party, Clement Attlee. The no.1 company of the battalion was renamed the Major Attlee Company after he promised to try to end the government's policy of non-intervention.

One man who wrote about his experiences fighting with the British battalion outside Teruel was Laurie Lee, in his book *A Moment of War*, published more than fifty years after the battle. The only problem with his account is that it is fictitious: he wasn't there. It was while preparing an article for *The Spectator* to mark the sixtieth anniversary of the Battle of Teruel in December 1997 that I went to see Bill Alexander to ask him about his memories of the battle. I had a copy of Laurie Lee's book with me, and as soon as I produced it, Alexander growled: 'He wasn't at Teruel; he never got beyond Barcelona. That book is mostly pure fantasy.'

The article caused a bit of a stir when it was published, even including a radio interview on *The World at One*. Lee had died earlier that year and his widow was naturally upset. Several writers came to Lee's defence, saying that it really didn't matter whether his experiences were historically true, and that it was naïve to expect a poet's version of events to be historically accurate. No one, of course, should object to a bit of artistic licence—and Lee was writing half a century after the events. But the book does purport to be a memoir of his few months in Spain (it was probably no more than nine weeks) during the war, and he does claim to have had his moment of war in the snow outside Teruel. Reviewers of the book were impressed by its honesty: in the *Times Literary Supplement* Valentine Cunningham wrote that 'what Spain did for Laurie Lee was to bring home the importance of, and to enable, truthful words, truthful art, in the face of the liars, rhetoricians and propagandists'. Perhaps so, but he was not very truthful about his own experiences.

In her biography of Laurie Lee, published in 1999, Valerie Grove writes that his account 'remains touching and vivid (as to atmosphere) and imaginative (as to hard fact)'. From an Irish historian who had been examining the files of the International Brigades in Moscow's Comintern archive, Grove was able to learn more about Lee's movements in Spain. Alexander was wrong to say that he had never got beyond Barcelona. He was transferred from Figueras to Albacete, the military base camp for Brigaders, and then probably to the training centre at Tarazona de la Mancha, west of Valencia (though Alexander

141

said that Lee's description of life there 'bears no resemblance to the experience of others at the time'). But it is doubtful if he ever joined the International Brigades. He had failed his medical examination due to epilepsy, and he was soon repatriated without going to a war zone.

There are many things—names, dates—that make no sense in *A Moment of War*. But it is the chapter entitled 'The Frozen Terraces of Teruel' which, while a fine piece of writing, is pure fantasy. The cover illustration for the book shows the author, in an overcoat and with a rifle slung over his shoulder, standing in the snow and looking towards the bombarded city of Teruel—'all dusted with a silver, shimmering light', as Lee describes it. It was here, he wrote, that he joined a Welshman and some Spanish soldiers, spent several days in a frozen bunker and was shelled by enemy tanks.

> Our machine-gun blew up, and we pulled back down the gully, scrambling and falling over the ice. First, I remember a running close-up of the enemy—small, panting little men, red-faced boys, frantically spitting Moors. There was the sudden bungled confrontation, the breathless hand-to-hand, the awkward pushing, jabbing, grunting, swearing, death a moment's weakness or slip of the foot away. Then we broke and raced off, each man going alone, each the gasping centre of his own survival.
>
> I headed for the old barn where I'd spent my first night. I lay in a state of sick paralysis. I had killed a man, and remembered his shocked, angry eyes. There was nothing I could say to him now. Tanks rattled by and cries receded. I began to have hallucinations and breaks in the brain.

After Lee crossed the Pyrenees at the beginning of December 1937 he was held prisoner for two weeks, because he had no papers. On the way home he was, according to his account, arrested in Barcelona as a deserter and spy and jailed for three weeks, then rescued by Bill Rust, correspondent for the *Daily Worker*. However, the Barcelona archives held in Moscow contain no record of Lee's imprisonment, and Valerie Grove concludes that it must have been imagined. Why did he also invent the episode at Teruel? He had endured great hardship in getting to Spain and as far as the International Brigades' training centre, but his poor health disqualified him from active service with the British battalion. Perhaps he was so disappointed not to have fought in the Republican cause, not to have had his moment of war, that he pretended, and may even have convinced himself after so many years, that he had. After the war he declined to associate with Brigaders or attend reunions. The Imperial War Museum tried to get him to join a forum on the Civil War with Stephen Spender, but he refused. And when I asked Lee, in 1995, to talk to me about Teruel, he said the memories were too painful.

A journalist tried to bring Lee together with Peter Kemp, a young Cambridge graduate who had fought with the Nationalists at the Battle of Teruel, but he turned that down too. Kemp joined the Carlist *Requetés* in 1936 and transferred to the Spanish Foreign Legion in Aragon. On 5 February 1938 he was watching the aerial and artillery bombardment of Republican forces in the Sierra Palomera north of Teruel, and counting himself lucky to survive 'friendly fire' from Nationalist aircraft. Five Nationalist divisions were part of a great enveloping movement which in three days would inflict huge casualties on the Republicans around the city and seal its fate. Kemp's *bandera* suffered only half a dozen deaths from enemy fire, but an equal number died from cold. He spent several nights on a snow-covered ridge four thousand feet up; as they were in full view of the enemy, no fires were permitted. After forty-eight hours' leave in Saragossa, which he spent with a Cambridge contemporary, Kemp rejoined his unit in another mountainous sector north of Teruel, where the legionnaires were involved in heavy fighting with a much larger number of Republican troops, consisting mainly of members of the International Brigades. Kemp survived, but knew that had he been captured, he would have been shot.

He was one of the very few Englishmen to fight for the Nationalists—not for the fascists, he would insist, but against communism. One of the only Englishwomen to work as a nurse on the Nationalist side was Priscilla ('Pip') Scott-Ellis, who joined a medical unit in the bombed-out village of Cella, five miles from the city and the nearest hospital to the front. In her diary she expressed her horror at some of the surgical procedures she witnessed, often without anaesthetic and with scant regard for hygiene.* On the day, 22 February, that Teruel was finally recaptured by the Nationalists, Pip walked through the remains of the city, finding it 'utterly destroyed. I didn't see a single whole house, they are all covered in bullet holes and shot to bits by cannons with great gaping holes from air bombardments. The filth was incredible…'

Several British nurses were helping to look after Republicans wounded during the Teruel battle. Charlotte Haldane, who came in January 1938 to visit the British Battalion, was accompanied by the Negro singer and political activist Paul Robeson, who visited field hospitals and sang in the wards. (Later that year he went to Wales to sing in a concert to commemorate the Welsh Brigaders who had died in Spain.) Perhaps the most remarkable incident involving foreigners at Teruel was the shelling of a car on the last day of December 1937 which contained four members of the press. They were reporting the war from the Nationalist side and had stopped in the village of Caudé, north of Concud, on their way to observe the battle for the city. A Republican shell exploded in the square, killing three of the occupants of the car: Dick Sheepshanks, who was representing Reuters, and two American journalists. The fourth, who escaped with minor head wounds, was Kim Philby, reporting the war for *The Times* and already a Soviet agent. When the Battle of Teruel was over, he received a decoration from Franco and went on to report from the Battle of the Ebro.

Among those fighting for the Nationalist cause, and forcibly merged with the Falangists in the spring of 1937, were the Carlists. As passionate opponents of liberalism and republicanism, they were natural allies of Franco. They were also traditionalists, fervently loyal to *Dios, Patria y Rey*, and they took as their inspiration the nineteenth-century claim to the throne of the Infante Carlos, brother of Ferdinand VII. Having two daughters and no son, in

---

* The diary was published in 1995 under the title *The Chances of Death*, edited by Sir Raymond Carr.

1830 Ferdinand had published the Pragmatic Sanction (first introduced though not enacted by his father, Charles IV) to enable his elder daughter Isabella to succeed him. Under the previous Salic Law, which restricted the succession to the direct male line, Ferdinand's brother Carlos would have become king. But on Ferdinand's death in 1833 his widow Maria Cristina became regent (Isabella was barely three years old). Carlos insisted the throne was his, the country divided and embarked on three so-called Carlist Wars which continued, on and off, for more than forty years.

The Carlist militias were most active in the Basque country, Catalonia and Aragon. (A hundred years later they would rise again, in Navarre, donning their red berets and shouting their old battle cry, '¡Viva Cristo Rey!' as they joined the Civil War in what they saw as a crusade against secularism.) One of the most committed Carlists was Ramon Cabrera, who had trained initially for the priesthood and whose extraordinary life was divided into two very distinct parts: the first as savage warrior, the second as English country squire. He joined the Carlist guerrillas in Morella, a fortress town which stands on top of a cliff in the hinterland known as the Maestrazgo, between Teruel and Tortosa (where Cabrera was born). For the next seven years, having risen quickly to the rank of *comandante general* of Carlist forces in lower Aragon, he controlled this wild and desolate region with extreme ruthlessness and brutality. The shooting of prisoners of war was fairly standard practice in those times, but when Cabrera's mother was taken hostage by government soldiers (known as Cristinos, fighting for the Queen Regent), he wreaked terrible revenge. He began by shooting two local mayors and, when his mother was executed by firing squad, his merciless reprisals included the murder of civilians, also the wives or daughters of Cristino officers whom he was holding hostage. *The Times*, in a leading article, did not seek to condone Cabrera's cruelty but reserved its condemnation for the murder of Cabrera's mother by a government which Britain was actively supporting through the supply of arms, ammunition and volunteer soldiers.

Atrocities continued on both sides, Cabrera acquired the nickname of El Tigre del Maestrazgo, and he established his headquarters in the small town of Cantavieja, situated 4,000 feet up in mountainous country and like Morella another fastness with walls built into the cliff face. Here he set up a gunpowder plant, a foundry for making weapons and a factory to make uniforms and boots for his troops. Today there is little evidence of Cabrera's time in Cantavieja: a Plaza de Cabrera and the ruins of his house behind the church, a Salon General Cabrera in the local hotel, and a museum of the Carlist wars. Cabrera's life is described in a booklet on the town's website which, with simple colour illustrations and lines of doggerel, is intended as a history lesson for children. But the children are not spared a picture of the general, on his horse, thrusting spears into the naked bodies of his enemies.

Cabrera captured Morella—his troops scaled its walls at night with ropes provided by partisans within the town—and moved his centre of operations there in 1838. This magnificent stronghold is surmounted by a castle which has been variously occupied, attacked and rebuilt over the centuries by Romans, Visigoths, Moors and Christians. Outside the castle entrance there stands today a statue of El Tigre on his horse, wearing a beret and a cape over his shoulders. Black vultures are often to be seen circling above the fortress. The pretender Don Carlos granted Cabrera the title of Count of Morella, but it remained his stronghold for less than two years. He was ousted by General Espartero, commanding the government forces, who added insult to Cabrera by appointing himself Duke of Morella. (Espartero then ousted Queen Maria Cristina and made himself regent.)

The Tiger of the Maestrazgo left his mountain fiefdom for good, sought refuge in France, and returned briefly to Spain a few years later where he fought his last battle on the banks of the River Ter in Catalonia. Despite losing it, he was given the additional title of Marquis del Ter. Now in his early forties, he laid down his arms, came to England and surrendered to the charms of a young Protestant woman called Marianne Richards. Marriage in London followed, and the murderous Spanish warlord became an irenic country squire, living out the rest of his life in Surrey. With his wife's considerable fortune (her father was a large landowner and successful QC), he bought a large castellated house in Virginia Water which had been built for the Duke of Wellington's brother-in-law. The house became the clubhouse for the Wentworth golf course in the early twentieth century; by an enjoyable coincidence the Wentworth PGA Championship was won, in 2005, by an Argentinian golfer called Angel Cabrera.

The Cabreras, or the Count and Countess of Morella, as they were known, had five children, one of whom joined the German Army and became Kaiser Wilhelm's Master of Ceremonies shortly before World War I. The ageing field-marshal (the rank was bestowed on him by Alfonso XII, when Cabrera recognised him as king, much to the fury of the Carlists) was known as a benevolent patriarchal figure in that part of the Home Counties. His name is perpetuated in the Cabrera Club at Wentworth, in Cabrera Avenue (which has a Methodist church) and Cabrera Close in Virginia Water, and a riverside walk along the wooded banks of the River Bourne which is cared for by the Cabrera Trust. He also helped to fund the building of the Catholic Church of St Edward the Confessor in Windsor, where a Mass is still celebrated for him every year on the anniversary of his death. On either side of the altar are two stained-glass windows erected by two of Cabrera's children, in memory of one of their brothers. An inscription reads: 'Pray for Don Leopoldo Carlos Cabrera y Richards, 1860-1909.'

When El Tigre died in 1877, two British generals attended his funeral, at Christ Church, Virginia Water, and a railed corner of the churchyard was set aside for his grave, surmounted by a cross on a four-step podium. On the top step there is a relief carving of the classical tools of war—helmet, sword, spear, shield, together with a laurel wreath—and the words from St John: 'I am the Resurrection and the Life.' The tomb was listed Grade II in 1988. Lime trees stand over the grave, and a plaque to his memory is set in the wall behind the cross, with the not inappropriate words from the Book of Job: 'There the wicked cease from troubling, and there the weary be at rest.' Beyond the churchyard, on the other side of a hedge, are two cottages, dated 1901 and 1906, built by Cabrera's widow. Stone plaques on the brick facades of the houses give their names as Cantavieja Cottage and El Ter Cottage, with the chiselled crown of Morella above. Today's owners of Cantavieja Cottage, no doubt finding that a bit of a mouthful, have renamed it Victoria House. Between the two cottages a small modern building now stands, with the predictably unsuitable name of Lone Pine.

Marianne Cabrera provided the funds for a number of houses to be built in her husband's memory, with names associated with his life—Ebro, Morella, Tortosa—but not all of them have survived. When she died in 1915 aged ninety-four, the respect accorded to her husband forty years earlier seemed to have dissipated. The local newspaper referred to him as 'the Carlist desperado' who had killed more than a thousand of his enemies. But in Wentworth and Windsor his name is rightly remembered as a local benefactor. Very few people in Virginia Water could tell you today of the ruthless military career of the Spanish Tiger. But I was amused to note that the neighbouring town of Sunningdale has an Indian restaurant called The Tiger's Pad.

MÁLAGA

The central market in Málaga is an iron-clad, nineteenth-century building, but with a name, Atarazanas, and an arched entrance which recall its Moorish origins five hundred years earlier. A century before Ferdinand and Isabella besieged and took the city, the Nasrid ruler Mohammed V built a shipyard (*atarazanas* in Arabic) with seven imposing horseshoe-arched gateways, of which only one remains today. As the Andalusian housewives pass through the entrance each morning, some of them having already attended Mass at the cathedral nearby, they may not be aware that the Arabic inscription within two small shields above the arch reminds them that 'only Allah is great, glory be to Him'. It is difficult to believe that this market was once at the water's edge, and that in the eighteenth century local fishermen were still casting their lines into the sea from here. Ships were moored in what is today the Alameda Principal, with its long avenue of mature ficus trees.

Foreigners, principally from Britain and Germany, began to arrive in Málaga, to trade and to live there but, if they could possibly avoid it, not to end their days in Andalusia. Until the nineteenth century all non-Catholics who died in Málaga had to be buried on the beach, at night, with feet first in the sand and their faces towards the sea. Their bodies were often unavoidably exposed by the action of wind and sea and then mutilated by dogs. These degrading scenes were witnessed by an Englishman, William Mark, who had served with Nelson and later at Gibraltar during the Peninsular War. Arriving in Málaga in 1816 as prospective British Consul, he resolved to remedy the situation and provide a decent burial-place for English Protestants.

It was ten years before Mark was appointed consul, whereupon he decided on his initial strategy: to embarrass the city authorities by drawing public attention to a Protestant burial. When one of his consular clerks died, he formed a funeral cortege to process through the streets to the beach, not after dark as prescribed but in broad daylight.

Mark and his fellow mourners took off their hats as they passed some canons of the cathedral, who felt obliged to show respect and so stood bare-headed until the cortege had passed.

The government in London was reluctant to encourage Mark to pursue the matter any further. So he wrote to the governor of Málaga who, having fought in the war under Lord William Bentinck, was well disposed towards the British. Within months a plot of waste land had been granted for a Protestant cemetery, Mark took possession of it 'in the name of King George the Fourth for ever', and a royal order from King Ferdinand VII confirmed the handover. Three acres of waste ground on a steep hillside below the Gibralfaro castle were now British territory. Lord Aberdeen, then Foreign Secretary, agreed to provide £200 to build a wall round the area which, with the burial of its first inmate in 1831, became known as the English Cemetery.

Mark's friend, the Hispanophile traveller and diarist Richard Ford, commented that the cemetery provided 'snug lying for heretical car-cases' and, in view of his wife Harriet's ill health, joked somewhat tastelessly that Mark had 'tried all in his power to get me to Málaga to have a pretty female specimen in his sepulchral museum'. (She died seven years later and was buried in Hertfordshire.) When Ford's baby son died and was buried in Seville, he wrote that 'I doubt if Mark will ever forgive me'. However, Mark's cemetery did not remain empty for long, most notably with the burial there of a young Irish officer, Robert Boyd, who joined a rebellion against the Spanish king and was executed on the beach at Málaga with his Spanish fellow conspirators. Mark had pleaded for mercy on Boyd's behalf with the Governor of Málaga, but in vain; and he was deeply shocked that Boyd was shot without trial. He was unlikely to have been amused when his friend Ford wrote to Henry Addington, British Plenipotentiary in Madrid: 'In his heart I believe [Mark] was as glad as a young surgeon to get a subject for his new churchyard.'

On a steep hillside below the Gibralfaro castle, the English Ceme-tery remains a beautiful place, one hundred and fifty years after Hans Christian Andersen came here and wrote of 'this charming garden, a little paradise of myrtle hedges and tall geranium bushes'. The cemetery gates in the Avenida de Pries, opposite a restaurant and next to the Centro de Estetica y Relajacion, are guarded by two lions beside a Victorian lodge with gabled roof and Gothic windows. A path lined with trees leads up to the garden, a haven of peace where visitors are able to inspect the graves among mimosa, bougainvillaea and a profusion of plumbago.

The city council decided in 2003 not to permit any more burials, on grounds of its own interpretation of 'health and safety'. At that time the cemetery was still British government property, though it had provided no financial support for several decades. A recently retired British consul, Bruce McIntyre, applied to register the cemetery as a charitable foundation and, after four years of bureaucratic prevaricating, ownership of the cemetery was transferred by the British government, with the formal approval of the city authorities, to the English Cemetery in Málaga Foundation. In 2012 the place was declared a 'Bien de Interés Cultural'.

The principal problem, of course, is lack of funds to maintain the cemetery. Concerts and other fundraising events have been held there, but were seldom attended by British tourists or any of the expatriate community living on the Costa del Sol. One Englishwoman resident of Benalmadena, invited to join a tour of the cemetery, said it clashed with her bingo night. A Greek Revival sandstone lodge-temple, built in the cemetery grounds in 1840, was converted fifty years later into St George's Anglican Church. Services are held every Sunday, but the congregation is small, consisting mainly, and somewhat surprisingly, of Nigerians. The foundation is obliged to rely almost entirely on private donations, and on the fees charged for the interring of ashes, which is still allowed by the city council. (In 2014 the charge for a plot was €1,000 and for a niche in one of the walls €650.) There is no shortage of British money along Spain's south coast—some of it from ill-gotten gains—but very little is diverted to the English Cemetery.

There are about twelve hundred graves in the cemetery, not all of them containing the remains of British Protestants. One area is reserved for Roman Catholics, both British and Spanish, and there is a memorial to the officers and men of the Imperial German Navy who were drowned when the training ship *Gneisenau* sank outside Málaga harbour in 1900. Four Allied servicemen from World War II are buried in Commonwealth war graves. The original inner cemetery, surrounded by a wall in need of repair, contains graves covered with shells, many of them now broken. Where the names and dates are legible, they are mostly of children who died of fever during the nineteenth century.

Inscriptions on gravestones are seldom light-hearted, but there is one exception here:

Here lies Stephanie Hespeler
Then Boultbee, then Freeze, then Benn
So many men, never The Man...
Arg-h, men!

Geraniums grow by the monument to William Mark, 'consul for the kingdom of Granada at Málaga' and founder of the cemetery. The memorial to the Irish officer Robert Boyd describes him as '*heroe romantico*'. Dr Joseph Noble MP is buried here: after he died a victim of cholera in 1861, a hospital was established by his family in his memory, to treat the seamen and fishermen of Málaga. The red-brick building still stands, near the cemetery and adjacent to the bullring, but is now occupied by municipal offices. Other distinguished residents of the cemetery include several foreign ambassadors, a Finnish author of detective stories, the Spanish poet Jorge Guillen, Sir George Langworthy and Marjorie Grice-Hutchinson.

Langworthy is described on his gravestone as *hijo adoptivo y predilecto* (adopted favourite son) of Torremolinos, for having built the first hotel in what was then no more than a fishing village. But it didn't make him a fortune: he died a pauper in 1946. Marjorie Grice-Hutchinson, the last person to be buried in the cemetery, was a distinguished academic who wrote papers on monetary theory in sixteenth-century Spain and has a street named after her near the airport, where her family used to own a large estate, which she donated in the 1980s to Málaga University.

However, the best-known name in the English Cemetery is that of Gerald Brenan, described on his headstone as '*Escritor Ingles: Amigo de España*'. He lived in Andalusia on and off for more than sixty years, during which he wrote of his life in the village of Yegen in the region of Las Alpujarras in the 1920s (*South from Granada*) and one of the best books on the background to the Spanish Civil War (*The Spanish Labyrinth*). In Yegen he entertained members of the Bloomsbury Group—Virginia Woolf, Lytton Strachey—and in 1931 his Spanish maid gave birth to a daughter by him. In the same year he married Gamel Woolsey, an American poet whom he had met in Dorset, and they moved to Churriana, on the coast outside Málaga. Two months after the outbreak of the Civil War in 1936, they returned to England but went back to their Spanish house in the early 1950s. Frances Partridge, in her diary, mentions a visit to the English Cemetery with the Brenans, when he told her they were going to the British Consul to book their places: 'It's the nicest cemetery I know, but it's very difficult to get into now. It's got a lovely view—that's very important.'

During these years there was quite a community, both literary and artistic, of mostly English and Americans in Churriana. The Partridges rented a house there, near the Brenans; Augustus John, Bertrand Russell and V. S. Pritchett stayed, and Cyril Connolly was a frequent visitor. He introduced the Brenans to a gregarious American couple, Bill and Annie Davis (she was Connolly's first wife's sister) who kept almost open house at their large property, La Consula. Here they often entertained Ernest Hemingway and his favourite bullfighter, Antonio Ordoñez, together with a variety of friends and others who were passing through and whom they sometimes hardly knew. There was plenty of lively intercourse, both social and sexual, a bit of drug-taking and games of cards played for high stakes. The Brenans would sometimes accompany the Davises on their annual expedition across the Guadalquivir river to the Coto Doñana for the Whitsun festival of El Rocio.

When Brenan died in 1987, he donated his body for medical research to Málaga University, but none of the students wanted to dissect such an illustrious corpse, which was kept in formaldehyde for fifteen years. When his body was finally cremated and placed next to his wife (she had died and was buried in 1968), one resident commented that she would have turned in her grave knowing that the remains of her husband, who had been guilty of many infidelities with younger women, were next to hers.

Very few British residents stayed on in Málaga when the Civil War began. One who was most reluctant to leave was a remarkable seventy-one-year-old Scotsman, Sir Peter Chalmers-Mitchell, who had recently retired after more than thirty years as secretary of the Zoological Society (he was responsible for creating the Whipsnade Park Zoo). Though never a soldier, he could be ranked in distinction with two Scottish warriors who made their mark in Andalusia: Sir James Douglas, comrade-in-arms of Robert the Bruce, who joined forces with Alfonso XI in 1330 and was killed at the Battle of Teba, north of Ronda; and General Sir George Graham, who defeated the French in the Peninsular War at the Battle of Barrosa, outside Cádiz.

Chalmers-Mitchell was born in Dunfermline, the son of a Presbyterian minister. While at the London Zoo, he published an anonymous article, 'A Biological View of English Foreign Policy', in 1896, which caused quite a stir at the time, positing his theory of the inevitability of war between Britain and Germany and the necessity for Germany to be destroyed. He contributed to scientific journals and covered a number of biological subjects in the 1911 edition of the *Encyclopaedia Britannica*. During World War I, while working at the War Office, he translated a play by Pierre Louys, who was noted for the lesbian themes in much of his work; and in 1920, representing *The Times*, he took part in an attempted flight from Cairo to the Cape.

This range of interests did not deflect him from his responsibilities at the London Zoo and his ambition to establish a wild animal park, which opened at Whipsnade in Bedfordshire in 1931. Four years later, Chalmers-Mitchell decided to retire—he was succeeded by Sir Julian Huxley—and buy a house in Málaga where he went to spend 'what I expected to be a peaceful old age'. But civil war in Spain was only months away when he took up what he hoped would be permanent residence at the Villa Santa Lucia on the outskirts of the city in December 1935.

Chalmers-Mitchell, together with a number of British acquaintances who had come out to Málaga to avoid the winter at home, seemed blissfully unaware of what was brewing and took little interest in the politics of the country. They enjoyed the beautiful spring weather, lunched and dined together and talked of investing in plots of land for the future. Bridge was played every day at the English club; a new golf course had just been opened; and the wandering fiddler Laurie Lee, who had recently arrived in the city, observed 'English debs wearing little hats... while sipping glasses of pallid tea'. So apparently unconcerned were the members of the English club by the dangerous political instability and the critical elections won by the Popular Front, that they were discussing the purchase of larger premises. As Chalmers-Mitchell wrote in his memoir *My House in Malaga*:

> The chief difference of opinion was whether [the club] should be moved to commodious rooms in the centre of town, near the harbour (a few months later the building that was being discussed was completely destroyed by rebel bombs), or to a separate house with a garden nearer the two chief hotels.

The retired secretary of the Zoological Society cut a striking figure as he walked along Calle Marques de Larios in the city centre, dressed invariably in a white suit with waistcoat and bow tie. Nor did he moderate his appearance after the Civil War had begun. Gerald Brenan and Gamel, living in Churriana in 1936, would sometimes meet Chalmers-Mitchell when they came into Málaga to buy provisions and inspect the damage caused by air raids. As Gamel recorded in her book of their experiences at the time, *Death's Other Kingdom*, there was 'Sir Peter, dressed as usual in immaculate summer clothes with fresh flowers in his buttonhole'.

When the rebellion began in mid-July many of the principal cities in Andalusia fell quickly to the Nationalists, but Málaga remained with the Republic for almost another seven months. Not only did Chalmers-Mitchell support the elected government, he made a point of keeping in with the various Republican committees which controlled Málaga and in particular with the Federacion Anarquista Iberica (FAI). He denounced the Nationalists for their indiscriminate bombing of Málaga from the air during the second half of 1936, and the British government for failing to support the Republic. But his political views were not 'of the extreme Left', as they were described by *The Times*'s reviewer of *My House in Malaga*; nor was he an anarchist, which Gerald Brenan's biographer, Jonathan Gathorne-Hardy, called him. The tendency to anarchism in the Spanish temperament and tradition certainly appealed to Chalmers-Mitchell, and he admired their concepts of free will and individualism and, he said, their good manners. Of course he would not have condoned the anarchists' destruction of churches and murder of priests; but he agreed with Brenan, writing in *The Spanish Labyrinth*, that they were 'uncompromising moralists' who would never have submitted to the rigid control and demands of communism.

The great majority of the British residents and visitors to Málaga left Spain as soon as possible after the rising, travelling home via Gibraltar. They took with them stories of atrocities committed by the Republicans—children killed, nuns raped, dead bodies mutilated—which Chalmers-Mitchell was anxious to refute. When he returned to London in October he wrote a letter to *The Times* in which, while acknowledging that summary executions had taken place—prisoners shot in jail, men taken from their houses at night and shot by the roadside—he denied that there had been atrocities. 'There were no outrages in the ordinary sense of the word, no torturing, mutilation or other horrors.' This elicited a response from Mr S. Burdett-Coutts of Tunbridge Wells: 'Some of us are sufficiently old-fashioned to regard these nocturnal murders as "outrages in the ordinary sense of the word", and the mental anguish inflicted upon victims, potential victims and their families as the subtlest form of torture.'

While Nationalist sympathisers would certainly have exaggerated the scale and circumstances of the hundreds of killings which did take place while Málaga was still under Republican control, one must conclude that Chalmers-Mitchell was seeing the situation through partially 'Red'-tinted glasses. The Brenans had left Spain in September, and would not return until after World War II, but Chalmers-Mitchell went back to Málaga at the end of 1936. 'It was my home; I had come to love and respect the people who possibly were going to face more terrible things, and I was unhappy about my garden and flowers.' He took with him, as a gift to the hospital, a supply of hypodermic needles and morphia.

Both he and the Brenans, while sympathetic to the Republican cause, had given shelter to prominent pro-Nationalist families and helped them escape from Málaga. Chalmers-Mitchell's neighbour was Tomas Bolin, an enthusiastic monarchist and passionate supporter of Franco, who was clearly at risk of arrest by the Republican committees. He asked if his family might take refuge in Chalmers-Mitchell's house, where they stayed for many weeks. When Bolin was taken away and imprisoned, Chalmers-Mitchell not only dissuaded the FAI from killing him but went frequently to the prison to find out how Bolin was being treated and to bring him a few things which he was allowed to receive. By a supreme irony, when Nationalist troops entered Málaga in February, Chalmers-Mitchell was arrested by Bolin's nephew.

Before that, the bombing of the city continued from the air and from warships outside the harbour. Windows in Chalmers-Mitchell's house were shattered, plaster fell from the ceiling and metal bomb fragments lodged in his garden. But he remained unperturbed: 'I was far from unhappy. I was much occupied, getting on well with the arrangement of material for my book, and before I was taken from my house I had the notes and extracts tied in bundles... and part of the actual first chapter written.' In fact, during the thirteen months he lived in Málaga, from the end of December 1935 to February 1937, under great stress for much of the time, this redoubtable septuagenarian wrote two volumes of memoirs (*My Fill of Days* and *My House in Malaga*, published 1937-8) and translated three books by Ramon Sender, novelist and journalist, whose wife was murdered by Nationalists during the war.

By mid-January 1937 Chalmers-Mitchell was almost the only Briton left in Málaga. But there was a Hungarian, to whom he offered the hospitality of his house if things became critical. This was Arthur Koestler, then a communist journalist attached to the *News Chronicle*, who was already a man marked by the Nationalists for having deceived them the previous summer in Seville into thinking he was a supporter of Franco. On the evening of 7 February, hours before the Nationalist rebels entered Málaga, Koestler turned up at the Villa Santa Lucia with its Union Jack flying over the front door, to find the Grand Old Man of Málaga, as Koestler called him,

> sitting at his writing desk in the light of an oil lamp, apparently oblivious of what is going on outside—a perfect Victorian idyll in the midst of the apocalyptic flood... I feel conscience-stricken because I am late for dinner and my clothes are dirty—on the way here there was another air raid and I had to grovel among the furrows.

At dinner—two sardines, some jam and two bottles of wine—Koestler tried to convince Chalmers-Mitchell, who was more than twice Koestler's age, that he should leave Málaga while he could. But the old man was having none of it. He thought that his presence in the city, as a distinguished observer of events, might dissuade the rebel forces from killing as many people as they would otherwise have done. From the terrace the two men could see a row of shining points of light: the Nationalists' tanks approaching from the mountains to the north. Chalmers-Mitchell gave Koestler a metal case containing a hypodermic syringe and a tube of morphine tablets, and kept one for himself. He had no intention of being taken alive and tortured. They continued to talk and, having finished the wine, switched to gin and vermouth. It was rather like the last days of Pompeii, Koestler said; the band playing on the *Titanic* after it had struck the iceberg may also have come to mind. Their conversation was occasionally interrupted by rifle shots or the rattle of a machine-gun.

Chalmers-Mitchell was having his breakfast bowl of porridge the next morning when warships appeared on the horizon and steamed towards the port. But they did not open fire: the rebel troops were about to enter Málaga from all directions. The first of them to reach the neighbourhood of the Villa Santa Lucia were Italian Blackshirts, whose officers, Chalmers-Mitchell commented, behaved correctly and courteously to him. This was the only courtesy shown to him that day.

A little later, three Spanish men, armed and in uniform, entered the house and, ignoring Chalmers-Mitchell's protests, began to search it. They soon came upon Koestler, who immediately recognised one of them and knew the game was up. It was Luis Bolin, Franco's chief press liaison officer in the south, who had learnt since their encounter the previous summer in Seville that Koestler was a Comintern agent; he was not going to let him go again.* What was remarkable was that Bolin knew of Chalmers-Mitchell because his uncle, Tomas, lived next door and he had visited Chalmers-Mitchell's house as a boy when it belonged to the British Consul. But he did not know that Chalmers-Mitchell had sheltered Tomas and his family in his house, visited him in prison and helped them to escape to Gibraltar. Back in Málaga with the invading Nationalist forces, Tomas now appeared at the house in uniform and, with what might in other circumstances have been a comic interruption, asked for the return of his suitcases which Chalmers-Mitchell had been looking after for him.

However, in spite of all that Chalmers-Mitchell had done for the Bolin family, Tomas appeared distinctly unfriendly and ungrateful, while his nephew Luis had his former protector under armed arrest. As he and Koestler were taken away in a car, Tomas did ask his neph-

---

* Luis Bolin was London correspondent of the newspaper *ABC* when, in July 1936, he hired a plane and pilot to fly from Croydon, pick up Franco in the Canary Islands and transport him to Morocco. He also helped organise a fundraising group in London calling itself the Friends of Nationalist Spain. As Franco's press officer, Bolin intimidated and threatened foreign journalists who strayed from the Nationalist line. After international pressure to release Koestler from jail, and his account of his experiences in *Spanish Testament*, Bolin fell from favour. His highly partisan account of the war, *Spain – The Vital Years*, was published in 1967. Sacheverell Sitwell dedicated his book, *Spain*, published in 1950, to Bolin in gratitude for the assistance which Bolin had given him in his travels round the country.

ew to ensure that Chalmers-Mitchell came to no harm. While they waited at the police station, and before they were separated, Chalmers-Mitchell recited to Koestler some lines of Swinburne:

Live thou and take thy fill of days and die
When thy day comes: and make not much of death
Lest ere thy day thou reap an evil thing.

Koestler said he found these words very comforting when he was imprisoned and expecting to be shot.

Chalmers-Mitchell was taken not to jail but to the Hotel Caleta Palace, a few hundred yards along the road past the English Cemetery where, he knew, neither he nor Koestler would be buried. In fact, the Bolins, nephew and uncle, wanted only to be rid of this distinguished, if tiresome, British gentleman by expelling him from Nationalist Spain. But that was achieved the following day by Chalmers-Mitchell's own initiative. Left to himself, he paid a member of the hotel staff to take a message to a friend of his, the former American consul, informing him that he was detained in the hotel.

Then, showing true British phlegm, Chalmers-Mitchell selected a few novels from a bookshelf and settled himself in an armchair. Later, as he recorded, he

dined early and abundantly. I finished two of the novels and took a third to my room... Two sentries paced outside my door and followed me to the lavatory... I slept well, rose early, shaved and washed in cold water, had coffee and milk in the dining-room. Then I went into the lounge, found the veranda open and took a chair into the brilliant sunlight, and sat down to wait events.

Having received no word from his American friend, Chalmers-Mitchell may conceivably have begun to feel nervous about what was going to happen to him, as indicated by what he wrote next: 'Possibly under strain it was good to have some obsession; mine was that in the hurry of getting night-things under Bolin's revolver, I had forgotten handkerchiefs, and had only one clean one in my pocket.'

But all would be well. On his way to the hotel the following morning, the American had met the acting British consul, Mr Clissold, and the commander of a destroyer, HMS *Basilisk*, which had just arrived from Gibraltar. Chalmers-Mitchell was taken on board, and Clissold was given permission by Luis Bolin to go to the Chalmers-Mitchell villa and pack a couple of suitcases for him which, he was relieved to find, included some clean handkerchiefs. The destroyer took him as far as Gibraltar, and from there he returned to London on another ship. An English newspaper reported that bluejackets of the Royal Navy 'brave death to save knight about to be shot'. It was not quite as dramatic as that, but Sir Peter Chalmers-Mitchell had been fortunate to escape unharmed. (During the first six and a half months of the war the Republicans were responsible for killing one thousand people in Málaga, while in the first week of the Nationalists' occupation of the city they murdered or executed three thousand five hundred.)

He had sent a cable from HMS *Basilisk* to the editor of the *News Chronicle* warning him that Koestler was in great danger. Having been summarily tried and sentenced to death, he was transferred to prison in Seville, where he spent the next three months in conditions of squalor and constant fear, with executions of other prisoners taking place in the middle of the night. Back in England, Koestler's wife arranged for newspaper articles to be published, questions were asked in the House of Commons, MPs sent letters of protest to Franco, Winston Churchill wrote to the Foreign Office and members of the International PEN Club—including J.B. Priestley, Aldous Huxley and E. M. Forster—added their voices. In May Koestler's release was negotiated by the International Red Cross in exchange for Señora Haya who was held by the Republican government in Valencia.

She was the wife of the Nationalist pilot Carlos Haya, who also served as Franco's personal pilot and who now flew Koestler from Seville to La Linea, where he crossed the border to Gibraltar. The following year he published *Spanish Testament* and dedicated the book to Chalmers-Mitchell, who continued to lead an active life, standing as Independent Progressive candidate in a Scottish Universities by-election in 1938. He died aged eighty at the end of World War II.

Koestler's life continued on its erratic path until he brought it to an end, committing suicide with his wife in 1983. Haya was killed when his plane collided in the air with a Republican fighter during the Battle of Teruel. But his name has lived on, in the Hospital Carlos Haya in Málaga founded in 1956.

Fifty years later, the Law of Historical Memory required that all names and symbols associated with Franco and the Nationalists during and after the Civil War should be removed from public buildings and streets. When the hospital's name was changed in 2009 to Hospital Regional Universitario de Málaga, everyone still referred to it by the name of Franco's pilot. Some said that he had been involved in bombing refugees fleeing towards Almeria; but many others simply did not know who Carlos Haya was. The president of Málaga's College of Physicians said that the hospital was known nationally and internationally as Carlos Haya, and that it would lose its identity among the medical profession if the name was changed. In 2016 the hospital entrance still announced the name of Carlos Haya, and the street running past the hospital was still marked as Avenida de Carlos Haya on the city's maps.*

The Caleta Palace hotel in which Chalmers-Mitchell was detained overnight became a hospital in the 1940s and is now a regional government building. But it still retains the ochre façade, brick arch lintels over the windows and balustrades at roof level which appear in old photographs of the hotel. It was designed in the late nineteenth century by the same architect, Eduardo Strachan, who was responsible for what *malagueños* will tell you is one of the finest streets in Spain, Calle Marques de Larios. The street is marble-paved and pedestrianised, all the buildings are of similar height and some have French windows and wrought-iron railings on the upper floors.

The Churriana of Gerald Brenan's day is no more, though his house, built by one of the Larios family in 1840 and now extensively renovated, was opened as a museum and cultural centre in 2014. The Davises house, La Consula, is now a cookery school and restaurant and the village is almost overwhelmed by the hugely expanded air-

* There is also a Calle del Capitan Haya in Madrid.

162

port. Of the more than 2.5 million people from Britain who flew to Málaga in 2013, the vast majority head at once to the coastal resorts east and west of the city. So they miss the delights of the city: the Moorish Alcazaba and Gibralfaro castle, with magnificent views over the port and into La Malagueta bullring; the Picasso museum (he was born there); the Pompidou Centre on the waterfront, opened in 2015; the Renaissance cathedral, which Ferdinand and Isabella ordered to be built after they conquered Málaga in 1487, but was not begun until after their deaths; and the historic English Cemetery. Richard Ford would surely now wish to revise his opinion, written in the mid-nineteenth century, that one day in Málaga 'will suffice. It has few attractions beyond climate, almonds and raisins and sweet wine'.

GIBRALTAR

Sir Joshua Hassan, Chief Minister of Gibraltar for twenty years in the last century, was a Moroccan Jew whose family, having joined the diaspora following the expulsion of Jews and Moors from Spain at the end of the fifteenth century, came to Gibraltar in 1728. This was only fifteen years after the Treaty of Utrecht had provided that 'no leave shall be given under any pretence whatsoever either to Jews or Moors to reside or have their dwellings in the said town of Gibraltar'. A more significant article of the Treaty—in which Spain ceded Gibraltar to Britain 'to be held and enjoyed absolutely with all manner of right for ever, without any exception or impediment whatsoever'—has been taken, at least by Britain and Gibraltarians, rather more seriously.

I saw a graffito scrawled across a faded poster in Governor's Parade, under the canopy of dragon trees: 'We don't know where we come from, and we don't know where we're going.' The people of Gibraltar come from a variety of countries, most of them around the Mediterranean. Rose Macaulay, visiting the Rock in the late 1940s, wrote in *Fabled Shore*: 'In complexion they range from the coffee colour of Indian and Moor, through the lighter brown of the Genoese, the sallowness of the Jew, the uncertain fair-to-dark of the British-Spanish (an Irish-Spanish cross is very common) to the ruddy fairness of the English.'

When Anglo-Dutch forces captured the Rock in 1704, during the War of the Spanish Succession, they indulged in an orgy of drunken rape, plunder and destruction—churches and convents were favourite targets—of a sort which would be repeated in the Peninsula War by Wellington's soldiers a century later. Most of the Spanish population fled to the town of San Roque six miles away, which Philip V called 'my city of Gibraltar resident in its Campo'. (The town was greatly enlarged by building with stone quarried from the nearby ruins of the ancient Phoenician and Roman city of Carteia.) New immigrants, many of them Jewish, came to Gibraltar from Genoa, Malta,

Portugal and Morocco; in the 1750s Jews made up a third of the civilian population. From time to time during this century, British government ministers proposed handing Gibraltar back to Spain but were overruled in Parliament. By the nineteenth century Spaniards were returning to the Rock and intermarriage was taking place. Today all Gibraltarians speak Spanish, albeit as a second language, and the great majority (about 85 per cent) are Catholic. They all have British nationality but relatively few have a British background. Little wonder that they have often been referred to as a mongrel race.

The division between the British military forces who manned the garrison of Fortress Gibraltar and the 'British' civilians who lived there was rigidly maintained until well into the twentieth century. There was no formal segregation but the local population was marginalised and regarded with patronising amusement which often bordered on contempt. Several nineteenth-century authors simply ignored the existence of the natives when writing about the Rock, while others mocked their inability to speak 'proper' English. But the remarks were not always light-hearted. It is extraordinary to find the Governor of Gibraltar, Sir Archibald Hunter, saying in 1913: 'English is no better spoken here in general than by Kaffir-rickshaw men in Durban and nothing like as well as by a donkey-boy at Suez or Cairo.'

Byron must have had a bad experience when he called Gibraltar 'the dirtiest and most detestable spot in existence'. Nor did the Hispanophile Richard Ford have any love for the place: commenting on the houses occupied by Gibraltarians, he wrote that 'they breed vermin and fevers in this semi-African hotbed; they are calculated to let in the enemy, heat, and are fit only for salamanders and "scorpions", as those born on the Rock are called.' 'Rock scorpions' was the pejorative term commonly used when referring to Gibraltarians. Some writers went further and compared them to the Barbary apes which inhabit the Rock. As recently as the 1960s, the novelist Anthony Burgess, who was stationed in Gibraltar during World War II, was using terms such as 'apelike' and 'simian' to describe the local people in his novel *A Vision of Battlements*. Undoubtedly many people in Britain, and British military personnel in Gibraltar, have looked down on the 'Gibbos' as English-speaking spicks or dagos, southern European Catholics and therefore inferior to the northern European Protestant Britons. However, the separation between the two populations, military and civilian, came to an end in 1991 when the British Army garrison was withdrawn from the Rock. Without this historical division, relations between Gibraltarians and the remaining, and increasing, migrant British population were bound to improve.

Now the defence of the Rock is undertaken by the Royal Gibraltar Regiment, about three-hundred strong, made up largely of Gibraltarians, together with some 'Costa boys'—sons of British expatriates living in southern Spain. All its officers have been trained at Sandhurst. In addition, the Royal Navy Gibraltar Squadron consists of two Scimitar class patrol boats and three RIBs (rigid inflatable boats), which are suitably fast for the job of chasing smugglers and intercepting Spanish boats in Gibraltar's territorial waters. The Royal Air Force maintains the airport as a forward mounting base. Following the closure of HM Dockyard in the 1980s, it is operated as a commercial ship repair facility, with a submarine berth still available. It was interesting to learn that Spanish ferries based in Algeciras prefer to use the Gibraltar dockyard for maintenance and repairs.

The naval docks remain as a base and port of call for NATO. While I was in Gibraltar for a few days in 1993, a visit by the aircraft carrier HMS *Ark Royal*, en route to the Adriatic during the Bosnian war, provided an insight into the change since World War II in one aspect of life on the Rock. At morning service in the King's Chapel, the preacher was *Ark Royal*'s chaplain, who paid generous tribute to the Chapel choir, comparing them to the choir at King's College, Cambridge. He also alluded to the traditional delights of 'a run ashore', at Gibraltar, quoting from Ecclesiastes 9:7—'Go thy way, eat thy bread with joy, and drink thy wine with a merry heart.'

I had seen hordes of sailors the night before eating very little except for packets of crisps, but drinking large quantities of draught English beer, served unpleasantly cold. They seemed merry enough, on one of their last nights ashore for perhaps several months, but something was missing. One would not have expected Ecclesiastes to mention it, but sailors the world over, when they are in port, are accustomed to expect a little female company—a few moments with 'a lady of the night' in a dark street or upstairs room; at least the sight of a bit of bare flesh in some back-street bar. In Gibraltar, however, there was no sex for our boys.

Some residents talked nostalgically of the days of the Trocadero and Uncle Tom's Cabin, part of which used to be run as a gentleman's club and brothel. Gib Liz was well-known to visitors for years, but had long since retired. There were no striptease clubs, no loose women to be seen, not even an 'adult' magazine. This was said to be because a young Gibraltarian, Carmen Gomez, had appeared naked in *Playboy* magazine, prompting the Catholic Bishop of Gibraltar to demand the banning of all clubs and magazines deemed by him to be unsuitable. So the sailors of HMS *Ark Royal* were unable to enjoy all the delights of a run ashore. They walked the length of Main Street, down the narrow lanes off Irish Town, along Line Wall Road; but there was nothing to be had except for yet another pint of beer in yet another ersatz pub—the Angry Friar, the Horseshoe, the Wembley. One beer-filled Scottish rating, who had been wolf-whistling a Moroccan woman in a djellaba, asked me, 'Where the fuck do you have to go to get a fuck round here?' The irony was that, if he had had the time, and a passport, he could have crossed the border and found any number of clubs and brothels and indulged in a variety of Spanish practices helpfully advertised in the classified pages, under the heading 'Adult Relaxation', of the Costa del Sol's newspaper, *Sur in English*.

Two centuries ago naval officers and seamen in Gibraltar were quite likely to die, if not in or as a result of battle, then of malignant fever, as recorded on many headstones in the Trafalgar Cemetery here. A tablet in the King's Chapel commemorates a junior officer who died of a 'fatal pestilential disorder'. Life was chancier then, but at least there was female company to be had on the Rock.

Gibraltar's red-light district was then to be found in dark alleys off Governor's Street: Serruya's Lane (now called New Passage), Castle Street and Hospital Ramp were notorious as the haunts of prostitutes in the nineteenth century. The majority of them were Spanish, others native Gibraltarian, and they were generally accepted and regulated by the colonial authorities. But British prostitutes were a different matter. They were considered 'undesirable and derogatory to the prestige of British rule', and there was the awful possibility that they might sell their bodies to the natives. With around a hundred prostitutes plying their trade in the Serruya's Lane area in the 1880s, it was unsurprising that venereal disease was rife (the British military then had the highest rate of VD of all the European armed forces).

Forty years later prostitution in Gibraltar was outlawed and most of the women decamped across the border to the neighbouring town of La Linea. The Alameda Gardens along Europa Road became a popular place for soldiers and sailors after dark, and unattached women frequented some of the taverns, ostensibly dance halls, with bizarre names such as Jack up the Ramps and Right Shoulder Forward. The only haunt from those days which was still there in the twenty-first century was the London Bar in Governor's Street, a gloomy place offering its few customers the delights of Sky Sports television, with fish and chips or jacket potatoes.

Along the street, where prostitutes used to loiter in the doorways, today Muslims, Hindus and Jews coexist happily. There are two synagogues nearby, a Hindu temple and a mosque at Europa Point, on the most southerly tip of the Rock. Standing above this inter-racial community is the Moorish castle built soon after the Berber general Tariq-ibn-Ziyad crossed the Straits in the eighth century and began the Islamic conquest of the Iberian peninsula. He gave his name to the place where he first landed: Jebel (Mount) Tariq, hence Gibraltar, which stands opposite Jebel Musa, behind the Moroccan coast. The two rocks or mountains were once known as Calpe and Abyla and, according to Greek mythology, formed the Pillars of Hercules.

Gibraltar was under Moorish occupation for considerably longer than it has been under the sovereignty of Britain. When the Moors finally left in 1462, they had been on the Rock, with a short break in the fourteenth century, for more than seven hundred years. As soon as the Moors had been expelled, a church was founded on the site of the principal mosque and rebuilt in Gothic style. Today it is the Catholic cathedral of St Mary the Crowned. Among other buildings which predate the British occupation is a sixteenth-century Franciscan friary and adjoining chapel. The friary, known as The Convent, has long been the residence of the Governor; the chapel became an Anglican church for the military garrison and was renamed the King's Chapel. (A Catholic Mass is still held there on Saturday evenings, beneath a stained glass window depicting a former head of the Church of England, King George VI.) The eighteenth-century traveller Francis Carter noted disapprovingly that this was 'the only one in town, all the other chapels and places of worship having been turned into store-houses, to the great scandal of the Spanish and inconvenience of the Protestants'.

Many churches and religious houses had also been sacked and destroyed by British soldiers and sailors in the aftermath of the 1704 invasion. It took the British more than a century to build their own church, and when they did so they gave it, the Cathedral of the Holy Trinity, Moorish arches over the main entrance and the windows, including the stained-glass east window behind the altar. With so many different places of worship within this small community, it was no wonder Richard Ford wrote that 'the Rock, in religious toleration, is the antithesis of Spain'—adding that Mammon was Gibraltar's god.

During the eighteenth century Gibraltar experienced four sieges. George III wanted to be rid of his British possession at the bottom of the Iberian peninsula, but after the Great Siege had continued for three and a half years, the Spanish and French forces finally admitted defeat in 1783. It was not long afterwards that the Garrison Library was founded, a handsome building which today houses some forty-five thousand books, maps and lithographs; and in the Trafalgar Cemetery the bodies were buried of those who had died following that 'great and memorable seafight'. Life on the Rock continued with few major interruptions until the mid-twentieth century, when two events not only brought the Gibraltarian community closer together but distanced it, in differing degrees, from Britain and Spain.

In 1940 the British government decided to evacuate the civilian population of Gibraltar, in the first place to French Morocco and later in the year to London, Ulster, Madeira and Jamaica. They were mostly accommodated in camps, in miserable conditions, and their discontent did not end when they were repatriated. The whole wartime experience, a rude awakening to the lack of control exercised by Gibraltarians over their own affairs, soon led to demands for greater self-government in the future. The closure of the border by Franco in 1969 lasted for more than fifteen years, until ten years after the *caudillo*'s death. Adopting a sort of siege mentality, instilled in them over the centuries, the Gibraltarians' sense of identity strengthened as their isolation from Spain continued. Nor did relations between the British and Gibraltar governments show much improvement. The crafty chief minister, Sir Joshua Hassan, was succeeded by the truculent trade union leader, Joe Bossano, who introduced an immigration law which discriminated against Britons living in Gibraltar who had not acquired Gibraltarian status.

Anglo-Spanish relations, generally good, always fall down over Gibraltar. It is the one subject on which all Spaniards are agreed. It is part of the Iberian peninsula, it rightfully belongs to Spain, its status as a British overseas territory is an indefensible anachronism. When a foreigner dares to draw parallels with the Spanish enclaves of Ceuta and Melilla which are on the mainland of Morocco, he is brusquely told that the situations are quite different, because those places are part of metropolitan Spain. Gibraltarians continue to vote overwhelmingly against any transfer of sovereignty to Spain and in favour of retaining the full British citizenship which they were granted in 1981.

Relations were further soured in that year, this time between the royal families of Britain and Spain, when the Prince and Princess of Wales took the insensitive decision to begin their honeymoon from Gibraltar, on the royal yacht *Britannia*. King Juan Carlos felt obliged to refuse his invitation to attend the wedding. Some years before, in the year after her coronation, the Queen paid a visit to Gibraltar, but she has never been back. Four months before her visit, violent demonstrations took place across Spain, with damage to British embassy property in Madrid and to consulates elsewhere in Spain. The Spanish consulate on the Rock was closed a few days before the Queen arrived; it has never reopened. In 2012, due to strained relations with Britain, Queen Sofia cancelled a planned trip to London to attend the Queen's diamond jubilee celebrations.

How different it all once was. Not long after the Battle of Trafalgar, the birthday of George III was celebrated with fireworks in Tarifa, and Ferdinand VII's birthday was marked by a royal salute on the Rock, with the Spanish ensign flying above Signal House. Good relations between Gibraltar and Spain were particularly in evidence during royal visits. When Queen Adelaide, widow of William IV, spent a few days at Gibraltar in 1838, she rode out to the Spanish cork woods accompanied by an escort of Spanish lancers. George V and Queen Mary, calling at Gibraltar in 1912 on their way back from the Delhi Durbar, received King Alfonso XIII's young son, whose mother was Queen Victoria's granddaughter. On the occasion of the British monarch's birthday, it was customary for the Governors of Gibraltar and Algeciras to march together through the town.

Perhaps the outstanding example of Anglo-Spanish cooperation in Gibraltar and the adjacent *campo* across the border was provided by the Calpe Hunt. For one hundred and twenty-five years a pack of hounds, kennelled on the Rock, would hunt the fox—and sometimes deer, rabbits and wild boar—over Andalusian country extending from San Roque and Los Barrios north to Castellar. Known as the Calpe Hunt, it became 'Royal' in 1906 when the kings of England and Spain became its joint patrons. Alfonso XIII remained as patron until hunting came to an end in 1939, though for the last eight years he was in exile.

The Reverend Mark Mackereth, chaplain to the Governor, is credited with having founded the hunt in 1813.* The English foxhounds,

---

* The Duke of Kent was officially Governor at the time, though absent for most of his tenure. The hunt often met at Duke of Kent's Farm, so named after he bought it for his French mistress. His only legitimate child was born a year before his death and would become Queen Victoria.

which had arrived by way of Cádiz, were soon hunting the cork woods and open country across the border, where, after the part just played by Britain in expelling the French invader from the peninsula, the Spanish were more than happy to let the officers of the Gibraltar garrison indulge their curious passion.

The Calpe was essentially a British hunt, dependent always on maintaining friendly relations with local Spanish landowners and farmers. In his invaluable history of the hunt, *Hounds are Home*, Gordon Fergusson appends a map of the hunting country in which features are identified mostly with English names—Mansels Thicket, Railway Covert, Herringbone Crags, Bailey's Bank, Pablo's Gorse. Pablo was Pablo Larios who, more than anyone, was responsible for keeping the hunt going on Spanish soil. The Larios family had several British connections: English and Irish officers had married Larios girls, the young Pablo had been partly educated in England, and he had hunted in Yorkshire and the Cotswolds. More significantly, the family owned huge estates along the Andalusian coast and in the hinterland which was the Calpe's hunting country. Pablo had ridden with the Calpe since he was eleven years old, he whipped-in for eight seasons and when the mastership became vacant in 1891 he was elected—the first master not to be a British officer. The appointment was supported by the Governor if not universally welcomed by the Gibraltar garrison, but it ensured that the Calpe could continue to hunt without restriction across country much of which was owned by the new master. With a short break, he remained master until his death in 1938.

Pablo's mother was a Gibraltarian and his father a Gibraltar resident who had bought a large building in the centre of the town, known as Connaught House, after the royal Duke who lived there briefly in the 1870s. (It was sold to the British government in 1920 and is now the city hall.) While it belonged to the Larios family, Pablo would preside over hunt suppers there, with much goodwill shown to the master by the resident officers and Calpe staff. The annual hunt ball was often held at The Convent, where a grand dinner would take place in the banqueting hall, surrounded and overlooked by the coats of arms and shields of Spanish monarchs before 1704 and of British monarchs from the reign of Queen Anne.

At the beginning of the twentieth century Pablo Larios got married and built a house at Guadacorte, a few miles from Gibraltar between the Guadarranque and Palmones rivers. It looks from one side as if it should be in Scotland, and on the other like an Edwardian retirement home on the English south coast. In 1906 he approached the palace in Madrid, and the hunt committee wrote to Edward VII, to petition both kings to become patrons of the Calpe. Their majesties were both pleased to accept, the hunt became known as the Royal Calpe Hunt and the crowns of England and Spain were added to the hunt buttons. Most appropriately, in the same year Alfonso XIII married Princess Ena, Queen Victoria's granddaughter.

The halcyon days of the Royal Calpe Hunt, and by extension of the relationship between Spain and Gibraltar, lasted for the next quarter of a century. Hunting did not have to stop for World War I—Spain was not involved—but the Calpe was proud to record three VCs awarded to its members. When hunt steeplechases were held on the Larios estate, special excursions were offered to Gibraltar residents. They went by steamer to Algeciras, then on to Guadacorte by train—a journey made possible thanks to the enterprise of a Scottish financier, Sir Alexander Henderson.

Henderson's idea was to provide a comfortable means of transport for members of the Gibraltar garrison to explore some of Andalusia without having to ride or travel by horse-drawn carriage over miles of road strewn with boulders and potholes. He started a ferry service across the bay to Algeciras, and from there built a railway line northwards, bridging river valleys and ravines and tunnelling through crags to Ronda. Beyond Ronda the line continued to Bobadilla, a junction with links to Madrid and elsewhere in Spain. Opened in 1891, the line was a triumph of British engineering which continues today, much of it on the same single track. At San Roque station a steel plate for hanging a platform lamp is inscribed 'Linley & Co. Birmingham', and in the station-master's office stands a 'Milner's Patent Fire-resisting Safe'. As the train makes its way through the old Calpe hunting country, then onwards to Jimena de la Frontera and past Gaucin, one can imagine hounds running through these delightful cork woods and river valleys which on other occasions would provide perfect picnic spots for military families liberated for a day from the confines of the Rock.

Knowing that the travellers would appreciate somewhere comfortable to rest and refresh themselves at the start and the end of their journeys, Henderson then commissioned the English architect T. E. Colcutt to build two hotels, the Reina Cristina in Algeciras and the Reina Victoria in Ronda.* They both survive today as hotels: the Reina Cristina was rebuilt in the same style after a fire in the 1920s, and the Reina Victoria maintains a room as a museum where the German poet Rainer Maria Rilke used to stay. The facades of both hotels still retain some of the atmosphere of early twentieth-century colonial outposts.

Problems for the Calpe began after Alfonso abdicated in 1931 and Spain was declared a republic. Hunting was stopped; 'a prudent decision', Gordon Fergusson comments in *Hounds are Home*, 'as within a few weeks the communist mob vent its destructive fury on the churches of Algeciras, Los Barrios and La Linea'. When hunting resumed, poachers were roaming the countryside and the foxes were driven to the hills. Care had to be exercised, especially as no one associated with the Royal Calpe Hunt was likely to be mistaken for a left-wing republican. A daughter of Pablo and Pepita Larios would shortly marry Miguel Primo de Rivera, son of the dictator general of the 1920s and brother of José Antonio, founder of the Falangist party.

While Spain was lurching from one government to another and towards the nightmare of civil war, the Calpe was having its own not so minor struggle, between the ageing master, Pablo Larios (now the Marques de Marzales) and the Governor, General Sir Alexander 'Lord God' Godley. Godley, who was not noted for his tact, thought and said it was high time that a young British officer took over from Larios;

---

* Colcutt also designed the Larios house at Guadacorte. Among his better known buildings are the Savoy Hotel, Wigmore Hall and Queen's Tower in London.

he was too old and the sport in recent seasons had been disappointing. The hunt 'was in danger of becoming altogether too Spanish, and too civilian an affair'. Larios resigned, a new master was appointed for the 1932-33 season and the hunt found itself warned off much of its hunting country. When Godley retired in 1933, George V, as patron, made it clear he was not impressed by the general's handling of this sorry affair. Indeed the King threatened to withdraw his patronage unless the new Governor, General Sir Charles Harington, made it up with Larios. This was done by the appointment of Lady Harington and Pablo Larios, Marques de Marzales, as joint masters. They shared the mastership for the next four years, until Larios's death, but by then the Calpe's days were almost over.

It was surprising enough that hunting continued at all during the Civil War. It did come to a halt for most of the 1936-7 season, but General Harington remained sanguine for the future. 'Everything at the moment looks as if the Whites will get the upper hand in this unfortunate civil war. If they do, things in this neighbourhood will settle down quietly...' There was no doubt where the sympathies of the hunt lay—though some were upset to hear the Nationalist execution squads at night on the Campamento polo ground, where they tied their victims to posts in the pony lines. At the start of the next season the Governor decided to seek permission from Franco, which he was delighted to grant, to resume hunting two days a week. A Labour MP raised the matter of contacts with Franco in the House of Commons, but was told by the Foreign Secretary, Anthony Eden, that the Royal Calpe Hunt's arrangements with the insurgent Nationalists were 'a purely local affair'.

The war continued to impinge on the Calpe's activities in small ways. Anti-communist feelings, still running high following the capture of most of Andalusia by the Nationalists, occasionally fastened on those members of the hunt whose red coats were thought by some locals to denote their political allegiance. When a man once shouted abuse at the 'Red' hunt staff hacking past his cottage, Lady Harington, whose ignorance of the Spanish language was notorious, was said to have thanked him for giving the hunt such a rousing welcome back after its enforced absence due to the war. In January 1939 Calpe hunt members joined Spanish soldiers to celebrate the fall of Barcelona.

Once Franco had achieved victory over the communist-backed Republic, his decided leanings towards Hitler and the imminence of world war made the continuation of the Calpe Hunt on Spanish soil politically unacceptable. The new Governor of Gibraltar, General Sir Edmund Ironside, who by 1939 had become the Calpe's joint master with Larios's son Pepito (a pilot with the Nationalist airforce), once commented: 'I sometimes wonder what would happen if war broke out on a hunting day. I hope to God it never does, for the Rock could be taken in a matter of minutes.' But there would be no more hunting days after April 1939. During the war Britain's principal objective in Spain was to preserve that country's neutrality and ensure that Franco did not permit German troops to march through Spain and seize Gibraltar. Franco was tempted to join the Axis in exchange for Hitler's offer to deliver Gibraltar to him (he probably would have done had Hitler promised him French Morocco as well), while Sir Samuel Hoare, British ambassador in Madrid, intimated that the sovereignty of Gibraltar would be discussed after the war if Spain remained neutral. When thousands of Allied troops launched the invasion of North Africa (Operation Torch) from Gibraltar in November 1942 without any interference from Spain, Britain could be fairly sure that Franco had decided to keep out of the war.

By this time all the Calpe hounds had been put down and the faithful kennel huntsman, José Pecino, after forty-two years with the hunt, went to join his family in Spain. (There is a photograph of him on a mantelpiece in the Garrison Library, where the Calpe archives are held.) An article in *The Times* in 1930, on taking the hounds with Pecino across the frontier for a morning's exercise, gives the flavour of Calpe hunting life as it used to be. From the North Front kennels, with the sun just touching the Spanish hills, they made their way towards the border which was still in chilly shadow.

> The policeman stopped the ingoing stream of gharries and black-shawled women, the sentry saluted and hounds pattered on to the neutral ground. The ponies capered across the sand. Behind them the Rock towered

rosily against the morning. As they cantered along the beach children scattered from their hoofs like coveys of partridges. Little green waves lapped round the wreck of a famous tea clipper, now dismasted. The Spanish sentry, bristling with weapons, grinned at them as they clattered over the cobbles into La Linea… They ploughed through the deep grey sand that paves La Linea's arterial roads. Aloes and cacti hedged the market-gardens on either hand. They found a flock of goats grazing the golf course, and a tiny beagle-sized hound gave chase. She was recalled by a howl from Pecino… The sun rose into the blue air that was not bluer than the distant corkwoods, as they halted at the inn to drink a glass of coffee.

Of course, such a scene will never be witnessed again. One might wistfully imagine that the best first step towards a resolution of the Gibraltar problem would be to revive the Royal Calpe Hunt, again under the joint patronage of the monarchs of England and Spain. However, apart from other, political considerations, the British officers aren't there any more, the sport would appeal to very few Gibraltarians, and it would hardly be practical nowadays to keep hounds kennelled on the Rock.

Agreements to agree on the future status of Gibraltar have been signed, in Lisbon in 1980 and in Brussels in 1984, but thirty years on an agreed solution is as far away as ever. The Lisbon and Brussels accords spoke vaguely of cooperation based on reciprocity and equality of rights between Gibraltarians and Spaniards, within the parameters of United Nations resolutions, which only convinced Gibraltarians that the ultimate objective was to return the Rock to Spain. Although Gibraltar today is almost entirely self-governing, it does not meet the requirements of the UN Special Committee on Decolonisation, though no great confidence is placed in a committee which includes Russia and Iran among its members. The Treaty of Utrecht continues to pose a problem because it provides, in Article X, that if Britain ever decides to relinquish the rights over Gibraltar which were ceded in perpetuity, the Rock should be given back to Spain. So, according to Spain, it can never be independent. But the future status of Gibraltar cannot be solved by handing the territory over from one country to another against the wishes of its people. It should not be beyond the wit of the three governments to agree to amend or even abandon the terms of a treaty signed more than three hundred years ago.

Nor should it be difficult for the governments to acknowledge that any long-term solution must lie within Europe. Sir Joshua Hassan foresaw this, expecting that in time Gibraltarians must be granted autonomy in Europe, if not nationhood. While probably never accepting that they be subject to the joint sovereignty of Britain and Spain, it would surely be possible to describe Gibraltar's future status more tactfully—joint authority?—in order to gain the agreement of all parties. There is the precedent of Andorra, a principality and effectively a sovereign state which accepts Spain and France (to be precise, the Bishop of Urgell and the French President) as 'co-principals'.

Gibraltar's position in the European Union has been unsatisfactory for years. Despite being a part of the EU (though outside the customs union and the Schengen Area) it was excluded from elections to the European Parliament until 2004. Since then its citizens have been able to participate in European elections only by voting in the South West England constituency. The 2016 EU referendum vote in Britain was swiftly followed by a demand from the Spanish government that joint sovereignty would be the price Gibraltar would have to pay for continued access to the European single market. While it was hoped that free movement between Spain and Gibraltar would continue—several thousand Spanish workers commute daily from La Linea—Britain's Foreign Secretary conceded that it would be more difficult to protect Gibraltar's interests in future.

Meanwhile Gibraltar continues to maintain its reputation for money laundering, tax evasion and smuggling, particularly of tobacco into Spain. Years ago, I watched one evening from a restaurant in La Linea as sacks of contraband cigarettes were dumped on the beach from a speedboat and rushed across the road to a tenement building where they would be safely hidden in flats usually treated by the Guardia Civil as 'no-go' areas. The Gibraltarian smugglers were known as Winston Boys (after the brand of cigarette most commonly sold to

Spain); when their RIBs were impounded in Gibraltar harbour they staged a riot and set fire to a police car in protest at this unwarranted restriction on their livelihood.

In the early 1990s, only a decade after 70 per cent of the economy had depended on the British military presence on the Rock, tourism and property prices were falling and development projects were failing. So the Gibraltar government was grateful to receive more than £10 million a year in duty on imported cigarettes, 90 per cent of which were exported illegally to Spain. Twenty years later Gibraltar was thriving as an offshore finance centre, new hotels were being built, one of them a large yacht berthed in the marina, and tourism was booming. However, there was little change in the age-old practice of smuggling. The Spanish government complained that the amount of tobacco brought into Gibraltar, if it were only for local consumption, would mean that every resident, including children, smoked nearly two hundred cigarettes a day.

Gibraltar's flourishing economy had been achieved without any lasting improvement in communications with Spain. The 2006 Cordoba Agreement between the three governments provided for flights to be resumed between Gibraltar and Spain—this had been agreed by Britain and Spain in 1987 but Joe Bossano, Gibraltar's Chief Minister, vetoed it. There were flights to and from Madrid for a while, but the service was discontinued after Spain's government changed in 2011. In 2015, apart from a weekly charter flight to Marrakesh, Gibraltar airport was used for passenger services only by airlines from Britain. It has been rumoured that the government pays a subsidy to these airlines to persuade them to continue flying to Gibraltar—a potentially dangerous airport which crosses the main road to the frontier and is often enveloped in fog—rather than land at Málaga.

Following the Cordoba Agreement, Spain opened a branch of the Instituto Cervantes in Gibraltar, to improve language and cultural links. It was a goodwill gesture, but it was no great surprise when the Spanish foreign minister announced the closure of the office in 2015, on the grounds that it was unnecessary on what was considered to be Spanish territory and that 'everyone there speaks Spanish except the apes'.

There seemed to be little improvement in relations between Gibraltar and Spain, despite the first ever official visit to the Rock by a Spanish minister in 2009. Three years later disputes over fishing rights in the area led to an increase in border controls and long delays for those entering and leaving Gibraltar. While David Cameron insisted that Britain would continue to respect the almost unanimous wish of Gibraltarians to remain British, their trust, at least in a British Labour government, was badly dented by Tony Blair's attempt in 2002 to do a joint sovereignty deal with Spain behind their back.

It was clear that any resolution of the Gibraltar problem in the future would depend on the people keeping their British citizenship. Even as a self-governing, almost independent state, they would still be reassured to think that, in the words of Lord Palmerston, 'a British subject, in whatever land he may be, shall feel confident that the watchful eye and the strong arm of England will protect him against injustice and wrong'. Those were the words of Britain's Foreign Secretary, in the mid-nineteenth century, in what was known as the Don Pacifico affair. David Pacifico was a Portuguese Jew who lived in Athens but—crucially—he had been born in Gibraltar and was a British citizen. Having been Portuguese consul in Morocco and in Greece, he stayed on in Athens for some years before his house was burnt down by an anti-Semitic mob. When the Greek government was dilatory about paying him compensation, Lord Palmerston sent a Royal Navy squadron to the Aegean where it blockaded the port of Piraeus and seized several Greek ships. Pacifico got his compensation and came to live in London. Of course nothing of the sort would happen today, but the memory of Don Pacifico may help the citizens of Gibraltar, fearful of a Spanish invasion, to sleep easier in their beds.

CÁDIZ & EL PUERTO

'Fair Cádiz, rising o'er the dark blue sea.' So wrote Byron in the first canto of *Childe Harold's Pilgrimage*, having visited the city in 1809. Someone else wrote that Cádiz can be best expressed by writing the word 'white' with a white pencil on blue paper. In *Voyage en Espagne* (translated as *A Romantic in Spain*) the French Romantic writer Theophile Gautier described the white as 'pure as silver, milk or snow, as marble or the finest crystallised sugar from the isles', and the blue as 'vivid as turquoise, sapphire or cobalt'. One need not go quite that far in confirming that today the predominant impression, looking over the sweep of the bay, is of white buildings, not all of them as pure as silver, milk or snow, gleaming in the sunlight against the blue of sea and sky. And the sun is replicated in the golden, mosque-like dome of the Baroque cathedral.

The city, originally Gadir, was founded by the Phoenicians more than a thousand years before Christ, when the ships of Tarshish traded between Iberia, Britain and the Near East. In Roman times Julius Caesar conferred the *civitas* of Rome on all citizens of the Spanish port, and Juvenal wrote of Jocosae Gades. Young *gaditanas* caught the eye of Martial who, having seen them dance, regretted in one of his epigrams that he had not enough money to pay for these 'girls from wanton Gades who with endless prurience swing lascivious loins in practised writhings'. When Somerset Maugham passed through Cádiz on his way to Morocco at the turn of the twentieth century, he was hoping to find a city devoted to pleasure and immorality but was disappointed. Comparing it to Naples, he wrote in *The Land of the Blessed Virgin* that Cádiz 'lacks that agreeable air of wickedness which the Italian town possesses to perfection'.

A century earlier, Byron wrote of Cádiz that 'the beauty of its streets and mansions is only excelled by the loveliness of its inhabitants'. He described the women whom he encountered as 'form'd for all the witching arts of love' and 'as far superior to the English women in beauty as the Spaniards are inferior to the English in every quality that dignifies the name of man'. Leaving aside his ungenerous backhanded comment, Byron's enthusiasms related specifically to an admiral's daughter whom he had accompanied to the opera and of whom he wrote to his mother that she was 'very pretty, in the Spanish style… by no means inferior to the English in charms, and certainly superior in fascination'. It was no doubt this señorita—with 'long black hair, dark languishing eyes'—whom he had in mind when he wrote his poem 'The Girl of Cádiz':

> Our English maids are long to woo,
> And frigid even in possession;
> And if their charms be fair to view,
> Their lips are slow at love's confession:
> But, born beneath a brighter sun,
> For love ordained the Spanish maid is,
> And who – when fondly, fairly won –
> Enchants you like the Girl of Cádiz?

Once married, according to Byron (though this may have been wishful thinking), the women of Cádiz 'throw off all restraint, but I believe their conduct is chaste enough before'. Gautier declined to comment on their virtue, confining himself to their physical appeal. 'They are very lovely and of a peculiar type: their complexions have a whiteness as of polished marble, which greatly emphasises the purity of their features… They also seemed to me plumper than the other Spanish women, and taller in stature.'

English travellers in Spain in the nineteenth century seemed particularly taken with the women of Cádiz. (Appropriately, they pronounced 'Cádiz to rhyme with 'ladies'.) Sir Arthur de Capell Brooke, in his *Sketches in Spain and Morocco*, enjoyed watching them on their balconies, 'luxuriously reclining amidst a profusion of odoriferous flowers, their warm cheeks flushed with the noontide heat'. A lady of Cádiz, he wrote, 'is a remarkably well-made person, not only from the beauty of her waist, but her general *tournure*… her swelling bosom and finely rounded limbs'. (Having spent a few years in the

Arctic, it was perhaps not surprising that he should get a bit carried away in the Spanish sun.) An Irish journalist, Michael Quin, used to sit in the Alameda gardens of a Sunday evening admiring the women as they passed by, with their 'hazel eyes, which are in themselves as dangerous as any other heavenly orbs, and almost as brilliant... Except in Kensington Gardens, I never saw such a congregation of beauty.'

While writing novels and before he embarked on his political career, the young Benjamin Disraeli visited Cádiz in 1830 during a tour of Andalusia. In letters home he wrote of 'las Espagnolas' walking in the evening *paseo* in their mantillas when, 'with their soft dark eyes dangerously conspicuous, you willingly believe in their universal beauty'. Admiring the city's 'white houses and green shutters [which] sparkle in the sun,' Disraeli imagined he saw 'Figaro in every street and Rosina in every balcony'.

Another English traveller of the time, Samuel Widdrington, enthused about the women's feet: 'The peculiar foot of Cádiz is short and round in the ankle, with a high instep, the ligaments being apparently compressed so as to give the springiness of step so admirable in their walk.' Richard Ford, writing of 'the descendants of those Gaditanae who turned more ancient heads than even the sun', also thought they had a fascinating way of walking. He called it *el piafar*, 'about which everyone has heard so much, and which has been distinguished by a competent female judge from the "affected wriggle of the French women, and the grenadier stride of the English, as a graceful swimming gait"'. Ford went on about the gait of the Cádiz ladies, also their feet, as he watched them walking along the Alameda 'with the confidence, the power of balance, and the instantaneous finding the centre of gravity of the chamois'. During three days of intensive research, along the Alameda, through the narrow streets of the old town, and in the open squares, I kept trying to identify a graceful swimming gait among the beautiful young ladies of Cádiz as they sauntered past, whether in swinging skirts or tight jeans. But I have to report a lack of success: not a hint of a breast stroke or a crawl. *El piafar*—a word which today usually refers to a horse pawing the ground—is no more.

Ford's other reason for going to the Alameda was to visit the British consul, John Brackenbury, whose residence was at number 83. His hospitality and his sherry were proverbial, according to Ford, while George Borrow also called on Brackenbury at his consulate, where he presided for twenty years. Borrow knew him to be a firm friend of the Bible Society. 'There is much dignity in his countenance,' he wrote, 'which is, however, softened by an expression of good humour truly engaging. His manner is frank and affable in the extreme.'

But there were drawbacks to nineteenth-century Cádiz. Ford called it a 'sea-prison' and referred to its 'detestable climate' when a warm easterly wind blows. 'The use of the knife is so common during this wind that courts of justice make allowances for the irritant effects.' This was still the case, or so I was told, a century later in Tarifa, at the southern tip of the Atlantic coast. If a man was charged with beating his wife, he could plead in his defence that the wind known as Levanter was blowing at the time and affecting his actions. This wind is said to be responsible for Tarifa having one of the highest suicide rates in Spain—and for being the country's most popular resort for windsurfing.

Augustus Hare's mood may have been depressed by the Levanter, or perhaps he was confined to his sickbed, when he visited Cádiz and recorded his impressions in *Wanderings in Spain*. Apart from a painting by Murillo, he wrote, 'there was literally nothing else to see'. How could he have missed the hauntingly memorable painting of St Francis by El Greco in the Hospital de las Mujeres, or the three Goya frescoes in the Oratorio de la Santa Cueva? In one of them, *The Last Supper*, some of the faces of Jesus's disciples seem to anticipate the faces he would paint in his dark canvases of the victims of the war against France. The Murillo painting which Hare admired is not the one he was working on in a Capuchin convent when he fell from the scaffolding and died shortly afterwards. It is an *Immaculate Conception* (of which he painted quite a number) in the Oratorio de San Felipe Neri, where the debates were held which led to the proclamation, in March 1812, of a liberal constitution for Spain.

For much of its character—its baroque buildings, its layout of straight, narrow streets and spacious squares, its more than one hundred watch-towers (*miradores*) looking out to sea—Cádiz has an eighteenth-century Irishman to thank. Alexander O'Reilly was one of those 'wild geese' who left their native Ireland to serve in the army of another Catholic country, usually Spain. He was charged with strengthening the Spanish fortifications in Cuba and Puerto Rico, he rose to the highest military rank, married into a prominent Cuban family and was made governor of Louisiana before returning to Spain and spending the last twenty-five years of his life in Cádiz. Among his other improvements to the city, he initiated the building of the Academia de Nobles Artes. Following his death the city responded by naming a street after him. There were quite a number of Irish merchants, financiers and naval officers living in Cádiz in the late eighteenth century. One of the latter, Enrique MacDonnell, was imprisoned on a rocky island in the bay for having struck and wounded a Frenchman before a bullfight. But the incident did his career no harm: he became an admiral of the Spanish navy and fought at Trafalgar (although, once England and Spain were on the same side, he took no active part in the Peninsular War).

Until the early nineteenth century, Cádiz had nothing to thank the English for. Following Columbus's discovery of America, it became the headquarters of the Spanish treasure fleets and the most prosperous port in Europe. A century later, however, Drake famously 'singed the King of Spain's beard' in 1587, destroying more than thirty ships anchored in the bay of Cádiz in preparation for the Armada's invasion of Britain, which had to be delayed until the following year. Then, partly in reprisal for Spain's failed attack, and to forestall another, Queen Elizabeth instructed the Earl of Essex in 1596 to do a bit more singeing. He not only equalled Drake's score of ships destroyed, but went on to burn most of the city of Cádiz as well, having first pillaged its churches and houses (and desecrated a statue of the Virgin Mary which was rescued and revered as La Vulnerata. It can be seen today in the English College in Valladolid.)

Thirty years later Charles I, thinking to inflict further humiliation on the Spanish, sent a fleet of one hundred ships to Cádiz under Sir Edward Cecil. No Spanish treasure ships were captured, most of the English soldiers got drunk when they went ashore, and the expedition was a fiasco. Admiral Blake blockaded the harbour in 1656, and Admiral Rooke commanded an unsuccessful attack in 1702. Cádiz then enjoyed a century of uninterrupted trade, particularly in gold and silver, with Spanish America, until the British once again blockaded the city, effectively for four years, after the Battle of Cape St Vincent. Admiral Horatio Nelson, having been involved in the Battle of Cádiz in 1797, returned a few years later for his final and most famous victory. The combined Spanish and French fleets left the bay of Cádiz in the early morning of 21 October 1805 and sailed south until they met some thirty ships of the Royal Navy that same afternoon off Cape Trafalgar.

In 1808 Spain and England came together in alliance against the occupying French, expelling Napoleon's forces across the Pyrenees some five years later. Admiral Purvis blockaded the harbour mouth at Cádiz; the French under Marshal Victor laid siege to the city for two years but failed to take it. In 1811 an Anglo-Spanish force advanced from Gibraltar and Tarifa to raise the siege, but the subsequent Battle of Barrosa, south of the city, was inconclusive and Victor reoccupied his siege lines. It is difficult today to imagine Barrosa as the site of a battle in which about three thousand were killed. It is a place of seaside *urbanizacion* facing a long white-sand beach: modern holiday housing, hotels, swimming pools and golf.

In his series of novels chronicling the career of Richard Sharpe in India and during the Peninsular War, Bernard Cornwell devotes *Sharpe's Fury* to his seemingly indestructible character's exploits on the Guadiana river, in the city of Cádiz and at the Battle of Barrosa. Sharpe finds in Cádiz a number of influential Spaniards who would rather make a rapprochement with Napoleon than continue the alliance with Britain, fearing that their ally intends to make of Cádiz another Gibraltar. Memories of Nelson's bombardment of the city in 1800, and five years later of his defeat of the Spanish and French navies off Cape Trafalgar, are all too recent and painful for many *gaditanos*. At Barrosa Sharpe turns up towards the end of the battle and, in an act of personal revenge, assaults and wounds a French colonel who has surrendered to him. An inquiry is called for, but Sharpe is exonerated by the commander of the British force, General Sir Thomas Graham.

Graham had four thousand soldiers at Barrosa, the Spanish twice that number, and unfortunately it was the Spanish General Manuel La Peña who had overall command. Graham's troops were largely un-supported by La Peña who, in the words of the military historian Sir William Napier, showed 'contemptible feebleness'. Despite being heavily outnumbered by the French, however, Graham saved the day by a bold counter-attack, forcing them to fall back to the town of Chiclana. But nothing was really achieved as a result of the battle: the siege was not broken and Cádiz was not relieved until the following year. La Peña was subsequently court-martialled and acquitted, but relieved of his command. Graham re-entered Cádiz and was voted the title of grandee of Spain by the Cortes, but he declined the honour.

Having served with Sir John Moore in Spain—he was at his side when Moore was mortally wounded at La Coruña—Graham commanded under Wellington for much of the rest of the Peninsular campaign. One of the most impressive of Wellington's generals, he was ennobled as Baron Lynedoch and died at the age of 95. The other principal historical character in *Sharpe's Fury* is Henry Wellesley, Wellington's younger brother, who was Britain's ambassador in Cádiz, remaining in his post in Spain until 1821. He was cuckolded by Henry Paget who, as the Marquess of Anglesey, went on to lead Wellington's cavalry at Waterloo—and to marry his commander's ex-sister-in-law. Bernard Cornwell attributes to Wellesley (fictitiously) an affair with a woman to whom he has written compromising letters, which are being used by an *afrancesado* admiral and his chaplain, both of whom were taken prisoner at Trafalgar, to blackmail Wellesley. The ambassador calls on Sharpe for assistance, and he of course deals successfully with the problem, employing a bit of violence and murder in the cathedral.

It was after Wellington's victory at Salamanca, and Joseph Bonaparte's order to abandon Andalusia, that Cádiz was finally relieved in the summer of 1812. The British commander-in-chief was feted in Cádiz: a ball was held in his honour, at which he upset several members of the local aristocracy by taking their wives to supper and closing the doors so that their husbands were unable to join them. He also attended a bullfight and addressed the new national legislative assembly. This momentous event took place to celebrate Spain's new constitution, promulgated in Cádiz, which was the Spanish seat of government during the years of the French occupation of Madrid and the reign of Joseph Bonaparte.

Drawn up in March 1812, it established the principles of constitutional monarchy, limiting the power of the monarch and the influence of the Church and the nobility. Universal male suffrage and land reform were promised, and the rights of citizens were to be protected when threatened by a foreign invader. It was a first and significant step towards liberalism in Spain, and its conception and birth took place while Cádiz was under siege and effectively under British protection. However, when Ferdinand VII was restored to the throne in 1814, he was having none of it, and he swiftly decreed that the constitution be abolished—a move applauded by Wellington. His absolute monarchy was reimposed, although six years later rumblings of revolution were heard from the army. Ferdinand briefly restored the constitution, but then the French, alarmed at all this dangerous liberalism south of the Pyrenees, intervened in 1823 in support of the Spanish king. He had been held for a short time in the Cádiz customs house; having been freed by French forces led by his cousin, the Duke of Angouleme, Ferdinand turned on the constitutionalists in furious revenge. Four decades later his daughter, Queen Isabella, was obliged to go into exile as a result of a revolution starting with a naval rising in Cádiz and leading to six years of chaos and anarchy. Occasional *pronunciamentos* in favour of the Cádiz constitution would flicker briefly into life, though it was never restored for more than a few months.

But the liberal atmosphere in the city was decidedly more evident than elsewhere in Spain. Women held get-togethers similar to French salons, where they drank coffee instead of the previously popular hot chocolate, and books by banned authors such as Voltaire and Rousseau were readily available. In *The Bible in Spain*, George Borrow records how in the 1830s two English Methodist missionaries were allowed to preach in the city for a year, until they were banished by some higher ecclesiastical authority in Andalusia. In a country where the Inquisition was only just coming to an end, it was extraordinary that such heresy was permitted at all. Had the Methodists not been silenced, Borrow mused somewhat fancifully, 'not only Cádiz but the greater part of Andalusia would by this time have confessed the pure doctrines of the Gospel, and have discarded for ever the last relics of popish superstition'. That great enemy of tolerance, General Franco, liked to boast that he had liquidated the nineteenth century, and took instinctively against anyone who came from Cádiz, believing that all *gaditanos* were liberals, if not communists or freemasons, who would seek to undermine his dictatorship.

Cádiz's century was unquestionably the eighteenth. The wealth pouring in from Spanish America benefited the city even more after the River Guadalquivir silted up and the treasure ships could no longer reach Seville. Large quantities of foreign goods, re-exported through Cádiz, gave the city a distinctly cosmopolitan aspect. In 1786 Haydn was commissioned by the canons of the cathedral, which was then under construction, to compose an orchestral work, 'The Seven Last Words on the Cross'. (The ungenerous comment has been made, more than once, that this is the only interesting thing about the cathedral, built over many decades in the Baroque/Neo-classical style with a golden dome of Moorish appearance.) There were more than thirty churches—and still are in the old city today—and the tallest watch-tower, the Torre Tavira, was built in 1778 (it now contains a camera obscura). Travellers from Madrid to the south noted that—thanks in part to Governor O'Reilly—Cádiz was a more prosperous city than the capital, with superior shops and cafés.

One man who turned up in Cádiz in the late eighteenth century was the Reverend Joseph Townsend, making a tour of Spain which took him nearly two years and which he recorded in his three-volume *A Journey through Spain*. He was a remarkable polymath: rector of Pewsey in Wiltshire, a distinguished geologist, a physician, and a social reformer who wrote a critical treatise on the English Poor Laws. In Cádiz he was impressed by the *hospicio* (poorhouse) which he visited, but thought that its eight hundred inhabitants were rather too well looked after, being given too much food and too little work. A pre-Malthusian, he was of the opinion that the population was in danger of multiplying 'beyond the means of sustenance'. During the nineteenth century, however, the death rate due to poor drainage and polluted water was unusually high in Cádiz and the population went into decline. An English company set up a waterworks in the city, but its citizens failed to appreciate the need for it and the company soon failed.

Trade with southern America fell away as those countries became independent, and the Spanish empire came to an end when authority over Cuba, Puerto Rico and the Philippines was ceded to the United States in 1898. Cádiz and Havana had had a particularly close relationship. Both commercial and passenger ships were sailing regularly between the two cities in the nineteenth century. To some travellers they were not dissimilar, one describing Havana as a larger and hotter Cádiz. Location shots of Havana in one of the early James Bond movies were filmed in Cádiz. Much of the music and dance at the city's annual carnival in February apparently has its origins in Cuba.

Bullfights have never featured in the Cádiz carnival—the season does not begin until March—but they used to be held in the city every Sunday during the summer. However, the size and importance of the bullring across the bay in El Puerto de Santa Maria—the largest in Andalusia—meant that the plaza de toros in Cádiz was always struggling to survive. The original arena, with wooden stands, was replaced in the 1920s by a larger and more handsome one, close to the beach. But after the Civil War many people could not face going to the bullfights because their relatives had been executed by firing squads against the walls of the plaza. By the 1960s salt spray from the Atlantic was eating into the fabric of the building and major work was needed to restore it and to strengthen the stands. The *ayuntami-ento* (city council) would not agree to provide the funds; and so Cádiz held its last *corrida* on 16 July 1967. Cádiz remembers its bullfighting years in a little museum in the old town. The Museo de Vinos y Toros (it also has a bottle of almost every sherry ever made) displays some Picasso drawings of the bullfight, old suits of lights, and posters of *corridas* going back to the nineteenth century, when the bulls were dramatically described as *toros de muerte*.

To remember other aspects of the past life of Cádiz, one need only walk round the old city. The Alameda promenade and gardens and the waterfalls of the Parque Genoves have not changed much since the days when Richard Ford and other British travellers would sit there admiring the legs of the young *gaditanas*, before taking a stroll along the seafront, past the buildings perhaps not quite as gleaming white, 'like a line of ivory palaces', as Ford saw them. Living among the poor and down-and-outs of Cádiz in 1935, Laurie Lee described the city as 'a kind of Levantine ghetto entirely surrounded by sea—a heap of squat cubist hovels enclosed by medieval ramparts... a rotting hulk on the edge of a disease-ridden tropic sea'—though he did say that from a distance it sparkled with African light. A less jaded observer— Lee was writing more than thirty years after his trek through Spain— might comment on the narrow, mostly sunless streets enclosed by tall shuttered houses which give on to delightful, open squares such as the tree-lined Plaza de Mina, where Manuel de Falla was born, and the Plaza de Topete, with its colourful stalls selling fresh flowers.

Many of the Baroque churches of Cádiz have Italian marble on the facade and within the building. Two hundred and fifty years ago, more than 10 per cent of the population of Cádiz were foreign trad-ers—not only from Italy, but from France, the Netherlands and Brit-ain. Its days as one of the principal marine cities of the world are long gone; but it is pleasing to record that it has not become a prime foreign tourist destination instead. Perhaps the main observable dif-ference in Cádiz between the eighteenth century and today is that the foreigners are not there anymore.

Take the ferry across the bay from Cádiz to El Puerto de Santa Maria, at the mouth of the Rio Guadalete, and you find yourself in a more typical Andalusian town. Columbus set off from El Puerto on his second voyage to the Americas, taking with him, as navigator, Juan de la Cosa, who had been on the first voyage as master of his own ship, *Santa Maria*. At the end of the fifteenth century, in El Puerto, de la Cosa produced a *mappa mundi*, painted on parchment; it was the first to map the New World of the Americas which they had discovered. During this period the ships of these adventurers were frequently to be seen in El Puerto, setting out for, or coming back from, the New World.

Today this delightful little port has three more relevant claims to fame: seafood, sherry and bulls. The freshest of fish, especially shellfish, can be sampled in all its glorious variety at Romerijo, which is more of an institution than a mere restaurant. Close to the waterfront, it is spread over a large area on both sides of the road, and includes a long counter selling all sorts and sizes of shrimp, prawn and crab, not all of them locally caught. These may be taken, wrapped in paper bags, to a table where a plastic bucket is provided for the shells. Alternatively, you take a table and order from a menu which illustrates some of the lesser known crustacean treats, with names that are unlikely to be found in a Spanish dictionary. On past visits I have noted, and much enjoyed, *quisquillas* (shrimps), *camarones* (baby shrimps, often cooked in a thin tortilla), *navajas* (razor-clams), *cañaillas* (rather like whelks with a spiky shell, of the same family of shellfish used by the Phoenicians to extract purple dye), *ostras* (oysters), *carabineros* (large prawns with a dark red shell, very delicious and very expensive), *boquerones* (fresh fried anchovies), *acedías* (baby soles), *ortiguillas* (a kind of sea anemone, fried in batter), and *puntillitas* or *chopitos* (minuscule squid, also fried in batter). You may not get through all these at one sitting, but a meal at Romerijo is always a memorable, if sometimes slightly chaotic, experience.

The classic wine of this region, roughly forming a triangle which extends from Jerez to Sanlucar de Barrameda and Cádiz, is of course sherry. It was first introduced into England around the time of Henry VII, whose alliance with Ferdinand and Isabella was cemented by the marriage of his sons (first Arthur, and after his death Henry) to their daughter Catherine. At the end of the sixteenth century, when Cádiz was plundered by Drake and Essex, they brought home quantities of Sherris sack, or Jerez *seco*, which immediately became fashionable in England, not least with Sir John Falstaff. Two hundred years later a Devon man, Thomas Osborne, founded the sherry house which bears his name and owns most of the bodegas in the town. El Puerto, then known to the English as Port St Mary, was the centre of the sherry trade before it moved to Jerez.

No less renowned than the Osborne sherries, brandies and wines is the Osborne bull. It was originally designed in the 1950s to advertise Osborne's Veterano brandy. Soon the billboards which were erected on Andalusian hillsides—depicting a black fighting bull, noble and aggressive, with a pair of threatening horns and cojones well displayed—were regarded as much more than a sherry company's logo. They came to represent an iconic image of Spain. When legislation was passed banning the display of advertising billboards in open country, the Supreme Court made an exception for the Osborne bull, acknowledging that it was a cultural symbol. The only stipulation was that the name of Osborne be removed. Today about eighty of the famous black bull silhouettes, all of them constructed in El Puerto, can be seen on the highways of Spain, and in every region—there is even one in Catalonia and one in the Canary Islands, where bullfighting has been abolished.

Bulls have been fought in El Puerto since the eighteenth century. The present bullring, built in 1880, is, after Madrid, one of the largest in the country. For a town of fewer than a hundred thousand people, it is a remarkable size, having a greater capacity—up to fifteen thousand seats—than the bullrings of the much larger cities of Seville and Jerez. Inside the entrance to this magnificent building mounted bulls' heads, posters of past *corridas* and portraits of famous matadors are displayed to record the history of the bullring. There is the head of the first bull to be killed on the inaugural day in 1880, and a sketch of the Cordoban torero Rafael Molina, 'Lagartijo', who dispatched it. (Later in his career he and his great rival 'Frascuelo' caused a sensation when they performed at a bullfight in Paris in the Bois de Boulogne.) A coloured ceramic plaque records a slightly enigmatic comment from the legendary matador Joselito: '*Quien no ha visto toros en El Puerto, no sabe lo que es un dia de toros.*' (In loose translation: 'If you haven't seen a bullfight in El Puerto, you don't know what a day at the bulls is really like.') Prominently placed outside the plaza is a dramatic memorial to Paquirri, who was killed in a small Andalusian bullring in 1984. It is a black iron sculpture, on a stone base surrounded by water, showing the matador on his knees and the charging bull narrowly missing him as he executes a pass with the cape swirling over his head.

For one of the most memorable, and gruesome, occasions in El Puerto's bullfighting history, it is necessary to go back to 1857 and the town's old wooden bullring. The matador in question was Manuel Dominguez, who became known for his reckless bravery. He interrupted his career to go to South America for fifteen years, where his various activities included bullfighting and a spell in the Uruguayan army. He made a lot of money, lost it in a revolution and returned peseta-less to Spain. He wanted to get back to the bullring, but few remembered him and the contracts were not forthcoming. So Dominguez decided that desperate measures were called for. He sought out the famous matador of the day, Francisco Arjona, 'Cuchares', insulted him in a bar in Seville, and challenged him to fight *mano a mano* with Concha y Sierra bulls, the largest and most notorious breed at the time. The *corrida* took place in El Puerto in the summer of 1857; Dominguez was now forty-one years old but had not lost his nerve, determinedly following the precept of the School of Tauromachy that 'more can be done in the plaza with a pound of bravery and an ounce of intelligence than the other way round'.

Dominguez's first bull was a monster which he passed several times on his knees with the cape, as the horns came ever closer to his body and face. (He may have been the first torero to pass the bull while kneeling.) For the next fifteen minutes the spectators cheered and screamed as he demonstrated to them that, while Cuchares might better him in terms of artistry and fancy tricks, no one could deny that Dominguez was the braver. When he came to kill the bull, he lined up with his sword, then stood still waiting for the animal to charge and impale itself (a very dangerous technique known as *recibiendo*). The sword thrust was perfectly placed to receive the bull's charge, but it wrenched its head to the right, knocking Dominguez to the ground, then lowered its head and horns to his face as he lay defenceless.

A sketch of this moment shows the matador grabbing the right horn as it is about to penetrate his jaw. But it doesn't show what happened next. When his peons, rushing to his aid, managed to draw the bull away with their capes, and he was able to lurch to his feet, he presented a terrible sight. The horn had missed his jaw but had gouged out his right eye which, in the words of the American taurine writer Barnaby Conrad describing the scene, 'hung down on his cheek like a peeled grape'.

The story may have been embellished over the decades, but we are told that Dominguez then flicked away the dangling eyeball as though he were wiping sweat from his brow, and stumbled towards his adversary with his arm raised. The bull, with the sword buried between its shoulders, swayed backwards and fell dead. When he reached the infirmary and showed the doctors what remained of his eye and its socket, he said to them: '*Estos no son mas que desperdicios*' ('bits of garbage'). From that day he not only assumed heroic status, but he was now known as Desperdicios. Three months later he returned, one-eyed, to the bullring in Málaga, insisting that the bulls should be from the same Concha y Sierra breed which he had fought on that memorable day in El Puerto. His career went into gradual decline, but he lived on for another thirty years, enjoying his fame and his name. When they passed him in the street, passers-by would recall the story of Desperdicios, saying one to another: '¡Allí va un hombre!'

From time to time he would ride from Seville to El Rocio, in the Coto Doñana, to pray at the shrine there and give thanks for his survival. His route would take him through the village of La Puebla del Rio, on the banks of the River Guadalquivir, which today is incorporated in the professional name of one of the most stylish and highly-paid matadors, Morante de la Puebla. Morante was on the cartel of a bullfight which I saw at El Puerto in the summer of 2010. So was Cayetano, son of the matador whose memorial stands outside the plaza. What was most remarkable about the occasion was that this huge plaza was about 80 per cent full. Twelve thousand people had turned out, on a Sunday evening in August, for what was clearly an occasion. In the shaded seats many men wore suits and ties, others were in long-sleeved shirts and dark trousers, while women wore smart dresses, some with the traditional Andalusian polka dots. It was part of the natural order of a summer Sunday and it was hard to believe oneself in the same country as the Catalans who, a few weeks before, had voted to ban bullfighting. Here in El Puerto de Santa Maria, and in Cádiz, Jerez and the surrounding area, families had gathered after midday Mass, for conversation and a *copa*, and a good lunch not before 3 p.m. There would be time for a glass or two of Osborne's Veterano brandy, and perhaps a siesta, before setting out for the plaza de toros to be there in good time for the 7 p.m. start. And anyone who asked where they were going would be met with the excited reply: *¡A los toros!* ('To the bulls!')

Byron attended a bullfight in El Puerto de Santa Maria and described it graphically in *Childe Harold's Pilgrimage*. While portraying the occasion as a chivalric contest between man and beast, it is the courage and dignity of the bull which he most admires, as in this stanza:

> Where his vast neck just mingles with the spine,
> Sheath'd in his form the deadly weapon lies.
> He stops – he starts – disdaining to decline:
> Slowly he falls, amidst triumphant cries,
> Without a groan, without a struggle dies.

The Englishmen who journeyed in Spain in those years—and became known as *los curiosos impertinentes*—seldom condemned bullfighting in the published accounts of their travels. The Reverend Joseph Townsend had seen a *corrida* in Madrid and was hoping to see another one in El Puerto. 'I had been solicitous to see the most famous matador of Spain, named Romero, but at this season [March] the bull-feasts are prohibited.' Another Anglican vicar, the Reverend Edward Clarke, chaplain to the British embassy in Madrid in the mid-eighteenth century, was also an enthusiastic follower of the bulls. Michael Quin, who wrote for Catholic journals in England and Ireland, was much impressed by the drama of the bullfight when he was travelling in Spain in the 1820s:

> Nothing can be finer than the entry of a fierce proud bull into the arena. He rushes in; astonished by the crowd of spectators, he stops a while, looks around him, but when his eye lights on the horsemen in the arena, he paws the ground with the majesty of a lion, and summons up all his fury for the contest.

In his *Sketches in Spain*, Samuel Widdrington interested himself in the different breeds of bull in Andalusia and wrote enthusiastically of the

> antique and now peculiar beauty of a well filled plaza... the picturesque variety of the costumes of the toreros... and the solemnity with which the whole is conducted, form[ing] an ensemble which retains its charm long after the novelty has ceased, and separate from the mere object of witnessing the destruction of a few animals, and the disagreeable sights which are constantly displayed in these spectacles.

For Richard Twiss the most disagreeable sight was not the cruelty which he witnessed to bulls and horses, but the bloodthirsty behaviour of the women attending the *corrida*. The fighting and killing of a bull in a public arena was seemingly more socially acceptable to an English spectator in the nineteenth century than it is to most people in this country today. Or perhaps the fascination expressed by these English *curiosos* derived from witnessing, in an alien land, a spectacle akin to the gladiatorial combats of ancient Rome.

'Our honest John Bulls have long been more partial to their Spanish namesakes than even to those perpetrated by the Pope.' Richard Ford, writing in the mid-nineteenth century in his *Gatherings from Spain*, was no doubt being a bit mischievous. But some form of bullfighting, or bull-baiting, had been known in England since the fourteenth century. When John of Gaunt married the daughter of Pedro the Cruel, he held bullfights for his wife's entertainment at his castle outside Burton-on-Trent. A panoramic map from Shakespeare's time shows a 'bolle bayting' arena in London, on the south bank of the Thames; and the sport was not declared illegal until 1835, shortly after Ford's return from his Spanish travels.

Spanish bullfighting terms began to appear in English publications in the late eighteenth century. By the time work started, in the 1860s, on the compilation of the Oxford English Dictionary, a number of references to bullfighting, using Spanish words such as *corrida*, torero, *estocada, cuadrilla*, had been appearing in newspapers—the *Morning Post, Morning Chronicle* and *Bell's Life in London and Sporting Chronicle*—and were incorporated in the OED. In 1858 an article describing a bullfight was published in *Household Words*, a weekly journal edited by Charles Dickens.* Senior political figures of the time were drawn to the bullring. Disraeli wrote that 'those who have witnessed a Spanish bullfight will not be surprised at the passionate attachment of the Spanish people to their national pastime'. And in his last years Lord Curzon attended the spring *feria* in Seville, where 'the entire performance filled me, as it has filled so many others, with alternate admiration and disgust'.

In 1870 an entrepreneur from Cádiz tried to communicate his countrymen's *afición* for the bulls to an English audience when he staged a sort of bullfight at the Royal Agricultural Hall in Islington, north London. The occasion was announced as 'without cruelty or danger', rosettes were planted on the bull's flanks by the toreros,

---

*   In France Théophile Gautier's book, *Voyage en Espagne*, published in 1843, had a chapter on the bullfight, while at the same time his fellow author and literary critic Prosper Merimée was writing the novella, *Carmen*, which Bizet would use as the basis for his opera.

a long pole was used to strike the animal on the head, and the performance ended with a small bouquet of flowers being placed on its shoulders. When the entertainment was repeated a few days later, the RSPCA moved in and the Spanish organisers were taken to court. Evidence was given that the bulls were provoked by darts tipped with steel points, and the magistrate opined that this was unquestionably cruel. 'Had the defendants been English and conversant with the law, I should have inflicted on them the heaviest penalty in my power.' Making allowance, however, for the defendants' Spanish practices and their interpretation of what was cruel, he fined them twenty shillings each.

Apart from Ernest Hemingway's *The Sun Also Rises* (originally called *Fiesta*), much of which is set in Pamplona during the *feria* of San Fermin, the first English-language book on the art and history of bullfighting, Hemingway's *Death in the Afternoon*, was published in 1932, and it has never been out of print. In the same year the poet Roy Campbell, who became a supporter of Franco during the Civil War, wrote *Taurine Provence*. Marguerite Steen published a well-observed novel, *Matador*, in 1934 and twenty years later *Bulls of Parral*. At that time, in the 1950s, a number of books on bullfighting began to appear: *To the Bullfight* by John Marks, *Bull Fever* by Kenneth Tynan, and *The Bulls of Iberia* by Angus Macnab. (Aficionados cover the political spectrum: Tynan was a left-wing theatre critic and Macnab a fascist follower of Oswald Mosley who was detained during World War II under Regulation 18B.) Vicente Blasco Ibanez's novel *Sangre y Arena* (*Blood and Sand*) was published in English in an admirable translation by Frances Partridge; and the American Barnaby Conrad published an encyclopaedia of bullfighting, among other taurine books. The interest generated by these books coincided with the dominance in the bullring of two matadors, and brothers-in-law, Luis Miguel Dominguin and Antonio Ordoñez, whose rivalry during the 1959 season was chronicled by Hemingway in his last book, *The Dangerous Summer*. A couple of years later I saw my first bullfight.

My own enthusiasm for the bulls began when I read *Bull Fever* and, in particular, Tynan's description of an afternoon in Valencia when

Litri and Ordoñez excelled in the rain-sodden ring. Of course, his account may have been exaggerated—Tynan admitted that he could not write coolly about a bullfight and preferred to use immoderate language—but I have reread it several times and often wished I could witness something as dramatic. I was staying on the north coast of the island of Majorca and was fortunate that my host, who was a passionate aficionado, would take his family and guests every Sunday to the *corrida* in Palma. To those who had never been to a bullfight before, he would give a talk over lunch, explaining that we were not going to a sporting occasion, where one side would win and the other would lose, but to a spectacle where six bulls would be killed in the ring by men whose name, matador, means killer. If a matador was gored and unable to continue, another matador would finish the job (which is the literal translation of *faena*, as the last stage of a fight is called). Bullfight is an inadequate translation of what Spaniards call a *corrida de toros* (running of the bulls), which is part of *la fiesta nacional* or *la fiesta brava*. It has to be understood, by those who wish to understand it, that reports of *corridas* in the Spanish press appear not in the sports section but with arts and culture, often under the heading *Espectaculos*.

My Majorcan host once wrote that 'cricket in England and the national fiesta of bullfighting in Spain are just about the only two civilised pastimes left in Europe'. It was an enjoyably provocative statement, comparing bullfighting not with modern international cricket but with the game as it was once played. His point was that the result in cricket was, or should be, unimportant—in a bullfight it is preordained—but what does matter in both is, in the words of the American sports writer Grantland Rice, 'how you played the game'. He also wondered mischievously if it was 'mere chance that the national flag of Spain is identical to the colours of the Marylebone Cricket Club'.

It may be presumptuous of those non-Spaniards who are aficionados to try to interpret what few Anglo-Saxons can ever fully comprehend. But it may be worth making a few points and dispelling a few myths. The Spanish fighting bull is thought to be descended from the wild aurochs (*bos taurus primigenius*) which in Neolithic times roamed throughout Europe and North Africa. It is certainly quite different from other forms of cattle and, some say, the only animal which can be relied upon to charge on sight. The opponents of bullfighting, in particular those ignorant 'celebrities' who seek publicity for themselves in defence of animal rights and talk about the number of bulls which would be saved from being slaughtered if the spectacle was abolished, completely ignore the fact that, without the *corrida*, this breed of bull would cease to exist. It is far too dangerous an animal to be bred only for meat and milk, and it is not a good converter of grass into protein. The bull ranches would probably be turned over to flower and vegetable production under plastic, and the wildlife which now flourishes on land grazed by fighting bulls would be destroyed.

The chances are that an animal bred for beef will have been removed from its mother at birth and castrated. It may then be penned up with hundreds of other animals and fed on processed meal. After perhaps twenty months, much less if it is to be killed for veal, it will be crated in darkness and herded to its death in the abattoir. Compare this with a Spanish fighting bull, which roams free on lush pasture for up to five years, with no human interference, is then taken to the bullring and meets death by the matador's sword in a contest which will not last more than twenty minutes. A professor of animal physiology has stated that a fighting bull suffers most stress while being transported to the bullring. Once there, and concerned only to attack its adversaries, it produces beta-endorphins in sufficient quantity to anaesthetise the pain of its injuries. If, at birth, an animal had the option to become a domestic or a fighting bull, there would surely be no doubting its choice.

One aspect of the *corrida* which most repels non-Spaniards is the use of horses, blindfolded and allegedly with their vocal cords having been cut, ridden by picadors who incite the bull's charge and then sink their pointed lances into its neck muscles. The purpose of this is to lower the bull's head, thus enabling the matador to place his sword correctly in order to kill the animal. The horses may be knocked down by the force of the bull's charge, but they are rarely injured, as their flanks are protected by padded mattresses. Orson Welles, a confirmed aficionado who was riveted by this phase of the *corrida*, would often stand to applaud the picador's work; but even he might have averted his gaze in the days before the protective mattress was introduced in 1928. (*Death in the Afternoon*, though published in 1932, contains photographs of the horses unpadded and close to death.) In the first chapter of his novel, *The Plumed Serpent*, published in 1926, D. H. Lawrence describes the bull's horns penetrating the horse's abdomen at a *corrida* in Mexico City. *Blood and Sand*, first published in Spain in 1909, contains graphic, not to say revolting, descriptions, of horses dying in the ring:

> The first bull showed itself exceptionally persistent in attacking the men on horseback. Within a few moments it had unseated three picadors, who were waiting for it with their lances ready, and of the horses two lay dying with dark gouts of blood gushing from the holes in their chests. The other was galloping round the arena, mad with pain and terror, with its saddle flapping loose and its stomach ripped open, showing the blue and red entrails like enormous sausages. As it dragged its intestines on the ground and trod on them with its hind feet, they gradually became disentangled as a skein is unravelled.

This sort of thing had to be ended. Until then the combat between bull and mounted picador was the essential heart of the fight, and the picadors' names were listed above those of the matadors on the *carteles*. The *muleta* (red cloth) was used principally in order to further weaken the animal before putting it to the sword. When Juan Belmonte came along in 1913, he revolutionised the spectacle in a number of ways. Instead of getting out of the bull's way, he was the first torero to stand still and make the bull get out of his way by means of a variety of passes, with both cape and *muleta*, which came to be admired as much for their artistry as for the bravery of the man directing the bull's charge close to and past his body. The modern form of bullfighting, with the passes linked in series, was developed by, among others, Manolete, who was killed by a bull in Linares in 1947.*

Confirming the place of bullfighting today in the life and culture of Spain, it—tauromachy or the taurine art—was formally given the status of *patrimonio cultural* in 2012. Ex-king Juan Carlos, speaking of what he called *la fiesta nacional*, said at the time of his accession that his only regret on becoming king was that he would have less time to go to the bulls. (On the day of the funeral in London of Princess Diana, who had been Juan Carlos's guest several times at his house in Majorca, he attended the annual *goyesca corrida* in Ronda.) One may not share the view of Spain's Minister of Culture who, when taking over responsibility for bullfighting from the Interior Ministry in 2010, called it 'a ritual which confronts us with the profound dilemmas of life'. But it should be acknowledged that Spain is quite different from northern Europe: its rituals are both Catholic and pagan, and the bullfight may perhaps be seen as a blood sacrifice which is too alien to be judged by those whose lives are governed by principles of 'political correctness'. Nor can our secular society appreciate the significance of religion in the bullfight. Almost all *ferias* are held in honour of a saint, or the Virgin, or a religious festival such as Ascension or Pentecost or Corpus Christi. In small towns bullfights are almost always held on the patron saint's feast day. Every matador prays before entering the bullring. And the first pass made with the cape is called a *veronica*, after the saint who proffered a cloth to wipe Jesus's face as he carried the cross to Golgotha.† This is replicated in the manner used to cite the bull.

---

* Shortly after Manolete's death, his mother received a letter of condolence from Winston Churchill. In 1944 Manolete had killed a bull with a pronounced 'V' on its forehead, and its Anglophile breeder had sent the stuffed head to Churchill at Chartwell. Churchill wrote to Manolete after the war, thanking him for 'this most agreeable expression of friendship and good will from Spain'.

† When Jesus handed the veil back to Veronica, it had on it an impression of His face, which inspired Zurbaran's painting of *La Santa Faz* (*The Holy Face*) and some to suggest, somewhat fancifully, that the word 'veronica' is derived from 'vera icon', the true image.

As a left-wing theatre critic and opponent of capital punishment, Kenneth Tynan must have seemed an unlikely enthusiast for the bull-fight when his book, *Bull Fever*, was published in 1955. He saw the spectacle in dramatic terms: quoting the classical scholar Maurice Bowra on the task of the epic hero, he neatly defined it as representing 'the pursuit of honour through risk'—which is just what it should be. Today the most successful toreros are honoured with cultural awards, along with other artists, and by dint of their courage and self-control are often considered as role models.

It is of course the risk to the matador which makes a bullfight so exciting. And let no one underestimate that risk, from a wild beast which may be the only one in the animal kingdom, and certainly the only species of bull, to charge unprovoked. Every year toreros suffer serious injury from bulls which turn abruptly, often as the sword goes in, and sink one of their horns into a man's thigh. Thanks to medical advances, there are fewer fatal gorings nowadays. In the past the proximate cause of a torero's death would probably have been blood poisoning, gangrene or septicaemia. No wonder that a statue commemorating Sir Alexander Fleming, who discovered penicillin, stands outside the Las Ventas bullring in Madrid. It shows a torero saluting Fleming with his doffed *montera*, and was unveiled by the Mayor of Madrid and the British ambassador in 1964.

For many years a few hundred passionate, some might say obsessive, British enthusiasts for the bullfight have been represented by the Club Taurino of London, which celebrated its fiftieth anniversary in 2009. It publishes a bi-monthly magazine, *La Divisa*, containing highly technical reports of various *corridas* and on occasion heated debates about the strengths and weaknesses of this or that torero. One of the club's admirable objects is 'to promote a truthful and wider understanding of the Spanish national festival (*la fiesta brava*) and to counteract existing misconceptions and misrepresentation'. What it does not do is indulge in the bizarre flights of fancy to which some would-be taurine experts have been prone.

Social anthropologists, no doubt under the influence of Freud, have seen the *corrida* as an Oedipal drama in which the matador defeats and kills his father (the bull); or as a sexual act in which the matador, initially adopting the feminine role, finally becomes a man and 'rapes' the bull as he kills it. In this analysis he penetrates the 'vaginal wound'—the bull's shoulders having been bloodied by the picador's lance—with his sword-phallus, tempting one to ask a matador if he is aware, at the moment of truth, that he is raping a menstruating woman. In his book, *Blood Sport*, the American anthropologist Timothy Mitchell devotes a chapter to 'Psychosexual Aspects of the Bullfight' and argues that the emotion felt by spectators of the *corrida* is essentially pornographic—'unconscious phantasmagorial onanism' in the words of the twentieth-century writer and republican activist, José Bergamin.

The relationship between matador and bull may be difficult to understand, but it is undoubtedly one of respect and, in some cases, almost of affection. Many matadors have spoken of the warmth that a great bull can inspire in them, and of their sadness at killing it. One is drawn irresistibly to Oscar Wilde's lines in 'The Ballad of Reading Gaol':

Yet each man kills the thing he loves,
By each let this be heard...
The coward does it with a kiss,
The brave man with a sword!

Does the *corrida* mirror Spain's social and historical traumas? It can surely be better understood in the context of a country which, in the last two hundred years, has suffered invasion, revolution and civil war. It is a country of blood and death, heat and dust, fierce light and deep shade, passionate love and tragic loss. Listen to the music of flamenco, with its Moorish and Romany origins, look at the *pinturas negras* of Goya, or the many portraits and sculptures of the crucified Christ with gaping wounds in his naked body, and you begin to realise that Spain is different. The cruelty and the beauty of the bullfight belong to Spain. In Britain, with a different experience of the past two centuries, a different mentality, different priorities, we can express revulsion at the *corrida*, and stay away from it; but that surely does not entitle us to seek to interfere with the cultural tradition of another country.

There is no denying that opposition to the bullfight within Spain has been growing in the past few years. More significant, though, for its future is the economic downturn in Spain, beginning in 2007 which, with unemployment above 25 per cent, became known as *la crisis*. Over the next seven years the annual number of *corridas* held at the twenty most popular bullrings fell by one third—though there were still substantially more annual bullfighting events than there had been fifty years ago. The leading matadors were fighting on twice as many occasions in 2000 as they were in 2015. Less than half as many matadors were entering the profession in 2015 and some bull breeders were going out of business. The decline is attributable in part to cuts in public funding and the decision of certain left-wing mayors to ban the bullfight in their towns (though the ban in San Sebastián was lifted in 2015 when a new mayor was elected). It is also the price of tickets and the lack of young people going to the bulls which threaten the future of *la fiesta brava*. While youth unemployment remains so high—at almost 50 per cent in 2015—and bullfight tickets are much more expensive than those for a football match, younger people are not going to follow the example of their parents, who might have gone to the bulls, as a matter of course, almost every Sunday during the season. According to a recent poll, only 25 per cent of the population had attended a bullfight in the past five years—and most of them were middle-aged or older.

Certainly, football is far more popular than bullfighting these days. A barber in Madrid was said to offer his customers a choice of conversation—the ball or the bull—but he stopped asking when the overwhelming majority wanted to talk football. However, it would be wrong to say that the popularity of football, and the great success which Spanish teams enjoy, will bring an end to the *corrida*. Only four decades after the first football club was founded in Spain (by two Scotsmen in Huelva) at the end of the nineteenth century, the head of the bullfighting family in Marguerite Steen's novel, *Matador*, was railing against 'this cursed futbol, which is corrupting the taste of young Spain'. The two enthusiasms continue to co-exist in the twenty-first century—but the long-term survival of bullfighting cannot be guaranteed.

PICTURE CREDITS

Duke of Wellington (ullstein bild/Getty Images)
Sir Harry Smith (Culture Club/Hulton Archive/Getty Images)
Sir John Moore (Hulton Archive/Getty Images)
Richard Ford (Michael Russell)
British-built houses in Huelva (Author's photograph)
English Cemetery, Málaga (*The Oldie*)
Duke of Berwick (Kachelhoffer Clement/Corbis Historical/Getty Images)
Robert Persons (Royal English College, Valladolid)
Queen Ena and Alfonso XIII (Hulton Archive/Getty Images)
La Vulnerata (Royal English College, Valladolid)
Clement Attlee and José Miaja (Hulton Archive/Getty Images)
POUM militia guards (Universal Images Group/Getty Images)
Ramon Cabrera (Alinari/Getty Images)
Miramar Palace (Author's photograph)
Kenneth Tynan (*The New York Post*/Getty Images)
Sir Peter Chalmers-Mitchell (Zoological Society London)
Roy Campbell (Guardian News & Media Ltd/Jane Bown)
Benjamin Disraeli (Culture Club/Hulton Archive/Getty Images)
Lord Byron (Archive Photos/Getty Images)
Duke of Kent (Popperfoto/Getty Images)
George Borrow (Hulton Archive/Getty Images)

BIBLIOGRAPHY

Alexander, Bill: *British Volunteers for Liberty* (Lawrence & Wishart, 1982)
Alford, Stephen: *The Watchers* (Allen Lane, 2012)

Beevor, Anthony: *The Spanish Civil War* (Orbis, 1982)
Bolin, Luis: *Spain – The Vital Years* (J. B. Lippincott & Co, 1967)
Borrow, George: *The Bible in Spain* (Oxford, 1842)
Brenan, Gerald: *The Spanish Labyrinth* (Cambridge, 1943)
  South from Granada (Cambridge, 1957)
Brooke, Sir Arthur de Capell: *Sketches in Spain and Morocco* (London,
  1831)
Burns, Jimmy: *Spain: A Literary Companion* (John Murray, 1994)
  Papa Spy (Bloomsbury, 2009)
Burrieza, Javier: *La Misión de Robert Persons* (Valladolid, 2010)

Campbell, Roy: *Flowering Rifle* (Longmans, Green & Co, 1939)
  Light on a Dark Horse (Hollis & Carter, 1951)
Carr, Sir Raymond: *Spain 1808-1975* (Oxford, 1982)
Chalmers-Mitchell, Peter: *My House in Malaga* (Faber, 1938)
Childs, Jessie: *God's Traitors* (Bodley Head, 2014)
Conrad, Barnaby: *Gates of Fear* (Michael Joseph, 1957)
Cornwell, Bernard: *Sharpe's Fury* (HarperCollins, 2006)
Courtauld, Simon: *Spanish Hours* (Libri Mundi, 1996)

Delibes, Miguel: *The Heretic* (Overlook Press, 2006)

Fergusson, Gordon: *Hounds are Home* (Springwood Books, 1979)
Fletcher, Ian: *Fields of Fire* (Spellmount, 1994)
Ford, Richard: *A Handbook for Travellers in Spain* (John Murray, 1845)
  Gatherings from Spain (John Murray, 1846)
Fyrth, Jim: *Women's Voices from the Spanish Civil War* (Lawrence &
  Wishart, 1991)

Garcia, Joseph: *Gibraltar: The Making of a People* (Panorama Publishing, 2002)

Gathorne-Hardy, Jonathan: *Gerald Brenan: The Interior Castle* (Sinclair-Stevenson, 1992)

Gautier, Theophile: *A Romantic in Spain* (Alfred Knopf, 1926)

Gilmour, David: *Cities of Spain* (John Murray, 1992)

Goodwin, Robert: *Spain: The Centre of the World 1519-1682* (Bloomsbury, 2015)

Grice-Hutchinson, Marjorie: *The English Cemetery at Malaga* (1964)

Grove, Valerie: *Laurie Lee* (Viking, 1999)

Hare, Augustus: *Wanderings in Spain* (London, 1873)

Harris, Benjamin: *The Recollections of Rifleman Harris* (London, 1848)

Heman Chant, Roy: *Spanish Tiger* (Midas, 1983)

Hemingway, Ernest: *Fiesta* (Jonathan Cape, 1927)
Death in the Afternoon (Jonathan Cape, 1932)
The Dangerous Summer (Hamish Hamilton, 1985)

Heyer, Georgette: *The Spanish Bride* (William Heinemann, 1940)

Hooper, John: *The Spaniards* (Viking, 1986)

Hopkins, Adam: *Spanish Journeys* (Viking, 1992)

Howse, Christopher: *A Pilgrim in Spain* (Continuum, 2011)
The Train in Spain (Bloomsbury, 2013)

Hughes, Robert: *Barcelona* (Harvill, 1992)

Ibanez, Vicente Blasco: *Blood and Sand* (Elek, 1958)

Ivanovic, Vane: *LX* (Weidenfeld & Nicolson, 1977)

Kamen, Henry: *Spain's Road to Empire* (Allen Lane, 2002)

Kemp, Peter: *The Thorns of Memory* (Sinclair-Stevenson, 1990)

Koestler, Arthur: *Spanish Testament* (Gollancz, 1937)

Kurlansky, Mark: *The Basque History of the World* (Jonathan Cape, 1999)

Lawrence, D. H.: *The Plumed Serpent* (Secker & Warburg, 1926)

Lee, Laurie: *As I Walked Out One Midsummer Morning* (Deutsch, 1969)
A Moment of War (Viking, 1991)

BIBLIOGRAPHY

Longford, Elizabeth: *Wellington – The Years of the Sword* (Weidenfeld & Nicolson, 1969)

Loomie, Albert J: *The Spanish Elizabethans* (Fordham University Press, 1963)

Low, Robert: *La Pasionaria* (Hutchinson, 1992)

Luard, Nicholas: *Andalucia* (Century, 1984)

Macaulay, Rose: *Fabled Shore* (Hamish Hamilton, 1949)

Macintyre, Ben: *Operation Mincemeat* (Bloomsbury, 2010)

Mitchell, David: *Travellers in Spain* (Santana Books, 2004)

Mitchell, Timothy: *Blood Sport* (Pennsylvania, 1991)

Morris, Jan: *Spain* (Faber, 1964)

Morton, H. V.: *A Stranger in Spain* (Methuen, 1955)

Oman, Sir Charles: *A History of the Peninsular War* (Oxford, 1902)

Orwell, George: *Homage to Catalonia* (Secker & Warburg, 1938)

Petrie, Sir Charles: *Philip II of Spain* (Eyre & Spottiswoode, 1964)

Preston, Paul: *Franco* (HarperCollins, 1993)
   ¡Comrades! (HarperCollins, 1999)
   Doves of War (HarperCollins, 2002)
   We Saw Spain Die (Constable, 2008)
   The Spanish Holocaust (HarperPress, 2012)

Pritchett, V. S.: *Marching Spain* (Ernest Benn, 1928)

Rawson, Andrew: *The Peninsular War* (Pen & Sword, 2009)

Robertson, Ian: *Richard Ford 1796-1858* (Michael Russell, 2004)

Ruiz Zafon, Carlos: *The Shadow of the Wind* (Weidenfeld & Nicolson, 2004)

Sanchez, M. G.: *The Prostitutes of Serruya's Lane and other Hidden Gibraltarian Histories* (Rock Scorpion, 2007)

Scott-Ellis, Priscilla: *The Chances of Death* (Michael Russell, 1995)

Sitwell, Sacheverell: *Spain* (Batsford, 1950)

Snow, Peter: *To War with Wellington* (John Murray, 2010)

Southey, Robert: *Letters written during a short residence in Spain and Portugal* (Bristol, 1797)
Steen, Marguerite: *Matador* (Gollancz, 1934)

Thomas, Hugh: *The Spanish Civil War* (Hamish Hamilton, 1977)
Townsend, Joseph: *A Journey Through Spain* (London, 1791)
Tynan, Kenneth: *Bull Fever* (Longmans, Green & Co, 1955)

Van Hensbergen, Gijs: *Gaudí* (HarperCollins, 2001)

Widdrington, Samuel: *Sketches in Spain* (London, 1834)
Woodworth, Paddy: *The Basque Country* (Signal, 2007)
Woolsey, Gamel: *Death's Other Kingdom* (Longmans, Green & Co, 1939)

INDEX

INDEX

INDEX

INDEX

INDEX